The Imagination

as a

Means of Grace

ERNEST LEE TUVESON

The Imagination as a Means of Grace

LOCKE AND THE AESTHETICS OF ROMANTICISM

GORDIAN PRESS
NEW YORK
1974

BOWLING GREEN STATE UNIVERSITY LIBRARY

ORIGINALLY PUBLISHED 1960
REPRINTED 1974

COPYRIGHT © 1960 BY
THE REGENTS OF THE UNIVERSITY OF CALIFORNIA
PUBLISHED BY GORDIAN PRESS, INC.
BY ARRANGEMENT WITH
UNIVERSITY OF CALIFORNIA PRESS

Library of Congress Cataloging in Publication Data

Tuveson, Ernest Lee.
The imagination as a means of grace.

Reprint of the 1960 ed. published by the University of California Press, Berkeley.
Includes bibliographical references.
1. Locke, John, 1632-1704. 2. Imagination.
I. Title.
[B1297.T8 1974] 192 73-21543
ISBN 0-87752-173-5

598769

192.2
Z9
T96im

CONTENTS

INTRODUCTION

The "crisis of the European consciousness" which occurred in the centuries after Copernicus produced in every aspect of culture changes so great and so deep that we are, even yet, far from capable of understanding them fully. This book deals with one of those changes: the revolution in the conceptions of art and of the artist. I concentrate on a central aspect of that change: the emergence of a new idea of the creative imagination. This process might be described as the epitome of the romantic revolution.

On one side, in the later eighteenth century, is Samuel Johnson, reiterating the classical definition of the imaginative faculty, which had been repeated for centuries: the practice of poetry is "an art of uniting pleasure with truth by calling imagination to the help of reason" (*Lives of the English Poets*). At the other extreme, in Johnson's own time, a host of theorists and poets were proclaiming that only so far as poetic imagination is divorced from the reason, only as the poetic creation produces an effect indefinable and *sui generis*, related to feeling and not to thought, can it do its proper work. A knowledge of this revolution is fundamental to any real understanding of what has happened in literature since the eighteenth century.

To understand why it occurred, we must realize that this aesthetic revolution was a projection of the complex of changes that took place in Western culture. It is a fabric composed of many threads, seemingly diverse and unrelated. They may, however, be classified under two main headings, which, indeed, comprehend the great interests and concerns of mankind: the idea of the nature and workings of man's mind, and the idea of the cosmos.

The profound importance of the Lockian epistemology, as I. A. Richards pointed out more than thirty years ago, has never been adequately assessed. Just what differences to artists and to theorists about art would the "new way of ideas" make? I have tried to analyze some of the consequences of Locke's new model of psychology: in particular, how the transference of the "locus of reality" to the perceiving mind made necessary eventually a radically new conception of art as effect; and how it was necessary to reconstruct "conscience" and the "means of grace" in terms of a theory of the mind that denied the possibility of occult and supernatural influences on the personality. By a natural process, I conclude, imagination came to be a means of grace within the world of actual, physical sense impressions.

To understand the content of imagination as thus reconstructed, moreover, it was necessary to turn to the effects in art of the other great revolution in thought: the emergence of a new conception of the universe, particularly of space—the process which Alexander Koyré has recently described in *From the Closed World to the Infinite Universe*. The "natural sublime," that obsessive form of romantic sensibility, was the symbolic projection of the new model of the universe just as the romantic imagination was, in a sense, of the new model of the mind.

Finally, I have discussed the emergent theory of imagination as it was presented by the aesthetic theorists of eighteenth-century England. There are two limitations. First, I have limited the scope of this study to the early period of romanticism, because there, in embryo, we see the rationale of much that was to follow. Second, I have not discussed at length the art, the poetry, that came out of this kind of theorizing. This subject I hope to take up later; but it seemed important first to get the theory straight—enough for one book. Theories of aesthetics are an interesting and significant part of the history of the human mind; but in the end they must be validated in terms of artistic creation. This study, therefore, I might describe as a prolegomenon, were it not that such a composition has a fatal habit of terminating the whole work.

This book was completed before I saw Marjorie Hope Nicolson's important new book *Mountain Gloom and Mountain Glory*. Her treatment of the changes in the attitude toward nature, especially toward the "great," necessarily in some respects parallels mine; but there are many differences between our interpretations. The two books, furthermore, are in most ways complementary: whereas Miss Nicolson is concerned largely with the outer world—the scientific and philosophical backgrounds of the new aesthetics—I am chiefly concerned with the inner one—the Lockian conception of the mind as that conception affected the theory of the imagination. I must also record my indebtedness to M. H. Abrams, *The Mirror and the Lamp*.

For reading the manuscript and for helpful criticisms I am indebted to the following colleagues: B. H. Bronson, J. R. Caldwell, Bertrand Evans, Arthur Hutson, and Josephine Miles. Several journals have generously given permission to use, in altered form, material I had previously published in their pages: *Modern Philology* (chapter i), *Modern Language Quarterly* (chapter iii), *English Literary History*, and *The Huntington Library Quarterly*. The director of the Henry E. Huntington Library and Art Museum has given permission to use quotations from letters in the Elizabeth Montagu Collection. I am grateful to the Folger Shakespeare Library for a fellowship and to its director and staff for much kind assistance while I was working in that scholars' paradise.

ERNEST LEE TUVESON

I THE NEW EPISTEMOLOGY

It has been said that "for Addison, and the men of letters of the eighteenth century, Locke was 'the philosopher,' somewhat as Aristotle had been for the schoolmen." [1] Another scholar, even more forthrightly, has asserted that "men of the early eighteenth century were not so much the beneficiaries of Locke as they were his prisoners." [2] The duo of Newton and Locke always appears as dominating the beginnings of the "modern" age at the turn of the century. Yet much of their influence on creative artists, as well as on ideas about art, remains obscure, for, like the larger part of an iceberg, it lies beneath the surface of expression. This book is concerned with some of the revolutionary changes in the idea of the imagination, especially that of literature, which Locke's new model of the mind brought about.

Locke—notably in his essays on the contract of society and on civil liberty—taught men new ideas, or rather confirmed what they had already been vaguely cogitating. In his epistemology, however, he did something that not even Newton had done: he taught them new ways of thinking, in the literal sense of that phrase. He inaugurated or made necessary a rethinking of every aspect of the personality: soul, conscience, reason, imagination, even immortality itself. All these concepts were destined to undergo metamorphoses as theories of how the mind receives sensations, how it deals with them, and how it is related to truth were transformed.

As one result of this general change, the inherited tradition of literature and its functions—a tradition with its roots in the classical world—ceased to be viable. The change, of course, did not occur with miraculous suddenness; but, even so, within an amazingly short period of time the assumptions about the human mind and the nature of character which poets and playwrights had made for thousands of years became antiquated. The century that, in its earlier years, saw the great codification of a modified neoclassical tradition, in Pope's *Essay on Man*, was to see at its end a kind of poetry and a kind of theory about poetry that relegated the great tradition to the limbo of ancient things as surely as Copernican-Galilean-Newtonian astronomy had relegated the astronomy of Ptolemy to the past. Change does not necessarily mean progress. Whether the transition has been good for art, so far as that can ever be determined, is still uncertain. What remains undisputed is that artists began to work in response to a set of conceptions about man, and the way he thinks, and the effect of experience on the psyche, which were radically different from those that had previously held sway. Before the eighteenth century, art had been considered a form of knowledge, an aspect of objective truth; afterward it tended to become a subjective impression—something that *happens to* consciousness. The vicissitudes of "imagination" reflect this change, for it was in this faculty that the problem of art, both of artist and of audience, centered.

When we survey the intellectual world of the late seventeenth century, we are impressed by the widening gulf between the "new philosophy" which Newton was bringing to classical formulation and the prevailing concepts of how the mind operates, of how experience actually occurs. The universe of Newton is preëminently quantitative. Atoms moving according to simple and universally applicable laws are the constituents of reality; the universe is without "up or down," it has no recognizable center, is unlimited in extent. Qualities and values are not intrinsic facts inhering in external objects. The whole idea of a beautiful parallel between physical and mental realities, between spiritual and physical, between great world and small world, became untenable.

Yet epistemology in 1690 still reflected the old qualitative idea of the universe. Reality is a combination of form and matter. The universe everywhere, in this opinion, is striving to realize a great and perfect idea, which is analogous to the living being. There is purpose behind motion. The question, according to a much-used formula, was "Why?" In the new philosophy it was "How?" This easy formulation, although it needs qualification, is essentially true, and helps explain why the discrepancy between epistemology and cosmology had become intolerable by the end of the seventeenth century. The peculiar distinction and importance of John Locke is that he constructed a system that bridged this gulf. That his formulations were overdue is demonstrated by the fact that the new epistemology, revolutionary and disturbing though it was, within a few decades became almost the only one accepted; and, it is not too much to say, modern psychology of whatever school shows its influence.

To understand the problem Locke tried to solve in his *Essay Concerning the Human Understanding* (which first appeared in 1690), we should go back to Hobbes. He had tried, in an overhasty effort, to explain all sensation, all thought, in terms of purely material, physiological changes of the body. He had tried to make the microcosm correspond exactly to the macrocosm of the atomic philosophers, with their impinging atoms, their laws of momentum and inertia, their wave motions through substances, and the like. It was, in fact, a reversal of the medieval attitude. The schoolmen had assumed that, since man is the center and the object of nature, the universe must present an analogy to the structure of the human mind and personality. Hobbes assumed just the opposite: the mind must be patterned after the physical universe. Particles of matter impinging on the organism give rise to modifications in the body which constitute the very substance of thought. Connections of these modifications, occurring in accidental sequences, in some way give rise to all our notions of relations. From these combinations, produced at random in the course of our ordinary experience, come all ideas, even the greatest and the subtlest. Nothing is involved, it seems, but "dead" matter; according to his theory, which represented the triumph of nominalism, there is no soul, no living self at the heart of it all, no center of consciousness to receive the material impression and to be aware of itself. The whole system was unconvincing, for it was false to the impression made by the very fact of living; the age rightly felt that it violated the integrity and dignity of man.

Yet the claims of Hobbes could not be entirely denied. His system, even if it failed to account for the wonderful phenomena of the mind in all its diversity and uniqueness, nevertheless had a certain fitness with the new ideas about the universe. For one thing, it recognized that the sense of qualitative differences—the belief that one object is higher and nobler than others—was becoming passé. The new model of the universe was to be horizontal rather than vertical. The matter of the sun is no more perfect than that of earth. The idea that the planets are ranged in an order of nobility, and may be guided by intelligences, was no longer believable. The theory of the universe that accounted for physical events by saying that a desire moves the elements—that fire ascends because it wants to return to its appointed place in the ether—was dissolving. The old philosophies assumed that a law had been established, that the elements making up the world had been given commands which like servants they obeyed. The universe was animated by souls, and a supreme soul in which, perhaps, the others participated—the anima mundi—provided the organic relationship of nature.

Man, alone among all creatures on earth, had free will and could obey or disobey. The history of physical as well as moral phenomena centered on this point, for the setting of man's life had been created to give him the potentiality for moral choice. The nature of man had suffered a great change, known as original sin, and that change was reflected in a certain imperfection of the macrocosm. Everywhere was the assumption that living beings, analogous to human personalities, carried out purposes. It was inconceivable that motion, growth, pattern, could be explained except by projecting thought and volition throughout the universe.

In the new cosmology the universe was explained in terms of the uniform operations of matter, which could be reduced to comprehensive and simplified natural laws. The moon moves as it does, not because it obeys a command to take part in the celestial dance, but because of properties of mass, position, and gravitational attraction. The wonderful art of the Creator is shown, not by His stage-managing the great ballet of the heavens, but by the economy whereby, with a comparatively simple master plan, He set matter in motion to operate as a machine. One atom is like another, and as good as another; it seems ridiculous even to raise the question whether the planets are "nobler" than the earth. God sees with equal eye the bubble and the world. The universe, although obviously designed and sustained by a divine energy, is nevertheless not of itself moral. Value must be found, not in things themselves, but in the way they affect sentient beings.

It is easy to assume that such a conclusion must have come as a severe blow to humanity. In fact, however, the triumph of the new philosophy seemed to release a tidal wave of enthusiasm and energy that carried mankind forward in the greatest creative activity of its history. The new system, we must remember, represented an apparent victory of order and common sense. In the late Renaissance a sense of dissolution, of beliefs going out with nothing to replace them, is common. Donne is a spokesman for the feeling of mutability triumphant, of hopeless paradoxes that can be accepted and resolved only by acts of courageous faith.

The movement of which Newton was the culmination presented a more comprehensible and securely ordered system. The hopeless paradoxes now appeared as mere illusions. Natural law robbed such omens as comets of their sinister qualities. Potentially, there were many terrifying problems, to be sure, but they did not confront mankind immediately; and, as we shall see, a new interpretation of the symbolic value of nature for a long time stood as a shield aganst these problems. A sense of literal enlightenment, of clearing away old mists, old confusions, was in the air when Locke, about 1670, meditated on the problem of the human understanding.

Locke was a true disciple of Bacon, with the master's overriding desire to aid men in solving their problems and in achieving a truer understanding of nature which would lead to a better life in this world. A pragmatic interest in relieving man's estate is the central motive for Locke's work. It was, therefore, in no mood of pure philosophical speculation that Locke considered the problem of the mind. For, if mankind was to benefit from the new philosophy, the concept of the mind's workings must be re-created. The situation in psychology, by the 1670's, was much like that of cosmology a half century before, when, as we can see from Donne's *Anatomy of the World,* there was an intolerable confusion about the model of the heavens, and coherence was gone.

The new philosophy had given men a satisfying idea which exorcised the cosmic ghosts. But, just as traditional physical philosophy had been quite inadequate to explain the flood of new observations of phenomena in the external world, so mental philosophy, in the latter part of the century, was unable to solve the problems of perception and thought. The average man must have been hopelessly bewildered by the chaos of theories. The nature of the planets could be explained, but the character of an idea in the mind remained mystical and obscure. In practice, epistemologies, like the old cosmology, simply moved the explanation one step farther back. We think because it is our "nature" to think. The old theory of forms still prevailed in an atomistic universe; the soul is the form of the body. Thought is the perfection of the rational being that dwells in the body. Thus universals maintained an uneasy tenure in a world where nominalistic philosophy was triumphing.

Psychological systems, except for Hobbes's, assumed that the human mind is an entity of an essentially different kind from the natural world it inhabits. Spenser depicted it as Alma, a great lady, mistress of the castle of the body, who remains in a state of alert. She is defended by a garrison—the five senses—and advised by reason. The mind, therefore, is intrinsically different from anything in nature, as the owner of a castle is distinct in kind from his fortress; and the soul is a being of another kind from the besiegers. Sensations have to be completely transformed—made into an "intellectible" mind-stuff. It was obvious that knowledge must begin with sensations, but then the mind must take these sensations and, using its innate knowing faculty, erect its own structure of thought.

Fewer than twenty years before Locke wrote the first draft of his *Essay Concerning the Human Understanding*, the Cambridge Platonist John Smith declared: "That the *Mental faculty* and power whereby we *judge* and *discern* is so far from being a *Body*, that it must *retract* and withdraw itself from all *Bodily operation* whensoever it will nakedly *discern* Truth." [3] Here we see a common principle of pre-Lockian epistemology: the soul, as a visitor in matter, participates in an order of truth to which the actual universe can never more than roughly approximate. The mind, even though it must utilize material impressions, is too fine, too perfect in itself, ever to be truly at home in nature. The highest idea, that of God, is completely removed in its essence from matter, even though reasoning from experience will confirm the proposition that the universe does have a Creator, and images will enable the soul to increase its imperfect understanding of the supernal reality. In this supreme knowledge, Smith goes so far as to say, imagination can only "breathe a gross dew upon the pure Glass of our Understandings"; this was an extreme position, but only extreme in degree.

A popular account of things mental and spiritual (there was always a connection between them) is given in Henry More's *Enchiridion Ethicum*, which was translated by Edward Southwell in 1690, the very year that Locke's own essay appeared. To go from one to the other of these works is to span the centuries, to go at a leap from the world of Spenser to that of Sterne. More starts from the assumption that the soul is an organic unity composed of hierarchical faculties. It joins the supranatural and natural worlds, as Ficino had postulated. Like a giant standing with head in the clouds and feet upon the earth, the soul lives in two levels. A good picture of what More assumes is given in one of the classical encyclopedias of medieval and Renaissance times, which discusses the internal powers of perception of the body as follows:

The first whereof . . . is feeling, and by that vertue the Soule is moved, and taketh heede to the bodylye wittes, and desireth those things, that belong to the bodye . . . The second power is wit: that is the vertue of the soule, whereby shee knoweth things sensible and corporall, when they be present. The third is imagination, whereby the Soule beholdeth the lykenesse of bodylye thinges when they bee absent. The fourth is "Racio," Reason, that deemeth and judgeth betweene good and evill, truth and falsenesse. The fifth is "Intellectus," understanding and inwit. The which comprehendeth thinges not material but intelligible, as God, Angel, and other such.[4]

More, characteristically, starts from the same kind of assumption. The virtues are arranged in a hierarchy of nobility and importance, representing an increasing remoteness from the divine source—just as are the planets and the social classes. Each power of the soul has its function and a certain autonomy: imagination (some authors refer also to a "common sense" that performs some of these functions) arranges and moderates the sensory perceptions, and thus prepares them for consideration by the highest faculties; it may also arrange new combinations of images, which the reason is called upon to judge. It may, indeed, run wild, and will do so unless the superior exercises its full authority, as the demos will run wild unless the prince and nobles control them. Nevertheless, all are members of one family, or branches of one tree.

John Davies represents the soul as "Being wholy in the whole, and in each part":

For as we hold there's but one God alone,
But yet three persons in the Deity:
So the Soule's parted (though in substance one)
In 't Understanding, Will, and Memory,
These Powres or Persons makes one Trinity,
Yet but one Substance indivisible,
Which perfect Trinity in Unity,

(Both beeing Spirituall and invisible)
Doe make the Soule, hir God so right resemble.

And like as one true God in persons three,
Doth rightly rule this great Worlds Monarchy,
So in Mans little World these Virtues bee,
But one Soule ruling it continually,
Yet in this lesser World, as well we try,
By sundry sorts of people; some there are
That be as heads, Some Rulers not so hie,
Some common Cittizens; and some lesse rare,
Those Ruralls bee, that still are out of square.[5]

How naturally it was taken for granted that the soul, like the universe itself, is organic, appears from such analogies. Henry More says that the intellectual part of the soul has Right Reason innately within it; it is not a possession so much as a constituent of the mind.

For Right Reason, which is in Man, is a sort of Copy or Transcript of that Reason or Law eternal which is registred in the Mind Divine. However this Law is not by Nature known unto us, than as 'tis communicated and reflected on our Minds by the same Right Reason, and so shines forth. But by how much it shines forth, by so much doth it oblige the Conscience, even as a Law Divine inscribed in our Hearts.[6]

Fulke Greville, in Sonnet I of *Caelica*, expresses the usual attitude when he writes that love, delight, virtue, and

Reason, the fire wherein men's thoughts be prov'd
Are from the world by Natures power bereft,
And in one creature, for her glory, left.

More says, uncompromisingly, "hence 'tis plain, that whatever is Intellectual and truely Moral, is also Divine, and partakes of God." [7]

Thus, while it was admitted that thought is set in motion by sensory experience, yet cognition and especially determination of values involve a supranatural intuition. The mind, as Lord Herbert of Cherbury suggests, might be like "a closed book, which opens upon the presentation of an object and reveals the characters already contained in it." [8] Or, as in Descartes, the mind and the body may be absolutely separated, the gulf between them being bridged by physical impressions transmitted to an agreed-upon point of contact (in the *konarion*) where the mind, thus aroused, begins its independent operations. These operations are strictly mental. "For I now know that, properly speaking, bodies are cognised not by the senses or by the imagination, but by the understanding alone. They are not thus cognised because seen or touched, but only in so far as they are apprehended understandingly." [9] In Meditation VI, he says that there is need of a "particular effort of mind in order to effect the act of imagination," whereas "intellection" is easy and clear. A pure intellection seems to be the proper activity of the mind, which can bring itself to deal in images only by an effort. Thinking has been so far separated from sense impressions that the latter seem afterthoughts.

And all these developments occur in the very age that witnessed an enormous increase in reliance on the senses, when science was calling for observation, for humility before nature. The proud tendency of the mind to rely on its independent reasoning was suspect. And, paradoxically, Descartes' own hypotheses of nature contributed markedly to this result. For he was no mystic, but a natural philosopher, concerned with explaining the operations of the universe in terms of the movements of atoms, his principle of vortices. To Henry More, as to others, Descartes appeared as a materialist. It was partly because of his interest in the material causes of phenomena that he found it necessary to postulate a gulf between body and mind.

Descartes' theory of sensation supposes an elaborate physical apparatus, with the body transmitting its impressions in wavelike motions. Other philosophers, except for the contemporary Hobbes, had vaguely talked of sense without worrying much about exactly how impressions are made, how they reach the reason, what consciousness is, and related problems. The concern was with values, and how the mind uses impressions. The general distrust of imagining and the confidence in the supranatural mooring of the mind tended to make philosophers indifferent to mere physiological machinery.

Descartes' preoccupation with the sensing apparatus shows that he was of the age of Harvey and the new physics. His violent separation of body from mind indicates, not denigration of the body, but a kind of despair; we are physical beings in an atomistic universe, but we think, and the best we can do is somehow to assert both facts at once, without logically reconciling them. He could not succeed, finally, in placing the mind within that natural world which was the center of his study.

Descartes' epistemology, moreover, led to the construction of "hypotheses"—attempts to explain fully, through reasoning from often scanty evidence, all aspects of phenomena. His test for the truth of thinking—"clear and distinct ideas"—encouraged a belief that by pure intellection a philosopher could, from his armchair, explain the history of nature; as his critics mockingly asserted, he could build whole new worlds—invisible, unfortunately, except to the philosopher! [10]

Before the 1690's, Descartes had become deeply suspect. Newton's celebrated rejection of hypotheses typified the distrust of this kind of thinking and, by implication, this kind of epistemology. Hobbes was right in assuming that men wished to believe that the mind deals directly with the "phantasms," the facts presented in sensory impressions. An age of experiment could no longer assume that the mind, with haughty independence, creates its own exclusively intelligible ideas and works with the guidance of intuitive knowledge. In short, thinking must work upward, from simple impressions, just as, in the state, it was becoming evident, authority must ascend—perhaps from a social compact—rather than descend from divinely established power.

Hobbes had overlooked another impelling need, and this oversight is one reason why Locke and not he was the presiding philosopher of the next century. The mind must be preserved as both living and moral in the sense of having responsibility. Earlier in the seventeenth century there had been, perhaps as a reaction against the growing reliance on material impressions, an influx of Neo-Platonic and Hermetic notions. Philosophers had stressed to an extreme degree the divine and hence suprasensory nature of thought; even ordinary mental operations took on an increasingly transcendent character. The ancient idea of preëxistence of the soul and reminiscence was revived; perhaps the soul's recollection of a heavenly world accounts for what the scientific-minded Glanvill called "those inbred fundamental notices that God hath implanted in our souls; such as arise not from external objects, nor particular humours and imaginations, but are immediately lodged in our minds." [11] In any event, the human mind participates in the divine. Henry More, despite his great interest in the work of the natural philosophers, gives a picture of the mind that is incongruous with any theory of experimental knowledge: "For this is the true Character of every intellectual Faculty; . . . that it cannot stoop, and as it were cringe, to particular Cases; but speaks boldly and definitively what is true and good unto all." [12]

There was, then, an acute need for a new model of the mind that would bring the intellectual processes into nature without making them wholly material phenomena, as in Hobbes's theory, in which the mind appears to be at the mercy of its unpredictable adventures with matter. There must be security and order in thought, which a "fortuitous concourse of atoms" could hardly produce. Locke's experiential epistemology seemed, at least to a majority of men, to leave religion and virtue secure. With it, the Enlightenment became a full reality.

The solution to the dilemma was to endow the mind, not with completed ideas, but with the power to make all its ideas out of impressions. Henry More had made a suggestion that could, with radical changes, lead to such a solution. In the soul, he says, is a power manifested in a "boniform Faculty," the very eye of the soul. Thus thinking is a matter of seeing relationships. But he regarded this eye as transcendent; the eye is there, but its earthy blindness must be cleared by a spiritual purgation.

Locke, also, makes the process of thinking a matter of seeing and "considering." In the center of the mind he places an observer, somewhat like the virtuoso who takes all the available data from experience and classifies and analyzes the facts into orderly groupings. This process involves nothing transcendent. Locke preserves Hobbes's intention to bring experience directly into the thought process, bridging the traditional gap between "phantasms" and "species." The mental power, instead of withdrawing from bodily operations to consider truth, as John Smith describes it, now performs what may be thought of as a bodily operation.

The material of all thought is—not merely derived from—sensations, which Locke calls "simple ideas." These impressions, arising from the impact of external physical objects upon the organs of the body, are conveyed by the "conduits of the nerves" directly to "their audience in the brain—the mind's presence-room (as I may so call it)." [13] These simple ideas cannot be resisted; we have no control over which ones enter the consciousness. In this way Locke (*Essay*, II, i, 25) maintained the humility before nature.

These simple ideas, when offered to the mind, the understanding can no more refuse to have, nor alter, when they are imprinted, nor blot them out, and make new ones itself, than a mirror can refuse, alter or obliterate the images or ideas which the objects set before it do therein produce. As the bodies that surround us do diversely affect our organs, the mind is forced to receive the impressions, and cannot avoid the perception of those ideas that are annexed to them.

This is a way of embodying in epistemology the belief that, as his pupil Shaftesbury was to say, man is made for nature and not nature for man. Experience parallels the concourse of the indivisible atoms. "For though the sight and touch often take in from the same object, at the same time, different ideas; as a man sees at once motion and colour; the hand feels softness and warmth in the same piece of wax: yet the simple ideas thus united in the same subject, are as perfectly distinct as those that come in by different senses . . ." (*Essay*, II, ii, 1). It follows that things exist in the mind, not as universals, but as conglomerations of experience-entities. The atoms of thought unite to form the objects of the mind as do those of matter to form material things.

Another source of simple ideas is the "reflection" of the mind upon its own operations. Again, reflection, like all thought, means considering perceptions (*Essay*, II, i, 4):

Secondly, the other fountain, from which experience furnisheth the understanding with ideas, is the perception of the operations of our own mind within us, as it is employed about the ideas it has got; which operations, when the soul comes to reflect on and consider, do furnish the understanding with another set of ideas, which could not be had from things without. And such are *perception, thinking, doubting, believing, reasoning, knowing, willing,* and all the different actings of our own minds.

The mind, then, is always the observer, even when the object is its own actions, which "pass there continually, . . . like floating visions." The intelligible, the noetic in thought, accordingly, has the nature of the visible and is made up of many pictures. This may be one source of the vogue for personification in eighteenth-century poetry. To personify Hope, Fear, or Melancholy is not to present an entirely poetical fiction, but to give an impression of the mind's "floating visions" of its own operations. Locke's emphasis on reflection or introspection, moreover, suggests the poetic "reverie."

The attentive observer within the mind, the understanding, goes on to construct out of these atoms of experience the combinations and trains of simple ideas that Locke calls "complex ideas." Here it is important to visualize the image of the mind as he describes it. When we do so, we appreciate the fact that this system is by no means really mechanistic. Cassirer voices a common opinion when he remarks that "reflection, as understood by Locke, is formed entirely on the pattern of sensation. It is not an active, but a purely passive principle . . . The mind behaves towards ideas like a mirror which can neither resist nor change nor extinguish the images that arise in it." [14] This is to confuse one step with another. Locke does indeed regard sensation as passive; so much he grants to the Hobbes side. And outside the active mind is a passive combination of ideas. But the looking-glass analogy does not apply to the "considering" the mind does. The mind, in contemplating the ideas it receives, acts like the Baconian observer I have mentioned. When we study a photograph, or a reflection in a mirror, noting details and comparing one image with another, we are not passive; but Locke visualizes the understanding as behaving in this way—as a living power, reflecting upon the continuum of experiences, arriving at combinations which present a fairly reliable correspondence to external reality. It possesses, too, the essential test for a living thing: it can refuse to consider. Thus did Locke bring the mind within the natural order while preserving its integrity, vitality, and self-awareness.

Constructing a satisfactory image of the mind in operation was a problem of great difficulty. At one time Locke talks of the understanding in terms that recall the camera obscura. External and internal sensations, he says, "are the only passages that I can find of knowledge to the understanding" (*Essay*, II, xi, 17):

> These alone, as far as I can discover, are the windows by which light is let into this *dark room;* for methinks the understanding is not much unlike a closet wholly shut from light, with only some little opening left, to let in external visible resemblances, or ideas of things without: would the pictures coming into such a dark room but stay there, and lie so orderly as to be found upon occasion, it would very much resemble the understanding of a man, in reference to all objects of sight, and ideas of them.

At first this would seem to be another version of Hobbes's mechanism. The pictures apparently enter the dark room and arrange themselves as sensation occurs, and the combination seems to be a passive process. But the words "and lie so orderly as to be found upon occasion" give quite another effect; for there must be something endowed with powers of acting and deciding, to "find" the pictures when they are needed. What Locke is describing here is really the setting of the understanding. And even the pictures have an irony of their own; for, alas, they do not always "stay there, and lie so orderly as to be found upon occasion."

Another image of the mind is clearer. It represents the sensations as conducted "from without to their audience in the brain—the mind's presence-room, as I may so call it." Locke, the spokesman of the first Lord Shaftesbury, was familiar with the audiences of great men and must have realized the implications of this figure. The understanding is seen as a judge, seated majestically within his presence-room, where ideas are ushered in for disposal. Like a ruler, he is powerful and autonomous, but depends absolutely on his retainers; with them he is a potentate, without them he is nothing. Unlike a sovereign, however, he cannot stir from the chamber, and cannot reject the intelligence he receives. He cannot go abroad to discover; unlike the bee in Swift's allegory of the ancients and moderns, he cannot range beyond the castle. He must perforce believe implicitly what he learns from retainers, even though by shrewd comparison he may get behind the sensations, as when the understanding suspects that colors do not really inhere in matter. And there is a hint that the ideas themselves may be spoken of as living and moving; for, if the impressions are nothing but looking-glass images, how can they have audience in the "presence-room"?

Yet it is equally true that we must not overrate the independence and scope of the understanding. Locke objects to the term "faculties" as meaning "some real beings in the soul that performed those actions of understanding and volition" (*Essay*, II, xxi, 6). His objection is really to the tendency of philosophers to make the mind a sort of persona, a fully equipped personality a priori. The understanding and the will Locke seems to regard as active, not automatons, but not fully endowed "souls." Spenser's Alma is a visitor who takes up residence in the body as chatelaine, but Locke's understanding is a part of the biological entity, the organism, an instrument for ensuring its survival and prosperous career. The proper word is the one Locke uses—"power," dynamic and self-guided, but not internally motivated. The sense of the soul as having truth in its very being, of Right Reason as inscribed on the tablets of the mind, is exactly what Locke distrusts; his attack on innate ideas is directed at precisely such notions.

We are told that even the most abstract and sublime ideas, such as the modes of power, infinity, and the like, even the idea of

God, are *composed of*—not refined from—discrete impressions, which retain their respective forms underneath, however much they may seem to be melted down in the mind or transformed into "mind-stuff." These impressions Locke usually thinks of as pictures. Unlike Hobbes, he has little to say about the imagination as a unique faculty. One reason is that the visual imagination is omnipresent, for it is the very medium of all thought. Indirectly it is the subject of all discussion. How naturally he falls into using the word! The understanding composes the most involved of ideas, the "mixed modes," "by enumerating and thereby, as it were, setting before our imaginations all those ideas which go to the making them up, and are the constituent parts of them" (*Essay*, II, xxii, 9). Locke does, to be sure, recognize that simple ideas of sensation come in through all five (and more) senses, but only sight is significant for the understanding faculty, for thought is seeing.

A principal source of error is obscurity, caused either by failure to observe attentively or by lack of illumination. The world of the mind should be flooded with a white light which reveals the ideas (*Essay*, II, xxix, 2):

> The perception of the mind being most aptly explained by words relating to the sight, we shall best understand what is meant by *clear* and *obscure* in our ideas, by reflecting on what we call clear and obscure in the objects of sight. Light being that which discovers to us visible objects, we give the name of *obscure* to that which is not placed in a light sufficient to discover minutely to us the figure and colours which are observable in it, and which, in a better light, would be discernible.

It follows that correction of error in opinion is largely a matter of bringing more light to bear on ideas, and of making people see, and want to see. Argumentation as it is generally understood—the syllogism, propositions, and chains of discursive thought—is of little use and may be harmful (*Essay*, IV, xvii, 4):

> [God] has given [men] a mind that can reason, without being instructed in methods of syllogizing; the understanding is not taught to reason by these rules; it has a native faculty to perceive the coherence or incoherence of its ideas, and can range them right, without any such per-

plexing repetitions. . . . Tell a country gentlewoman that the wind is southwest, and the weather lowering, and like to rain, and she will easily understand it is not safe for her to go abroad thin clad in such a day, after a fever; she clearly sees the probable connexion of all these, viz., southwest wind, and clouds, rain, wetting, taking cold, relapse, and danger of death, without tying them together in those artificial and cumbersome fetters of several syllogisms, that clog and hinder the mind, which proceeds from one part to another quicker and clearer without them . . .

Thus Locke constructed an acceptable epistemology which brought to a culmination the revolt against scholastic entanglements and metaphysics. And unless we understand this conception of simple seeing by a clear light as reasoning, we cannot understand in what sense the age that followed Locke, whose philosopher he was, is the Enlightenment; and we cannot fully understand, either, why description for its own sake, the setting forth of simple images, is a paramount activity of poetry.

Even abstraction is explained in this way. The word is likely to be misleading; we think that it means a kind of intellection whereby images are transmuted into a pure, figureless thought. To think of it so in the Lockian age is peculiarly misleading. For an abstraction, Locke informs us, is nothing other than a "particular idea," that is, a sensation, which is separated from all others that may come along with it in the melee of everyday experience, and which is taken as the representative of a large number of similar simple ideas, however combined with others those ideas may be. Locke's statement in the 1671 draft of the *Essay* is especially useful: ". . . the idea of white in the mind which stands for all the white that anywhere exists, and the word white which stands for that idea, though both these in their existence be but particular things, yet as representatives or in their significations are universals." [15]

Not all our thinking, however, can be conducted in the clear and inescapable manner whereby we perceive, as Locke says, that "a circle is not a triangle, that three are more than two." "This part of knowledge," he tells us in one of his memorable phrases, "is irresistible, and, like bright sunshine, forces itself immediately to be perceived, as soon as ever the mind turns its view that way; and leaves no room for hesitation, doubt, or examination, but the mind is presently filled with the clear light of it" (*Essay*, IV, ii, 1). The image of the mind filled with clear light, driving away the darkness and mists of past ages, is one reason for the great lift this age experienced and for its creative optimism.

For complex ideas, however, we need to draw inferences and to introduce intermediary ideas. We must often make combinations of ideas which obviously have no counterpart in nature: the word "philosophy" would be an example. Herein lies the great peril. For the understanding, swollen with pride in its power to combine ideas, may, like the spider in Swift's *Battle of the Books*, spin out of itself wondrous complex ideas which are in reality mere cobwebs. They may have an elegant and satisfying coherence, and so give a reassuring impression of solidity. "For it is plain that names of substantial beings, as well as others, as far as they have relative significations affixed to them, may, with great truth, be joined negatively and affirmatively in propositions, as their relative definitions make them fit to be so joined; . . . and all this without any knowledge of the nature or reality of things existing without us" (*Essay*, IV, viii, 9).

We seem to be imprisoned. If complex ideas consist of combinations of ideas made by the understanding, and airy nothings appear to be reasonable, how are we ever to blow them away and get to solid truth? The only escape, Locke asserts, is to return to the basic simple impressions which represent all we can really be sure of. "Whence we may take notice, that general certainty is never to be found but in our ideas. Whenever we go to seek it elsewhere, in experiment or observations without us, our knowledge goes not beyond particulars" (*Essay*, IV, vi, 16). The mind, like Antaeus, must constantly return to contact with the earth, with the physical world which conveys simple ideas to us. Unless we revert to this elemental experience frequently, we become weak; a sickness of the mind sets in, producing the darkness which artificial philosophy has so long mistaken for light. "Who knows not what odd notions many men's heads are filled with, and what strange ideas all men's brains are capable of?" The cry, with its telling emphasis on "many" and "all," is a veritable motto for Sterne.

Where the older philosophy saw the sense impressions as the starting point for intellection, and emphasized an ascent into the spiritual realm, the age of Newton and Locke desired a movement in breadth rather than height. Man is to gather in more facts continually, and to make sure that his mind is not setting up a barrier between reality and consciousness. The age desired a "great Instauration." In religion, the simple and obvious truth of the Gospels, it was thought, had been corrupted by priestcraft and superstition. In government, the original purity and simplicity of institutions had been confused and hidden. In knowledge, thought, and morality, the simple and saving realities of nature had been obfuscated by hard words "sealed up with Aristotle's arms." The desire to effect a reform by returning to the realities of nature was to dominate poetry as well as other aspects of intellectual activity.

Necessary as the understanding is, reliable as it is when allowed to operate properly, there runs throughout Locke's *Essay* a certain distrust of it. Dive into reality, he advises, throw out "substance," "essence," "rational," and all those other high-sounding and unfixed words. The "Age of Reason" distrusted Reason—as it had been understood for many centuries—far more deeply than did any preceding period. It is not strange that, a few years later, when Addison is considering the function of the imagination, he gives as one pleasure of that faculty the experience of new simple ideas. The moral value of simple experience affects every attitude in this time.

To establish the integrity and saving power of the simple sensation was the reason for the whole great structure of Locke's epistemology. And that structure guarantees the glorious hopes for utopia and perfectibility of the age of the philosophes. He seemed to have shown that good sense and common judgment—not the peculiar attainments of genius, but the average capacity of men—when released and allowed to move naturally will produce right opinions. What more could be desired?—unless indeed it was the natural desire to act on those opinions. Natural *virtue*, Locke had not established; but it was to be added unto him.

Two revolutionary concepts about the universe resulted from the astronomical innovations of the seventeenth century and earlier: the ending of the notion that the universe is geocentric, and the revelation that the heavenly bodies are not made of incorruptible matter. From Locke's epistemology emerged two conceptions of comparable importance, about the nature of the human mind.

One was the proposition that men know, not reality, but their own impressions alone. "Truth," Locke goes so far as to say, "seems to me to signify nothing but the joining or separating of signs, as the things signified to agree or disagree one with another." Yet through the ages men had assumed that the object of knowledge is truth—the real truth, whether of objects proper or of the transcendent ideas which the objects represent. Locke, on the contrary, asserted that the essences of things are unknowable, that all we can know assuredly is the ideas within our own circle of consciousness.

John Norris, one of the most acute early critics of the *Essay*, thus states the problem: "I very much wonder that our Author professing in the Title of the Chapter to discourse of Truth in general, and particularly of that Truth too which has been the Enquiry of so many ages, should yet confine his Discourse to Truth of Words and Truth of Thoughts, without the least mention of Objective Truth. Which indeed is the principal kind of Truth." [16] This, to be sure, is quite unfair to Locke, whose entire study was inspired by the rectification of opinion, of the ideas of truth. Norris is referring to the fact that, in the new epistemology, truth as an objective fact which confronts him and in some measure exists within him has disappeared. "The very principle of reality was shifted to the subjective human consciousness." [17] The mind that cannot look out of its dark room, that sees only the pictures, must indeed know its impressions only as substitutes for "truth" as Norris thinks of it.

Hence we see the importance of the mind's returning to the impressions that are closest to the world outside, the immediate, subrational sensations which Locke called the "simple ideas."

In the long run, literature also, whose object is the imitation of reality, was destined to undergo a shift of center. If truth is the joining or separating of signs, which represent ideas as impressions, then the study of truth is the study of experience within. This does not mean a flight from reality, but rather that the locus of reality must be found within rather than without. Locke's position is not to be confused with solipsism; the impressions of the mind—if we respect their integrity—may be presumed to have a high degree of correspondence with whatever is in nature, and we are not abandoned to completely private worlds. But our apprehensions of reality are private in another sense: our quality of awareness must be individual; and yet awareness is of the highest importance. It is not surprising that literature, from the eighteenth century on, has been drifting steadily toward contemplation of the world as seen by the mind rather than on "truth" per se; and, consequently, state of mind has assumed greater significance than objective fact. Nor is it strange that there has been an absorbing interest in abnormal conditions of the mind.

The paradox of what seems to be a subjective psychology in an age of objective science may be explained by several circumstances. First was the intense conviction that all nature is a great harmonious order, with each part operating according to simple, universal, and immutable laws. The natural world is no great cosmic dance or drama in which the individual participants may fail to perform their roles, but a machine, ideally constructed. The mind, as a part of that system, is assumed to be completely adapted to its physical surroundings. Yet, as Locke exclaims, of what strange ideas all men's brains are capable! This paradox is one of the great problems of the age, and is of the essence of Shandyism. Yet as an operating mechanism the mind is superb. Perhaps the personality is most completely natural, and therefore right and true, when it perceives, and when it is farthest from complex or abstract thought. The revival in the century of the ancient distinction between primary and secondary qualities, the latter belonging only to perception, far from upsetting the faith in the mind, finally became a proof of the divinely ordained adjustment of mentality to the great order. That our experience of color, heat, and the like should be purely subjective and yet reliable and predictable was evidence that man's nature has its own laws, as wonderful as those governing the movements of the planets.

St. Thomas Aquinas, describing this type of epistemology, rejected it, among other reasons, ". . . because the things we understand are the objects of science; therefore if what we understand is merely the intelligible species in the soul, it would follow that every science would not be concerned with objects outside the soul, but only with the intelligible species within the soul . . ." [18] Locke solves this difficulty in part by assuming that the mind deals directly with the "phantasms" rather than with "intelligible species" of things; in fact, he subjects the latter phrase to destructive criticism which seems to represent a triumph of common sense. Again, the experimental method, whereby the impressions of many individuals of a carefully controlled event can be compared, has negated the danger of subjectivism. But in the humanistic disciplines the prediction has not been without fulfillment, that concern is with things within rather than outside the soul.

The second point of the Lockian revolution concerned personal identity. Locke's opinion was that "*Self* is that conscious thinking thing, whatever substance made up of,—(whether spiritual or material, simple or compounded, it matters not)—which is sensible or conscious of pleasure and pain, capable of happiness or misery, and so is concerned for itself, as far as that consciousness extends" (*Essay*, II, xxvii, 17). The revolutionary force of the phrase in parentheses is evident, as well as the implication that the self "is concerned for itself" as its single nature. The pivot of the self, therefore, is the awareness of easiness or uneasiness, a state of mind rather than a single ego as a self-contained essence. Self, to use a modern expression, is a biological phenomenon. No enduring, unchanging soul is necessary to constitute the personality; the self is the understanding, the power of apprehending and responding in its dark room, together with the impressions as they group themselves or are grouped into patterns. The ego, therefore, is the sum of the matrix and of the simple ideas that come to it during the course of a lifetime—which is to say that the ego is constantly changing. If Socrates and the "present mayor of Queensborough" agree in identity of consciousness—that is, in the awareness of the same sensations—they are, Locke assures us, the same person. This was disconcerting enough, but, even worse (*Essay*, II, xxvii, 19):

> . . . if the same Socrates waking and sleeping do not partake of the same consciousness, Socrates waking and sleeping is not the same person. And to punish Socrates waking for what sleeping Socrates thought, and waking Socrates was never conscious of, would be no more of right, than to punish one twin for what his brother-twin did, whereof he knew nothing . . .

The germ of a new attitude toward penology, to mention only one problem of society, is here. Every phase of the traditional attitudes toward sin, immortality, and the nature of the soul would have to be reconsidered.

Above all, responsibility would have to be redefined. Before Locke, the soul was considered as engaging in a continuous negotiation with the world. It had within itself every potentiality, and could decide by its will whether to ascend or to descend in the cosmic hierarchy. It might weakly submit to the importunities and blandishments of the "lower" faculties such as the imagination, but it continued to have a separate and substantial and enduring individuality, as fixed and clearly marked as that of one of the atoms. Hamlet uses the word in this sense when he cries

> O heart, lose not thy nature; let not ever
> The soul of Nero enter this firm bosom: . . .

He certainly does not mean the "consciousness" of Nero, but the guilty ego, and the phrase may have a more heavily metaphorical character for us than it did for Shakespeare, to whom it meant an individual as representative of a separate, determinable type.

Locke in effect transferred the clear identity from the ego to the separate ideas, the simple impressions. They are the fixed elements, established as long as memory endures. The personality itself is a shifting thing; it exists, not throughout a lifetime as an essence, but hardly from hour to hour. For Socrates waking yesterday and Socrates today may be different, as the sensations which constitute the substance of consciousness, and therefore of personality, change. The oneness of the self is rather like that of a river, and in this sense "stream of consciousness" is an apt phrase, however poorly it may describe the actual process of experiencing.

Locke is a source of the phenomenon of modern thought which Joseph Wood Krutch has termed the "dissolution of the ego," wherein a "fluid" replaces a "hard core" individual personality. "The Christian, and to an almost equal extent the classic, conception of the 'persona' or the 'ego' seems to have been of a fully conscious unity, of a soul captain, born with us at birth and perhaps created by God. It is an ultimate, even *the* ultimate continuous reality persisting through time." [19] The word "persona" suggests an interesting ambiguity. The Latin word may mean "person," but again it may refer to a mask. So it may be an assumed character. In recent years the word has been applied to the fictitious personalities who are vehicles of Swift's satire. The question of identity was of great importance for Swift, and it haunts his creations—the "I" of *A Tale of a Tub*, Gulliver, Drapier. Who is the real Gulliver? At most he is an awareness continuing throughout the series of stories, but in each voyage he is, so to speak, re-created. He becomes a new being. Is the mask, the outward appearance, the reality, with no essential core behind it? Never, perhaps, after Locke has the problem of identity been really settled. It arises between us and our understanding of Milton's Adam and Eve. We think of them as beings that evolve, and we are fascinated by the subtle movement of experience we attribute to them. We can hardly think of them as beings guilty one moment, after being innocent a moment before, essences changed by independent action of the will; not so can we think of character.

For we have inherited Locke's rejection of the absolute decision. There is, he says, no will that makes decisions with splendid independence and authority. In line with Locke's opinions is the fact that such a writer as Proust, in the words of Krutch, "gives us the sense that the characters are not at any moment what they were at any previous time and that the conception which he first formed when he heard about them is much more enduringly real than the manifestations in the flesh which from time to time he encounters." [20] As in Locke, the impression is the enduring fact, and the theme of Proust is the recalling of impressions from memory into the arena of conscious awareness; as the unique impressions are recalled, an awareness of unique personality is built up in the mind. These impressions constitute individuality and enduring self. Proust, moreover, extends the dissolution of personality into the passions, which had been considered as entities. Love, he says, is no more than a succession of ephemeral states of mind. "The disintegration of the self," he remarks in an unpublished letter, "is a continuous death."

Goethe theorizes, in *Wilhelm Meister*, that the hero of a novel is more properly acted upon than acting. In other words, the response of the consciousness to its experiences, rather than those experiences objectively considered, is the proper subject of the writer. Let us consider, as a concrete example, the varying opinions of Hamlet. The transition from the kind of criticism represented by Dr. Johnson to Coleridge's theory is one from concern with the actions of a character in a situation, with primary interest in the moral consequences and values of those actions, to concern with the reactions of that character to a situation as it changes. The interest in public actions is succeeded by interest in states of mind of a sensibility, their sources, and the impressions felt within.

Coleridge himself reveals the opposition of views. Johnson, he points out, evaluates and condemns Hamlet's action in postponing his revenge when he sees the King praying; Hamlet's decision, according to the Johnsonian critique, is "atrocious and horrible." [21] On the contrary, Coleridge says, this action is merely "part of the indecision and irresoluteness of the hero," which in turn arises from the fact that Hamlet is a person in whom reflection is too strong. The criterion of the scene is the state of mind of the protagonist, rather than his own description of his motives. Coleridge's analysis, even in its phraseology, shows a Lockian ancestry. There is, we learn, a disorder of the apprehension. Hamlet suffers from deficiency in that immediate contact with primary impressions of reality that Locke feared: "the external world, and all its incidents and objects, were comparatively dim, and of no interest in themselves, and . . . began to interest only, when they were reflected in the mirror of his mind."

Such criticism demonstrates another facet of the dissolution of the ego. It does not involve the dissolution of personality; just as reality is not abolished but moved into a different locale, so personality does not cease to be. In a sense, "personality" is a modern conception. Just as the reduction of the earth to an insignificant speck in the new astronomy led to a great upsurge of interest in this same insignificant planet, so the reduction of the ego to inner responses led to an absorbing interest in the self as it was newly defined—in the individual being, a unique event as the older self could never be.

The characters of Shakespeare begin to step off the stage and to assume lives of their own outside the plays only after the revolution I have described. Attempts are made to reconstruct the early life of Hamlet, which Shakespeare neglected to describe in much detail: an enterprise that would have had little interest for audiences of the seventeenth century. Lady Macbeth is psychoanalyzed and Hamlet is studied as if he were the subject of a biography and not a play. To us, the heirs of Locke, Hamlet seems to *be* his mental history, and our interest focuses not on the public actions but on the states of mind producing those actions. To know the characters, we feel we must know the preconscious beginnings, the lurking impressions beyond the range of conscious thought, the motives below the level of reason, to be found in the totality of the fluid being. Above all, we desire to be carried out of our chambers of consciousness into another's, to *feel* his awareness of reality; and literature, better than any other medium, can make possible this vicarious experience by arranging the impressions so skillfully that we seem to be undergoing, from within another's dark room of perception, the sensations that go to make up another self.

It may be objected that much of what has just been said goes beyond Locke's own statements. Where do we find explicit study of the problem of what has *made* the character? The modern view, at least that of Freudians, Krutch remarks, is that "the character and the conduct of the individual depends, not upon his own free choice, but upon the experiences, traumatic or otherwise, to which he has been exposed and especially . . . those which he underwent in infancy."[22] To understand Locke's contribution to this opinion, which is characteristic of the modern world, we must turn to another side of his work. In the first versions of the *Essay*, Locke is exclusively taken up with the understanding, which he seems to treat as the center and dominating power of all consciousness to the point of being coextensive with it.

Yet even in the first edition of the *Essay* he intimates that there is something else in the mind. He states that children begin to receive simple ideas as soon as they live, perhaps even in the womb; those ideas remain in the memory and eventually influence adult behavior, though the mind awakens much later (*Essay*, II, i, 22). Norris pointed out the contradiction that this observation poses in Locke's theory of consciousness. Here we see a hint of the dilemma which was to become more and more important: consciousness is the essential condition of experience, but is it to be identified with awareness? Are there not deposited in memory ideas that emerge to affect our opinions and behavior, even though we may not remember having had such experiences, and even though the understanding has never dealt with them?

It must have seemed to Locke, in 1690, that he had reduced the complicated problem of the human mind to good sense and order. Questions that had long puzzled men's heads till they ached—the nature of reason in the soul, intellection, definitions of substance, and the like—had been simplified or swept away. The new model of the mind could give confidence to men as they went forward into the new age of intellectual freedom for which Locke was the spokesman.

Yet within so short a time as four years, Locke's correspondence shows, he began to realize that the new model was not complete. In the fourth edition (published 1700, although this part was written much earlier) appeared the celebrated chapter "Of the Association of Ideas." It transformed the nature of the work, and too often, even now, Locke's theory of the understanding is discussed without adequate recognition of the importance of this chapter. Locke had come to realize that the pictures in the dark room of the understanding do not always "lie so orderly" as could be desired, and we feel the stirrings of uneasiness about disorder in that narrow place.

Locke, of course, realized from the beginning that human thought is often inaccurate, obscure, confused. His purpose in writing the *Essay* was to lay the foundations for correction of opinion by showing how ideas, true and false, are really formed. He had attributed the common failures in ideation to lack of light, to failure to make careful distinctions between ideas, to remoteness from the source of all knowledge—sensation—to simple prejudice or failure to extend mental horizons, and to physical defects. All of these, except for the defects, could be corrected by energetic discipline. He had streamlined the concept of cognition, retaining a living power in the mind, although depriving it of independence and making it a plain, serviceable member of the community.

He appears to have understood later that the mind includes much more than the cabinet wherein understanding sits, making dispositions of and conclusions from its information. Round about this clearly outlined and brilliantly illuminated world is a murky land of ideas, dormant in memory and not subject to the control of the governor, yet very much a part of the total psyche. Locke faced this problem in the chapter on association which he defines as follows (*Essay*, II, xxxiii, 5):

> Some of our ideas have a *natural* correspondence and connexion one with another; it is the office and excellency of our reason to trace these, and hold them together in that union and correspondence which is founded in their peculiar beings. Besides this, there is another connexion of ideas wholly owing to *chance* or *custom*; ideas, that, in themselves, are not all of kin, come to be so united in some men's minds, that it is very hard to separate them; they always keep in company, and the one no sooner at any time comes into the understanding, but its associate appears with it; and if they are more than two which are thus united, the whole gang, always inseparable, show themselves together.

One important feature of this description is that the irrational—or, more precisely, unnatural—connections of ideas go together, are hooked so far as the mechanism of binding goes, in a manner similar to true ones: the trains of ideas, whether those of Bacon or of an eccentric humorist, associate and appear in the same way, and, as Locke pointed out, when one idea of the "gang" is recalled, the others, bound to it, come along. Again, no one is exempt; unfounded notions appear, not alone in the mind which is obviously deranged, but also in the solid and sane. Third, the associations of ideas are formed by or traced to external conditions over which we have no control. Locke's own examples show that these "shock" associations are usually the result of a unique episode rather than of habitual experiences. Fourth, these associations, having a life of their own, frequently come unbidden from their mysterious haunts into the illuminated realm of the understanding. When they do so, they may exert an irresistible influence on overt behavior. The incentives to action, as Locke says, are states of easiness or uneasiness. If these states are controlled according to real conditions, all is well, but the gangs from the mental underworld are likely to overturn the calmly ordered arrangements of the understanding.

The case histories (they must be among the very first, and it is only recently that we have had a name for them) which Locke presents are essential in appreciating his meaning. Many studies of melancholy had been made, with numerous examples of irrationality and madness. Locke's contribution was to trace these instances back to earlier experience, often to traumas incurred in childhood, rather than to demonic possession, physical disorder, judgment for sin, and the like. Locke cites the case of a man who, as a child, heard from a foolish maid stories which connect "ideas of goblins and sprites" with darkness. The result is that possibly "he shall never be able to separate them again so long as he lives, but darkness shall ever afterwards bring with it those frightful ideas, and they shall be so joined, that he can no more bear the one than the other." This association, made in early childhood through incidents the man has probably forgotten, is not truly an association producing "opinion," for the man may not be aware of having any notions on the subject, and he may in his understanding regard goblins as mere superstitions; yet he *is* uneasy in the dark.

In another example, a man associates his pain or sickness with a room in which he suffered; the connection is irrational; "yet when the idea of the place occurs to his mind, it brings . . . that of the pain and displeasure with it: he confounds them in his mind, and can as little bear the one as the other." Again, no conscious opinion, but a powerful association, lurking outside the lighted cabinet and producing a very real state of mind. Similar associations are, Locke fears, behind prejudices and superstitions, and are responsible for much unhappy history.

Reflection on the matter enhanced its importance. In the too often neglected *Conduct of the Understanding*, a later restatement, with some expansions, of the *Essay*, Locke gives a solemn warning that "this wrong connexion in our minds of ideas, in themselves loose and independent of one another," is so productive of evil, that "perhaps there is not any one thing that deserves more to be looked after." Here we encounter an authentic note of "modernism." From the elementary depth studies which Locke essayed to make, we can see that the old conception of lower faculties in revolt against the reason will not do. The wrong associations are a part of the history of what passes in man's mind, and we must reconstruct that history to find out the real causes of his mental malaise.

When Locke comes to consider what can be done about these wild complexes of ideas, he can only conclude that "When this combination is settled, and while it lasts, it is not in the power of reason to help us, and relieve us from the effects of it. Ideas in our minds, when they are there, will operate according to their natures and circumstances" (*Essay*, II, xxxiii, 13). With the last sentence, he deals the final blow to the traditional idea of the nature of personality and personal responsibility. His emphasis on environmental influences rather than on the inner will in the shaping of the self places him in the modern line. To "take care" of the association of ideas, we find, is a matter of seeing to it that the mind receives the right impressions, under the right circumstances; that is primarily a task for education, and it is no accident that Locke is a founder of modern pedagogical theory. To men who feel that society is sick and in need of a new start, it may appear, from these premises, that the solution is to bring up the child in the atmosphere of untouched nature, far removed from the contaminations produced by man.

It would seem almost inevitable that, after reaching this point, Locke should suggest that much could be done by way of fishing the associations out of the recesses beyond the immediate awareness, and subjecting them to the kind of historical reconstruction he makes in the case of the man who fears the dark. Then the false associations, inspected under the white light of understanding, might lose their despotic power. To take this step toward psychoanalysis, however, required almost two centuries.

It took a long time before an explicit theory of the unconscious emerged, even though it is implicit in Locke's discussion. Maurice Morgann made the point that character arises from a multitude of impressions which are outside the understanding. To appreciate the true nature of character—that is, the real motives of action—

is outside the scope of understanding alone. "The Understanding seems for the most part to take cognizance of *actions* only, and from these to infer *motives* and *character*; but the sense we have been speaking of proceeds in a contrary course; and determines of *actions* from certain *first principles of character*, which seem wholly out of the reach of the Understanding." [23]

Language, which is constructed to express the thoughts of the understanding, cannot communicate adequately the unique experience that constitutes character. The impression is "the separate possession of each, and not in its nature transferable; it is an imperfect sort of instinct, and proportionably dumb." "The reader will perceive," he emphasizes, "that I distinguish between *mental Impressions* and the *Understanding*." One consequence is the significant rejection of the theory of ideal imitation. Morgann considers most literature relating to character as unsound. The understanding loves the general and the logically organized. But these are the least satisfactory ways of dealing with the deeper and truer motives of human behavior. Morgann emphasizes the minute and the unique in opposition to the universal and the central. He makes the important point that a playwright who really succeeds—the model, of course, is Shakespeare—deals less in words than in symbolic action—tones and looks, images that convey to our instinct a different meaning from the ostensible one obvious to the understanding.

Another work that shows how the association of ideas would revolutionize literary theory and ultimately production is Walter Whiter's *A Specimen of a Commentary on Shakespeare . . . An Attempt to Explain and Illustrate Various Passages, on a New Principle of Criticism, Derived from Mr. Locke's Doctrine of the Association of Ideas* (1794). As the title indicates, and as Whiter specifically asserts, he goes to Locke directly for the meaning of association and has nothing to do with the associationist psychology of the followers of Hartley. This point is worth making, for it illustrates what is too often forgotten: the work of Hume, of Hartley, and of later theorists did not by any means entirely antiquate the *Essay Concerning the Human Understanding.* As Sterne proves, we must frequently return to Locke himself.

Whiter suggests that the "gangs" of ideas outside the understanding are important to the work of a creative writer. The theorists have taught us that association "operates on the faculties by a kind of fascinating control, which we sometimes cannot discover, and which generally we are unable to counteract." [24] This revelation has, however, remained mostly in the realm of pure theory; Whiter is trying to bring the action into relation with concrete realities. He does so by trying to unravel the associations, of which the writer himself was probably unaware, that a discerning observer may discover.

Whiter is torn by a division of allegiance, beyond which Morgann had succeeded in passing. Whiter is convinced that the greater a poet is, the more he will drop the minute and the unique, and depict the "broad and general views of our condition." Yet he is aware of, and devoted to, exactly those unique personal experiences which elude a contemptuous understanding. The problem that he does not solve is that of the value of these associations. The associations, he assures us, are not identical with the imagination regularly at work. Yet they form a valuable auxiliary to imagination.

Shakespeare, he says, must often have seen tapestries representing, in "wild and motley spectacles," stories from history, romance, and mythology.[25] Although the bard must rationally have been little pleased with these coarse and preposterous objects, yet they must have influenced him—he being unaware of how they found their way into his images. They would, despite their shortcomings, have enriched "the stores of his fancy with wild and original combinations, with a splendid train of lively and various imagery," and could "impart to his descriptions certain traits of a precise and definite colouring, which are adventitious and accidental, rather than general and characteristic, which belong rather to the impressions of the eye, than to those abstract and universal conceptions that are formed by the contemplation of the mind." This suggests Locke's respect for the visual simple idea, in and of itself.

This is, Whiter says, a new principle of criticism, but he never realizes its possibilities, and not until recent years have they been fully utilized by Shakespeare critics. Whiter himself applied the method only to detection of forgeries—the success of which was somewhat diminished by his acceptance as genuine, on the basis of image clusters, of Chatterton's Rowley poems. He never feels that in this deep and unique working of the mind is the true principle of imagination, or that in it are to be found symbolic projections which reveal truth inaccessible to the understanding.

The picture of the mind that emerges from Locke's discussion and that lies behind the essays of such writers as Morgann and Whiter is effectively described by E. S. Dallas, many years later.

> Outside consciousness there rolls a vast tide of life, which is, perhaps, even more important to us than the little isle of our thoughts which lies within our ken. . . . The thing to be firmly seized is, that we live in two concentric worlds of thought,—an inner ring, of which we are conscious, and which may be described as illuminated; an outer one, of which we are unconscious, and which may be described as in the dark. Between the outer and the inner ring, between our unconscious and our conscious existence, there is a free and a constant but unobserved traffic for ever carried on. Trains of thought are continually passing to and fro, from the light into the dark, and back from the dark into the light. When the current of thought flows from within our ken to beyond our ken, it is gone, we forget it, we know not what has become of it. After a time it comes back to us changed and grown, as if it were a new thought, and we know not whence it comes.[26]

Dallas, a pioneer in the use of the word "unconscious," develops a theory of creation that is rooted in Locke's division of the mind, and that adumbrates the "deep well of unconscious cerebration."

Critics have wondered why Locke did not refer to predecessors who dealt in association, notably Hobbes, who had made the connections of impressions imposed by experience the very fact of thinking. Aside from Locke's fear of being connected with the irreligious Leviathan, there was good reason to believe that his principle was really new, however much it might superficially resemble the older one. For Locke's association is quite different from that of the mechanistic psychologists. Hartley and his followers in the eighteenth century exactly reversed the meaning of association; what was to Locke irrational and outré became for the mechanists the central fact in rationality. Experience for Locke is not a mere automatic connection of impressions, as if an adding machine were being set up. He always has the sense of a living being, with inclinations of its own, responding in a myriad of ways to a world which affects it in as many ways. In the center is an autonomous organizing power; but its area is not sharply defined, and its boundaries expand and contract with the exigencies of the creature's total response to its ever-changing environment. The personality is potentially the whole of its experience, existing in a state of constantly shifting tensions.

The necessitarianism so characteristic of mechanistic psychology has no part in Locke's system. Rather, he puts the problem of freedom on a new foundation. The mind is neither absolutely free nor absolutely conditioned; but decision is a product of the vastly complex relationships among the facts of experience, modifying and influencing a living, acting power. The mind is neither a spirit existing within the body nor a mere machine, but the active, intelligent instrument of a complex organism.

The account of association is not complete unless we appreciate the force of Locke's frequent use of language and images that suggest ideas acting of their own volition. If associations are made outside consciousness, and remain passively in memory awaiting a call, the unconscious is limited. But Locke implies that the associations are far more complicated. He does give a physiological explanation for these combinations, but mostly he writes as if ideas were experienced from within. And from within, these combinations appear to be a voluntary "ganging"; in this sense, I suspect, he meant "association," and preferred the word to "combination." In *The Conduct of the Understanding,* he describes playful, "frisking" ideas that "set up an annoying chiming in our heads." An obsession may seize upon us, he adds, like the sheriff with his posse. To the experiencing consciousness, ideas seem to be endowed with autonomy; one "comes into the understanding" and the others, his associates, insist on coming along. A backstairs clique is intriguing, or perhaps merely having fun, while the serious work proceeds in the cabinet. This description of unconscious associations as vital is one of Locke's most fruitful suggestions for literature. Because of his sense of the living activity of the mind in all its phases he was far more useful to the writer and critic than were the mechanistic associationists.

Locke had made necessary a new kind of thinking and creating for the artist, the critic, and the theorist. As the eighteenth century progressed, it became more and more evident that the very foundations on which Western art had been founded were no longer adequate. It was as if a building were moved to another site and onto another foundation. Some beginnings of the new foundation are the subject of the ensuing chapters.

II THE ORIGIN OF THE "MORAL SENSE"

Locke intended to establish knowledge and opinion on firm foundations. His interest, like that of Bacon, was to relieve man's estate. He hoped to diminish the many evils and follies from which men had so long suffered, because of the luxuriance of their fancies and the pride of abstract and unfounded reasoning. Nothing, he came to realize, was more important than to show them how they think, how thinking matches the investigation of nature, and how dangerous it is to go beyond the certain material of experience.

It was natural that Locke, almost like his own example of the man who is absorbed in the play he witnesses within the narrow room of the understanding, should have been absorbed in studying one aspect of the mind. If only the mental life could be restricted to the precise operations of the unbiased understanding! But Locke could not ignore the area of associations that lie beyond conscious control, and their enormous importance. He was perforce led to construct "a history of what passes in a man's mind"; and the century that followed was to inherit this problem.

Concentrating on the understanding, and limiting it to cognition and opinion, produced another complication. Explaining how we know and how we arrive at opinions of fact, Locke never accounted for the sense of *value*. Previously, knowing and valuing had been similar functions. "Racio," according to *Bateman upon Bartholome*, "deemeth and judgeth betweene good and evill, truth and falsenesse." The relationship between these judgments is very close.

The understanding, in Locke, is a perceiving instrument which is capable of great efficiency—within a severely restricted field. What it perceives is empirical fact. How we happen to have a conscience, however, he never explained. The spring of action he placed in a sense of "easiness" or "uneasiness" of the mind as a biological whole, rather than in a determinative will acting as an autonomous agent and instructed by the sovereign of the mind, the reason. But if the understanding is only a determiner of opinion, if it is concerned with general probabilities only, how can we bring it into relation with the immediate situations of life and explain the direct incentives to action?

Locke explained the moral imperative in two ways. First, there is the reward and punishment of a future life, which any sober man will consider, as well as the opinion of society (*Essay*, II, xxviii, 8; also II, xxviii, 5). Besides the primary penalties-and-rewards motivation, there is a possibility of determining moral values by correct reasoning from the relations of things as perceived by the senses (*Essay*, II, xxviii, 10). Yet this determination is but theoretical; Locke was uneasily aware that the customs and beliefs of various societies show an incredible variety.

When Molyneux urged him to write a system of ethics demonstrated with mathematical certainty by reason alone, Locke begged off, asserting that we already have a perfect body of ethics in the Gospel. While moral knowledge is "as capable of real certainty as mathematics," Locke himself gives away the dilemma when he says that these moral ideas are archetypes only (*Essay*, IV, iv, 7). How can these archetypes be brought into relation to the self-interest that motivates human action? How can the apparently spontaneous, self-denying action be explained? Is it only self-interest, cleverly disguised by nature?

Again, what gives emotional drive to a decision, one justified by philosophical reflection? We suspect that even the philosopher, having reasoned himself into virtue, would not be very strongly motivated by an abstraction. In the older model of the mind, the reason guided the autonomous will, which in turn was both affected by and appointed to rule the emotions; these, in turn, supplied energy for action. Pope, in the *Essay on Man*, gives an image of the process:

> On life's vast ocean diversely we sail,
> Reason the card, but Passion is the gale;
>
> . . . .
>
> Passions, like Elements, tho' born to fight,
> Yet, mix'd and soften'd, in this work unite:
>
> . . . .
>
> Suffice that Reason keep to Nature's road,
> Subject, compound them, follow her and God.

Many if not most moralists of the century on occasion revert to this old hierarchical image of the personality. Yet, after Locke, it seems anachronistic. The mind responds in specialized ways, Locke implies, and understanding tends to be isolated from the awareness which impels to action. There is no immediate contact with higher truth and value, those "fundamental notices" not derived from any sensation, which guarantee that the honest man is sustained by a divine certitude.

Is man by nature good or bad? Locke's epistemology implies that he is neither. Although, as his own writing on the social contract shows, he had a rather optimistic view of human potentialities, his conception of the mind represents it as, intrinsically, neither moral nor immoral. The mind serves no transcendental end, and is conditioned by its experience, over which it has no control. Thus religion is useful. Clearly, the neutral moral potentialities of mankind require positive direction which ordinary experience cannot give. Locke regards the Scriptures as a body of instructions, made effective by threats of punishment and promises of rewards. His literalness, his practicality, and his sociological piety remind us of the legalistic interpreters of the Koran.

Yet even Locke thought of the "state of nature" as a rather pleasant one. By the end of the seventeenth century, there were growing doubts in regard to the traditional doctrine of original sin. To be sure, such preachers as Tillotson, Barrow, and Burnet could speak of the inherent depravity of man in terms that recall the sternest orthodoxy.[1] Yet Tillotson was a modernist for his time, and more often stressed the potentialities for good in human nature. Another Latitudinarian, Isaac Barrow, thus describes the natural virtues:

> . . . the wisest observers of man's nature have pronounced him to be a creature gentle and sociable, inclinable to and fit for conversation, apt to keep good order, to observe rules of justice, to embrace any sort of vertue, if well managed; if instructed by good discipline, if guided by good example, if living under the influence of wise laws and virtuous governours.[2]

Here is the germ of the Enlightenment's faith in perfectibility. The emphasis is on environment—the external influences. Salvation comes from without; the problem is to see that the personality grows along its native lines rather than to cure by supernatural means a spiritual evil. This becomes clear from Barrow's description of the causes of evils: "Fierceness, rudeness, craft, . . . do grow among men (like weeds in any, even the best soil) and overspread the earth from neglect of good education; from ill conduct, ill customs, ill example . . ."

There are, of course, many reasons for so drastic a reversal of attitude on this vitally important question. Perhaps the most important reason lay in a sweeping rethinking of the whole question of the natural world. Such a rethinking had been under way for some time. Neo-Platonism represents one aspect; the assertion that evil is only a negation of good softened the reality of evil. The second Lord Brooke's *The Nature of Truth,* with its description of evil as little more than illusion, shows what results this kind of thinking could produce.

But Neo-Platonism, despite its softening of the harshness of evil, still maintained the older opinion that ascent to the true and the good requires a purgation from the material element. The new philosophy, however, more and more tended to describe the physical universe as complete and harmonious in itself; it is not to be transcended, and it is not merely the first rung on a ladder of spiritual ascent. The system itself represents the *raison d'être* of nature, and the process described in natural law is itself the final cause of existence, rather than a means to the end.

This conception of the universe brings the corollary that the human being, as an operating part of the great whole, will fit harmoniously into the system if he behaves "naturally." Once the mind has been absorbed into nature, it takes on characteristics of the natural world; and when the cosmic order appears as a marvelously and perfectly contrived machine, each part working precisely with every other part, the mind too must appear as natural and (to use a modern term which had to be invented to express a new attitude) "normal": at least it is potentially normal, and departures from the norm are maladjustment rather than willful sin. The emphasis is on environment rather than on a hereditary tendency to disobey and to forget God, to yield to the temptations of a "lower" part of the cosmos as represented by the physical.

The epistemology of Locke could superficially be adapted (although not with his approval) to this evolving attitude toward human nature. As early as 1697, suggestions of such an adaptation appeared. Thomas Burnet (the Master of the Charterhouse, not the Bishop) had devoted his career to reconciling the new philosophy with Christianity. In *The Sacred Theory of the Earth*, he had attempted to show that a Cartesian philosophy of physics could account for both the Flood and the final destruction of the present earth without recourse to miracles.[3] Providence, he explained, is virtually synonymous with natural law.

Burnet's theory of human nature was described by implication in the *Ancient Archaeology*, written to defend the *Sacred Theory* against its many opponents. The accounts of the creation and fall of man, he said, were fables, children's stories, adapted to the apprehension of mankind in its childish new beginnings after the fall. And the fall itself may have been a gradual decline in society, rather than a sudden change in all mankind.

Burnet was disturbed by the fact that Locke's system left man morally neutral, dependent on arbitrary revelation for the understanding of right and wrong; again, Locke had eliminated from the mind the innate knowledge of God's existence.[4] As a pupil of the Cambridge Platonists (he admired and followed Cudworth), Burnet was convinced that the mind of man is an image of that of the Creator. Like the Cambridge Platonists, he could not believe that a Calvinistic doctrine of total depravity was consistent with this glorious condition; nor, on the other hand, could he believe that right and wrong are created by God's arbitrary fiat. There must be in the mind itself a "candle of the Lord" to cast light on the darkness of experience. This phrase of Whichcote's is an interesting touchstone. Locke uses it also; but for him it has only a technical meaning, referring to that light which illuminates the ideas so that the understanding can distinguish them, rather than to a spiritual and moral radiance which gives certainty in the dilemmas of life.

Yet Burnet, unlike his masters the Cambridge Platonists, could not readily find a transcendental source for that flame. He combined Whichcote and Locke, just as he had tried to combine Moses and Descartes in explaining the flood. He feels that he does not refute Locke so much as make good his shortcomings. The supranatural must be rediscovered as part of nature.

Could not Locke's own pattern be extended? The understanding is supposed to have the power of recognizing immediately that two and two make four; on the elementary level, it has the innate power of recognizing apparent differences between colors. If the mind has these powers, may it not also be able to see in complex ideas, representing human situations, the qualities of good and evil? May not value be perceived? The analogy was the more appealing because Locke had made knowledge a process of perception. May we not, then, perceive the difference between right and wrong by a kind of sensation, a function of an organism of the personality?

This I am sure of, that the Distinction, suppose of Gratitude and Ingratitude, Fidelity and Infidelity, . . . and such others, is as sudden without any Ratiocination, and as sensible and piercing, as the difference I feel from the Scent of a Rose, and of Assa-foetida. 'Tis not like a Theorem, which we come to know by the help of precedent Demonstrations and Postulatums, but it rises as quick as any of our Passions, or as Laughter at the sight of a ridiculous Accident or Object.[5]

Locke briefly took note of this pamphlet by stating that, once our understanding has arrived at the conclusion that there is a revelation from a good, just, and holy God, we have "all that reason and ground that a just and wise law can or ought to have." [6] In political theory, Locke conceived of a social contract which rests on a universal ability to reason and to arrive at right opinions in all matters, as well as to apply those conclusions. Yet, by a curious paradox, in moral theory he reverted to a reactionary, absolute-monarchy conception of duty. When we have established that there is a God and that He has issued a commandment, we have no business meddling with the "reason and ground."

Burnet developed his thesis in later pamphlets. Perhaps the clearest exposition is here:

This is the case we represent: Such a Principle as Natural Conscience, we say, is seated in the Soul of Man, as other original Principles are: which shew themselves by degrees, in different times, and differently accordingly to other circumstances. Whether you will call this Principle, *Knowledge*, or by any other name . . . is indifferent to us; but 'tis a Principle of distinguishing one thing from another in Moral Cases, without ratiocination; and is improveable into more distinct Knowledge. We can evidently distinguish *Red* and *Yellow* colours, and yet are at a loss how to define either of them, or to express their difference in words. And so in Tastes, Odours, Sounds, and other sensible qualities.[7]

This apparently is not so much an objection to Locke's theory as a complaint that he had not gone far enough. Thus Locke admits that "there are natural tendencies imprinted on the minds of men;

and that from the very first instances of sense and perception, there are some things that are grateful, and others unwelcome to them." In such a statement we have, I suspect, the seed of the moral-sense theory.

Here, in a very early form, the theory shows its characteristic and revolutionary features. It is completely divorced from ratiocination. In the traditional conception, conscience, as the etymology of the word indicates, was envisioned as an act of conscious reasoning and judging. From innate principles inscribed on the soul, the reason determines whether a certain action is good or bad. Locke himself, in commenting on Burnet's pamphlet, very correctly asked how a "power" can be a "knowledge." Moral philosophers from this time on increasingly spoke of conscience as a "sense"—truly a contradiction in terms. Again, the moral sense is located, it would appear, in what had been considered a "lower" part of the soul, for it is a way of sensation, the raw material of experience unworked by intellectual activity. Given Burnet's hypothesis, it would be difficult to say, with the older philosophers, that the *racio* which judges between good and evil may exist without the body; Burnet, denying the action of ratiocination, eliminates *racio* from moral activity altogether. From Burnet's position one could easily conclude that the understanding may intervene between the moral sense and its objects, and that the simple, instinctive awareness of good and evil, which should grow normally as the body itself grows, may be corrupted by elaborations of rational thought.

Why, then, if the sense of good and evil is immediate, is so much of human conduct evil? It is important at this point to correct a common misapprehension. The sentimental moralists, of whom Burnet may be the first, were not fatuous optimists, proclaiming that all is well and denying the existence of evil in men's action. Actually, they were keenly aware of the wrongs in society. Burnet, in his *Sacred Theory of the Earth,* was obsessed by the monstrous wickedness that had preceded the great Flood. But the explanations and solutions are novel: evil is found in external factors rather than in the intrinsic nature of man. One solution is hinted at in the passage quoted above: the moral sense grows, and, in the infancy of mankind, as in that of individuals, may be inadequate for complex matters. Locke's examples of peoples who do barbarous things without shame—those who eat their relatives, make human sacrifices, and the like—may be explained on such a principle. This idea is one source of the theory of the primitive mind. The eighteenth century was much taken with the notion of "pre-formation"—that living beings are present, as complete miniatures, in embryos, and need only to grow in size to become mature. So, perhaps, with a moral sense.

More important, the moral sense may be obscured, just as the sun may be hidden by clouds. Perhaps, Burnet suggests, one principle in human nature eclipses another, as self-interest may overcast the power of sympathy. May not reason itself sometimes trip up the moral perception? May not abstraction remove us from the immediate sense of real values? If this is true, man may have been most admirable in those periods of history when, having emerged from barbarism, he had not yet become a highly civilized, refined creature, living in an environment his reason had created.

The conflict of principles in human nature presents new problems. It is no longer possible to explain evil by assuming a rebellion of lower against high faculties, for the mind now appears to be compounded of various "senses," of which reason itself, metamorphosed and diminished into the understanding, is only one. The old model of the mind as a kind of army commanded by the reason is replaced by the idea of a group of specialists sharing responsibility. One controls the moral area; another, that of self-preservation, involving knowledge of the external world; and it is logical to add a third, which would respond to beauty. If, from birth, man is exposed to the natural shaping experiences, these "powers" will, like the planets in their orbits, operate in beautiful harmony. Per contra, since no central reason and will can be assigned blame for dislocation in the balance of powers, it must be the shaping experience that goes awry when there is disorder. The shaping of the mind by nature is Wordsworth's theme in *The Prelude:*

> Dust as we are, the immortal spirit grows
> Like harmony in music; there is a dark
> Inscrutable workmanship that reconciles
> Discordant elements, makes them cling together
> In one society. . . .[8]

The "workmanship" is, of course, the "means which Nature deigned to employ," a "ministry" of beauty and of fear.

The moral sense is for Burnet a naturalized version of what Cambridge Platonists, among them Henry More, called a "boniform faculty"—a "faculty of that divine Composition, and supernatural Texture, as enables us to distinguish not only what is simply and absolutely the best, but to relish it, and to have pleasure in that alone." But, More emphasizes, the "eye of the Soul," if it exists in all of us, nevertheless is covered by a veil of the material, and only by spiritual perfection can that veil be removed. When More speaks of "seeing" in spiritual terms, he uses a metaphor common to poets of mystical experience. Burnet, however, makes the metaphor a literal fact.

So More considers the moral vision, the immediate perception of good and evil, to be the final rather than original state. For Burnet, on the contrary, the moral vision is the primal, the truly natural endowment of man. To keep in the course of nature rather than to ascend to a state above nature is, then, the duty of mankind.

Burnet may, in terms of strict historical priority, deserve credit for originating the notion of a moral sense. As far as influence is concerned, however, the third Earl of Shaftesbury was undoubtedly the pioneer. This young man, inspired with an ardor for nobility, virtue, and spirituality which recalls the Cambridge Platonists in its idealism, was repelled by what he considered to be the degradation of man's nature that Locke's ideas suggested. Despite the intimate connection of Locke with the Shaftesbury line, the Earl expressed his abhorrence in violent terms.

> 'Twas Mr. Locke that struck at all fundamentals, threw all order and virtue out of the world, and made the very ideas of these (which are

the same as those of God) *unnatural,* and without foundation in our minds. *Innate* is a word he poorly plays upon; the right word, though less used, is *connatural.* For what has birth or progress of the foetus out of the womb to do in this case? The question is not about the *time* the ideas entered, . . . but whether the constitution of man be such that, being adult and grown up, at such or such a time, sooner or later . . . , the idea and sense of order, administration, and a God, will not infallibly, inevitably, necessarily spring up in him.[9]

What Shaftesbury wanted was assurance that, in the course of normal experience, the ideas of God, order, and the rest will spring up in the mind, and without the kind of "ratiocination" that Locke considered necessary. He wanted to be assured that the stream of impressions will shape themselves into the great moral ideas, without conscious effort or willed action. Clearly, Locke's understanding could not be the agency.

The issues Locke had raised could not, whatever one might think of Locke's own epistemology, be dismissed. The bogey of relativism had come to stay. "Thus virtue, according to Mr. Locke, has no other measure, law, or rule, than fashion and custom; morality, justice, equity, depend only on law and will, and God indeed is a perfect free agent in his sense; that is, free to anything, that is however ill . . ." [10] The eternal rightness of things, and the human participation in that rightness, must be reëstablished, but Locke had not shown the way.

Yet knowledge of good and evil must be accounted for just as any other knowledge derived from sensation. Shaftesbury does not go back to the Cambridge Platonist's *mens,* to a transcendent intuition of the mind; on the contrary, he follows the path already laid out by Burnet. Shaftesbury's initial attempt at a solution of the dilemma, in the first edition of the *Inquiry Concerning Virtue* is, however, more clearly based on Locke. It develops Locke's statement that one source of ideas is the mind's observation of and reflection on its own operations. Is there not an inner sense that responds to qualities as the physical sense responds to sensible characteristics?

In a Creature capable of forming general Notions of things, not only the sensible things that offer themselves to the sense, are the objects of the Affections; but the very *Actions* themselves, and the affections of Pity, Charity, Kindness, Justice, and so their contraries, being brought into the Mind by reflection, become Objects.[11]

He implies that a power, parallel to the understanding, responds to the actions, but this power is a "sense," for its response does not involve the perception of trains of ideas which is necessary to formation of opinion. In the following passage, the immediacy of reaction is stressed; the mind does not arrive at an opinion or formal judgment, but instantly "inclines to" or recoils from what it perceives.

And thus the several Motions, Inclinations, Passions, Dispositions, and consequent Carriage and Behavior of Creatures in the various Parts of life, being in several scenes represented to the Mind, which readily discerns the good and the ill towards the species or Public; it proves afterwards a new work for the affection, either virtuously and soundly to incline to, and affect what is just and right; and disaffect what is contrary; or, vitiously and corruptly to affect what is ill, and disregard or hate what is worthy and good.

Shaftesbury's account makes some advances on Burnet's pioneer statements. For one thing, the mechanism is described. Scenes appear before the mind; like a spectator at a play, the mind applauds or condemns as it observes the action before it. Here, perhaps, we see the beginning of a new attitude toward the drama. A function of a play may be to train the "sentiments" by presenting, realistically, scenes like the inner representations which reflection brings into the mind. The play then may serve to exercise and strengthen the moral sense. Diderot, who was especially influenced by Shaftesbury, called for a domestic tragedy that would perform such a function.

Thus, to use a term which philosophers influenced by Shaftesbury were to make famous, the awareness of right and wrong is manifested by a "reflex sense." A specific analogy with aesthetic impressions was added in later editions of the *Inquiry;* this was the version that was known to the eighteenth century.

The Case is the same in the *mental* or *moral* subjects, as in the ordinary *Bodys*, or common Subjects of *Sense*. The Shapes, Motions, Colours, and Proportions of these latter being presented to our Eye; there naturally results a Beauty or Deformity, according to the different Measure, Arrangement, and Disposition of their several Parts. So in *Behaviour* and *Actions*, when presented to our Understanding, there must be found, of necessity, an apparent Difference, according to the Regularity or Irregularity of the Subjects.[12]

Shaftesbury is following Locke in trying to make the understanding coextensive with the whole of the mental activity. But it is clear that the "understanding" of the Lockian type will have to be restricted in extent. Francis Hutcheson's essential contribution was to recognize this fact and to invent the phrase "moral sense." Shaftesbury at least dimly realized that the value area of the mind must constitute a world to itself, outside the process of cognition, and he suggested, with his aesthetic analogy for moral perception, that the response to goodness will be closely related with that to beauty. Finally, he had provided what seemed to be a sufficient explanation for the motivation of action—that drive toward the good —which Locke's picture of sterile consideration of ethical questions had left out.

In *The Moralists* Shaftesbury repeats the substance of this theory, and asks, "How is it possible therefore not to own, that as these Distinctions have their Foundation *in Nature*, the Discernment itself is *natural*, and from NATURE alone . . . ?" [13] There is no need for such a revealed law as Locke had required; the instrument of morality is within the make-up of the human being. The heart of the new kind of religion that Shaftesbury inaugurated is the idea that values and spiritual powers previously attributed to the supranatural are to be found within the natural order itself.

Culverwel, by contrast, in his *Discourse of the Light of Nature* (1652), sharply distinguishes the actions of the soul. Paraphrasing Lord Herbert of Cherbury, he says that it has "purer faculties" which "unclasp and disclose themselves, . . . being made in as harmonious proportion suitable to spiritual objects, as the eye is to colours, or the eare to sounds." When the soul comes down from the mount whereon it views the divine light, "it puts on the veile of sense, and so converses with material objects" (p. 94). The soul, he adds, "cannot sufficiently attend both to spirituals and corporeals." Shaftesbury's radical point is that attending to corporeals carries with it attending to spirituals. He has transferred to the "veile of sense" the glory from the mount; a new light shines over the world of everyday experience.

Thus was established the faith that in the unity of man there is

> One spirit over ignorance and vice
> Predominant, in good and evil hearts;
> One sense for moral judgments, as one eye
> For the sun's light.[14]

Yet the unity of man is everywhere broken. In the first edition of the *Inquiry Concerning Virtue*, Shaftesbury exclaims that, whereas we see all other creatures living in "so great a harmony, and such an adherence to Nature," man alone "lives at odds with his whole Species, and with Nature: so that it is next to a Prodigy to see a Man in the World who lives NATURALLY, and as A MAN." How can man be brought back to his lost harmony with nature? Is not nature —the external world, untouched by selfish human schemes—itself the means?

The development of the moral-sense theory was closely associated with another revolution. Perhaps the world of sensation provides a means of salvation for corrupted mankind. A mystique of nature accompanies Shaftesbury's ethical theory; and, as its instrument, a new kind of imagination evolves, another sense parallel to the other two powers of the mind. The steps whereby nature became a source of redemption and the imagination a means of grace may now be traced.

III THE RATIONALE OF THE "NATURAL SUBLIME"

Richard Glover, in his "Poem on Sir Isaac Newton" (1728), eulogized the great scientist as follows:

> . . . . from the darksome main
> Earth raises smiling, as new-born, her head,
> And with fresh charms her lovely face arrays.
> So his extensive thought accomplish'd first
> The mighty task to drive th'obstructing mists
> Of Ignorance away, beneath whose gloom
> Th'unshrouded majesty of Nature lay.

This is the mood of the early eighteenth century. Nature, obscured for centuries by the mists of scholastic ignorance, has once more been revealed in all her loveliness and majesty—a "spreading" scene, the vastness of the prospect giving evidence of its purity. The newborn earth thus revealed is transfigured, clothed in a radiance that rises to touch the heavens in the great mountains and in the endless horizon of the sea.

This transfiguration is to be taken as spiritual and moral. Glover, like the crowd of his fellow poets who "deified" Newton, saw in him the prophet of a new dispensation for the human race. Nature had become the symbol of a new hope and was to be the presiding myth of Western civilization for decades to come. How that myth arose, and how it achieved its vast import can be traced through a succession of writers beginning in the seventeenth century. In this chapter we shall be concerned with the emergence of the central image symbolizing that myth: the "great," later known as the "natural sublime." In succeeding chapters, the emergence of the "imagination" as the instrument of the new redemptive myth will be studied.

Among the currents of thought leading to the romantic preoccupation with the "sublime of nature" was physicotheology, which had already been given an institutional character by the Boyle Lectures. These endowed sermons, designed to prove from natural philosophy that a beneficent God created and sustains the universe, and to demonstrate the truths of Christianity from a study of nature, began with Bentley as preacher in 1692.

The ostensible and doubtless sincere purpose of the lectures was to defend a liberal but not very unorthodox Christian doctrine against the materialism which, it was feared, the scientific movement could encourage. The ultimate effect, however, was largely unintended. Unvarying emphasis on the evidences of divine idea perfectly realized in the laws of motion, gravity, the construction of animal bodies, and other phenomena, created a cumulative impression of the perfection and absolute completeness of nature. Here degree of emphasis is the key. Christian theologians had asserted that the "book of nature" demonstrates divine purpose in the universe, but that it was to be read in the light of the higher book, Revelation. An imperfection in the natural order, resulting from the fall, makes natural philosophy alone quite inadequate as the guide to heaven.

In the eighteenth century the emphasis gradually is reversed: the book of Revelation now is to be read by the light of stars and sun, and it is not surprising to find conservative church members, as if unaware of the significance of their actions, substituting communion with nature for communion in the sacrament. Elizabeth

Carter, for example, in a letter of 1762, remarks, "I am afraid I shall miss my church tomorrow, but the sea is to me a sermon and prayers, and at once doctrine and devotion." A reading of the letters she wrote over a long lifetime confirms the suspicion that the sea gave her far more vivid and powerful intimations of divinity than any she received in the parish church.

It is curious that the sea is "sermon and prayers." For the oceans had long been associated with the fallen state of mankind; the book of Revelation seems to promise that in the millennial earth they will no longer exist. Only a few years before Mrs. Carter wrote these lines, an active debate had raged as to how the seas had emerged—presumably as a consequence of the fall—and how they were to be eliminated in the redeemed world. This mystical attitude can hardly be attributed to the influence of physicotheology alone, although it helped prepare men to accept whatever is as right. We must look to another movement contributing to the formation of the myth of nature.

A word that had a hypnotic effect in the eighteenth century was "Immensity." Usually capitalized, it was like a bell calling the romantic age to devotions of natural religion. Moreover, it was the name not only of a quality, but of an object as well—the greatest object, the Deity. Here is Shaftesbury's expression of the idea: "Thy Being is boundless, unsearchable, impenetrable. In thy Immensity all Thought is lost; Fancy gives o'er its Flight: and weary'd Imagination spends itself in vain; finding no Coast nor Limit of this Ocean, nor in the widest Tract thro' which it soars, no one Point yet nearer the Circumference than the first Center whence it parted." [1]

Now a significant point is that anyone familiar only with the traditional language of mystics would be sure to miss Shaftesbury's meaning. Many who have aspired to identification with the divine have used this image; but it has always been a purely spiritual reality that they had in mind. The boundless immensity of God is said to be a "sea"—but a metaphorical sea, actually the nonmaterial supreme reality which one can attain only by transcending nature. Yet, we find on reading further, Shaftesbury is speaking of visible form. "In vain we try to fathom the abyss of SPACE, the Seat of thy extensive Being; of which no place is empty, no Void which is not full." "Immensity" then is "SPACE"; the ecstatic capitals indicate its divine and ineffable nature; space is spiritual and divine, and God is intermingled with the unlimited expanse of the firmament on high.

Behind modern man's obsession with the vast, the unlimited, and the suggestive rather than the sharply defined, is a long evolution of thought. The preoccupation with infinity was characteristic of the seventeenth century from the middle onward. Henry More voices the rapture that the conception of infinite space could elicit:

> Wherefore with leave th'infinite I'll sing
> Of Time, of Space: or without leave; I'm brent
> And all my spirits move with pleasant trembeling.[2]
> With eagre rage, my heart for joy doth spring,

More was by no means an exception; the idea of the unbounded was intoxicating to an age that exalted the individual, his will and power, even to infinity. The expansion of the physical universe represented by the new astronomy seemed to confirm the greatness of the human soul.

But yet "infinity" is not "Immensity." The transition is explained in Shaftesbury's description of space-Deity as the being in which no "one Point [is] yet nearer the Circumference than the first Center whence it parted." This is no mere effusion, but the statement of a powerful idea. The authors of the "negative theology," such as the extremely influential Dionysius the pseudo-Areopagite, had declared that the qualities of God are the opposite of anything we can know; for God, being infinite, must be the opposite of the limited and finite, and whatever is created is limited. We must accordingly be careful not to confuse attributes of the uncreated God with those of any created objects. There is no distinction in God's nature; in Him all opposites are reconciled, and His center is truly "everywhere and nowhere." When the mystic speaks of the "boundless sea" of God in which the limited self desires to be lost, he uses an image that represents the opposite of anything that actually exists; the physical image is only an imperfect way of hinting to the mind what reality is intended. Space, moreover, is no abyss, but is limited and bounded by the walls of a proportioned universe.

A first break with this dominant idea came in the fifteenth-century philosopher Nicholas of Cusa, who was a favorite of the Cambridge Platonists. His purpose was to reconcile God's immanence with His transcendence, through the attribute of the "unlimited." He regarded the universe, the sum of existing beings, as not the opposite of the infinite God, but His complement and (although necessarily imperfect) image. The infinite spirit, Nicholas reasoned, must have a concrete manifestation. The world of created things is not an emanation, a descent from the apex of divine perfection wherein the indwelling light is fainter on each level (as in Neo-Platonism); nor is it a workman's construction, evidence but by no means image of a planning mind (as in Augustine). Instead, it is an *explicatio* or unfolding of the divine essence. "So infinite truth," Nicholas wrote, "is the precision of finite truth; and absolutely infinite, the precision, measure, truth, and perfection of everything finite." [3]

Shaftesbury made an extreme statement of this idea. All originally existed, he says, in the Divine Mind, until "becoming productive, it unfolded itself in the various Map of Nature, and in this *fair visible* World." [4] The idea of pre-formation is, I think, suggested here. All the order of nature existed, as if in perfect miniature, in the Divine, until it grew into the universe which we behold and of which we are members.

What made speculations of this kind effective was the new cosmology. The image of the heavens after Copernicus did indeed represent an infinite universe. Perhaps it was Bruno who took the momentous step of fitting purely metaphysical opinion with the hypotheses of science. He may have been the one who identified the physical universe, which astronomers were beginning to envision as unlimited, with the metaphysical concept of unlimited divinity.[5] The traditional hierarchy of celestial spheres was quickly replaced by a universe of infinite or at least indefinite extent, having no center. Bruno could assert that the likeness of the divine cannot be attained any more completely by a man than by an ant, for the immutable levels of value, whereby one entity was proved to be more noble than another, inevitably vanished from a universe without "up" or "down." The magic word for the Middle Ages and the Renaissance was "ascent"; for the late seventeenth century, it is "comprehension." The desire to reach out into the vast universe, to comprehend quantitatively all its phenomena, to fly ever onward without barrier or end, is dominant. There may be a connection between the exaltation of liberty in politics and the vogue for immensity in philosophy and literature and painting.

The conversion of Henry More, that representative philosopher of the middle and later seventeenth century, illustrates the movement. In 1642, he still argues, with the negative theologians, that since only God can be infinite, the created world must have definite limits. But only four years later, "roused up by a philosophick Furie," he is transported by the conviction that both the world and time are infinite. A mystique of space appears. More is now convinced that wherever space is, there God must be; he equates the vast distances revealed by the telescope—the space in which planets seem to "float"—with the omnipresence of God. The nexus between the infinite Spirit and the world is space, or indefinite extension, independent of body. Thus spiritual omnipresence takes on a physical character, as in Shaftesbury's phrase "the Abyss of SPACE, the Seat of thy extensive Being."

The prospect of the heavens as seen through the telescope, which had been in use for less than half a century, had already produced an intellectual revolution:

> An inward triumph doth my soul upheave
> And spread abroad through endless 'spersed aire.
> My nimble mind this clammie clod doth leave,
> And lightly stepping on from starre to starre
> Swifter then lightening, passeth wide and farre
> Measuring th'unbounded Heavens and wastful skie.[6]

The revolution would not have occurred so suddenly, however, had the theoretical foundation not been laid. The *content* of a new idea was poured, so to speak, into the *form* of an older one, and the associations with the old belief became attached to the new. Thus the great traditional conception of an "anima mundi," Cudworth's "plastic spirit" of the universe, was transformed into that of a divine and yet *physical* omnipresence in space.

> . . . What ever is, is life and Energie
> From God, who is th'Originall of all;
> Who being everywhere doth multiplie
> His own broad shade that endlesse throughout all doth lie.[7]

Space, then, came to share some attributes of God. The empty places of the solar system took on a sacred character. An obscure country preacher, Ellis Bradshaw, in 1649 printed *A Week-daies Lecture, or Continued Sermon to wit, The Preaching of the Heavens,* which shows how great was the excitement over space mystique, even among the relatively uneducated. Bradshaw, in his simple enthusiasm for "place," "boundlesse, and unlimitable extensive, vastly circumventing, even the highest Heavens, beyond all thought, or imagination of man, or any finite being, and that on every side," anticipates the enthusiasm of Shaftesbury.

A powerful new idea had swum into the ken of Western man. The idea of absolute space in which bodies are located became, as E. A. Burtt remarks, "the true substitute, in terms of the geometrical view of the universe, for the Pure Form or Absolute Actuality of Aristotelianism." [8] But space, unlike the mysterious "Pure Form," is visible!—yet not so visible, so crassly material and solid, as to lack an ethereal quality.

How startling was the proposition that space is a visible divine attribute may be seen in an interchange of letters between More and Descartes. More explained his views as follows: "I maintain that the divine extension fills this space, and that your principle, that only matter is extended, is a false one; that as a matter of fact the sides [of a vase from which all the air has been pumped] would tend to meet by a natural, not an absolute necessity, and that only

God can prevent this meeting." [9] Descartes' reply clearly shows to what extent he clung, despite his atomism, to orthodoxy. "By an extended being one commonly means something which can be imagined," he says; but we must assume, of both the human soul and divinity, that "neither the one nor the other is subject to the imagination, but merely to reason, and one cannot separate them into parts, especially into parts which have magnitude and determinable shapes."

The new philosophy and the mystique of space demanded a new epistemology. Descartes spoke from the point of view of belief in innate ideas, and of reason as an intuitive, self-contained faculty. The conception of God must be purely spiritual and rational, and must be "uncontaminated" by the imagination, that is, by the physical sensations. Yet, as these quotations indicate, the enthusiasm about omnipresence does center in an "image." The idea of God, it would seem, arises from experience and is not given to the mind. The older epistemology was compatible with the old negative theology, with its premise that the mind cannot form a real image of God, that the infinite Deity is the un-"imagined" opposite of the finite, and that therefore no creature can derive from its worldly contacts alone any conception of the Supreme Being.

The crossing of this line—to the view that the whole idea of God arises entirely from sensory experience—is a momentous event. A preliminary step was to make the universe itself unlimited, an unfoldment of, rather than the opposite of, the infinite Deity. But the exact way in which the idea of God arises in the mind needed further explanation. Here again Locke served as purveyor of method. The essentials of his system were by no means new; but to get from scattered theories to specific process is a long step. To describe that process, Locke, with his meticulous, neat, above all common-sense understanding of the mind, was ideally suited. He accounted for a process that had been considered impossible: the way in which the idea of an infinite and transcendent and yet immanent Creator could arise from limited sense impressions. (This proposition must be distinguished from the commonly accepted point that contemplation of nature will confirm the innate idea of God; the origin of an idea is quite different from additional proof.) The necessity of revelation as a source of the idea of God is also in effect eliminated. The existence of revelation is, in fact, shown by the mind's prior reasoning.

Locke appeals to "every man's thoughts, whether the idea of space be not as distinct from that of solidity, as it is from the idea of scarlet colour?" (*Essay*, II, xiii, 11). Extension, then, must have an existence independent of that of bodies. With the epistemological difficulties in this statement we are not concerned. (It is hardly necessary to point out that modern physics has antiquated such a hypothesis.) Most interesting at present is the fact that Locke can appeal to common experience as authority for a notion which was established by cultural action, not by universal conclusion. What he assumes to be the common idea would not have been obvious to anyone a hundred years earlier, for, in the Aristotelian-medieval view, space and extension of objects are identical; and Locke could have had some difficulty with Hobbes, who held that space is a mere "fantastical," imaginary quality of bodies.

Yet, the new idea had gained such wide acceptance that Locke could seem to prefer common experience to "metaphysical subtlety," with the implication that the plain honest man is worth a dozen elaborate theorists. "For I would fain meet with that thinking man that can in his own thoughts set any bounds to space, more than he can to duration, or by thinking hope to arrive at the end of either; and therefore, if his idea of eternity be infinite, so is his idea of immensity; they are both finite or infinite alike" (*Essay*, II, xiii, 21). What is more "natural" than to think of the heavens as going on forever? Both Newtonian and Lockian systems owed much of their success to the enthronement of common notions. It seems obvious, once we consider the matter, that our minds somehow look directly at their impressions, and then proceed to construct combinations. Even the distinction between primary and secondary qualities—between appearances, like mass and form, which represent qualities that are really "there" in matter, and those, like color and odor, which seem to be subjective effects only —proves to be less upsetting than might be supposed. Few people have failed to notice vaguely some difference between the flickering of light, a possible unreality of color, and the apparent solidity of shape and mass.

Locke formalized and clarified the inchoate observations that had been made. By extending indefinitely impressions such as those of space, and then joining those impressions, we form the complex idea of God (*Essay*, II, xxiii, 35):

For it is infinity, which, joined to our ideas of existence, power, knowledge, &c., makes that complex idea, whereby we represent to ourselves the best we can, the Supreme Being. For though in his own essence (which certainly we do not know, not knowing the real essence of a pebble, or a fly, or of our own selves) God be simple and uncompounded, yet I think we may say we have no other idea of him, but a complex one of existence, knowledge, power, happiness, &c., infinite and eternal . . . originally got from sensation and reflection.

"Originally got from sensation and reflection" and "whereby we represent to ourselves . . . the Supreme Being"—these are the key phrases. For Locke's "ideas" always have a visual quality. If we do not "see" an idea, we do not really have it. Unlimited space, now revealed as the source of the greatest of ideas, naturally assumed a new dignity. Bishop Berkeley wrote that Joseph Raphson, the mathematician, in *De Spatio Reali seu Ente Infinite*, "pretends to find out fifteen of the incommunicable attributes of God in space." [10] Berkeley was concerned because this deification of space had become the fashion. Similar catalogues of divine attributes —even more extravagant—were associated with space in such works as More's *Enchiridion Metaphysicum*.

An amalgamation of ideas centering in a symbol thus takes place. In the mysterious depths of limitless space we see a kind of ethereal substance which is an attribute of the Deity. There is a meeting of supranatural and natural. "Immensity" is not a mere metaphor of incommunicable spiritual reality, but a physical-spiritual datum of experience. More exclaims:

That the perpetual Observation of this infinite Amplitude and Mensurability, which we cannot disimagine in our Phancy but will necessarily be, may be a more rude and obscure Notion offered to our Mind of that *necessary* and *self-existent* Essence which the *Idea* of God does with greater fulness and distinctness represent to us. . . . Whence, as I said before, the *Idea* of God being such as it is, it will both justly and necessarily cast this ruder notion of *Space* upon that Infinite and Eternal Spirit which is God.[11]

More, at heart a Neo-Platonist even in his enthusiasm for the new philosophy, thinks of the impression of immensity as a first rung on a ladder, a "rude and obscure Notion" from which we may ascend to a fuller and more spiritual idea of God. What Locke does is to cut off the top of the ladder. The "ruder notion of Space" is not merely the beginning of the idea of God, to be exalted and purified, but the very fullness of that idea itself so far as we may have it.

Sir William Jones, the Orientalist, may serve as a representative of Locke-influenced thought on this subject. In a translation of the "Hymn to Narayena" he anticipates a common practice of nineteenth-century romantics—reading the nature mystique into Oriental religious ideas. He represents God as the Being

> . . . who through ev'ry part
> Of space expanded and of endless time,
> Beyond the stretch of lab'ring thought sublime,
> Bad'st uproar into beauteous order start . . .

It is doubtful that "space expanded" fits Hindu concepts very closely. God, it appears, exists in a definite, physical immensity which is co-eternal with Him and therefore a quality of Him. And eternity has been calmly identified with infinite time in a manner quite foreign to otherworldly philosophy and religion. The tone is more Miltonic than Hindu; for Milton, apparently influenced by More, represents God as saying that He is the Being who "fills infinity, nor vacuous the space." Jones, moreover, suggests the depersonalization of God: He is "impervious, inaccessible, immense." Nature was to become a means of conquering the inaccessibility.

Berkeley was not the only one who objected to the deification of space and, by extension, the glorification of nature. Samuel Clarke, though an advocate of the new philosophy, was shocked by "the Weakness of such, as have presumed to imagine *Infinite Space* to be a just Representation or adequate idea of the Essence of the Supreme Cause." [12] The reason he gives for the error is significant: men fancy any substances "not Objects of their Corporeal Senses, to be, as it were, mere Nothings."

Here is the crux. As Newton observed, a thing to be real must have some kind of physical existence: "since every particle of space is *always,* and every indivisible moment of duration is *everywhere,* certainly the Maker and Lord of all things cannot be *never* and *nowhere.*" [13] This dismissal of the negative theology which had been closely interwoven with religious feeling for many centuries could, obviously, have led to extreme pessimism and disillusionment. As the universe became impersonal, material, terrifyingly vast and empty, it would seem that there *must* have been a breakdown of the sense of value in the cosmos, and of confidence in the dignity of man. Yet there was no Leopardi, no Melville, no Thomas Hardy in the eighteenth century, and it was biology rather than astronomy that produced nineteenth-century pessimism. The great crisis of change from an anthropocentric and geocentric cosmology, with a supranatural theology, to the Newtonian world machine produced no great spiritual upheaval. In this critical period of transition, a major support of confidence was the emergence of the ideas I have described. The delicate operation of moving the locus of divinity to nature was accomplished with wonderful ease and speed.

The deification of space and the glorification of nature may have served another purpose, less important but still large. The rise of nominalism, represented by the image of a universe of endless atomistic events, presented a problem of sheer monotony, with no one thing or event more noble, more important—or more interesting—than another. Immensity and eternity gave at least the illusion that supreme values were to be found in the endless continuum of commonplace thoughts and petty, selfish purposes which came to constitute the laissez-faire society. The natural sublime served to validate the actions of life, and thus took its place along with the idea of progress as a psychological prop of Western society.

The new ideas became viable with great speed, thanks to a remarkable series of developments in the arts, especially in literature. An imaginative symbolism was necessary to render usable the myth of nature, to bring it into immediate relationship with human thought. The process by which that projection was accomplished can now be traced.

The first stage was to extend the conception of infinity of space as a divine attribute to objects that give an *impression* of infinity. This extension gave a symbolic form to the idea of infinity and solved the problem of accounting for the great but terrifying phenomena of mountains, storms, and the like. To Christian thinkers, much—even most—of the earth had seemed alien and dangerous to man. Living in a world originally intended for his use and benefit, he must have committed a great fault to merit his present surroundings. The message of the new revelation, however, is that the universe is the unfoldment of God's original model. If man is a part of that great harmony, he must view the world in a new light. Western Europe, beginning with English thinkers, found a moral and spiritual use for mountains, waste places, and storms. Within half a century after Milton had described the curse upon nature that followed the fall, occurred

> the change from an age when men frankly hated and feared all those things in Nature which are neither sensuously pleasing, useful, safe, symmetrical, or gaily coloured, to an age when men love and actually seek out mountains, waste places, dark forests, cataracts, and storm-beaten coasts. What was once the ugly has become a department (even the major department) of the beautiful.[14]

In a morally and spiritually harmonious world, mountains and seas are images of God's being constantly before human eyes. They serve a purpose of the utmost importance; the awe, the very terror which they arouse, evokes emotions akin to those which the Supreme Existence itself should cause; their immensity evokes the concept of Immensity itself; and their horror and grandeur are immediate evidence—not merely symbols—of the existence and irresistible power of the merciful Creator.

Perhaps the feeling for the "great" emerges first in Thomas Burnet's *Sacred Theory of the Earth.* According to his theory, the earth originally was a paradise, with a smooth and unobjectionable skin marred by neither mountains nor oceans. In time, however, as corruption of human society increased, the earth (purely by natural process) dried out; eventually, just when sin reached its peak, a great eruption of the waters below the earth caused the Biblical flood. The mountains and oceans which came into being bear evidence that the present earth is but a "ruin." Formally, Burnet retained the Renaissance ideals of proportion and symmetry as necessary components of beauty. The landscape of the Alps will never do. But with what delight and enthusiasm he contemplates the "ruin"!

And yet these Mountains we are speaking of, to confess the truth, are nothing but great ruines; but such as show a certain magnificence in Nature . . . Look upon those great ranges of Mountains in *Europe* or in Asia . . . in what confusion do they lie? They have neither form nor beauty, nor shape nor order, no more than the Clouds in the Air.[15]

"A certain magnificence in Nature"—why, if they have neither form nor beauty? The reason Burnet gives in a passage that makes us feel we have passed over the line into a new sensibility, and that here, in the time of Dryden and Wren, romanticism appears in embryo, like those of pre-formation theories, a miniature of what was to come.

The greatest objects of Nature are, methinks, the most pleasing to behold: and next to the great Concave of the Heavens, and those boundless Regions where the Stars inhabit, there is nothing that I look upon with more pleasure than the wide Sea and the Mountains of the Earth. There is something august and stately in the Air of those things that inspires the mind with great thoughts and passions; we do naturally upon such occasions think of God and his greatness, and whatsoever hath but the shadow and appearance of INFINITE, as all things have that are too big for our comprehension, they fill and overbear the mind with their Excess, and cast it into a pleasing kind of stupor and admiration.[16]

The attitude here is unquestionably complex. We are certainly beyond the limits of neoclassical sensibility. The *Sacred Theory*, furthermore, reflects the characteristics that art historians have identified as late baroque: affection for contorted form, fascination for greatness as the manifestation of great power, the taste for "a certain Strangeness in beauty." Important, also, in Burnet, is the "aesthetic of the ruin" of the Renaissance and the seventeenth century; Burnet applied something of this sensibility to the "ruin" of the earth. Yet, granted these points, the remark that the mountains lack order and form, and yet are the most pleasing to behold, is in conflict with the heart of post-Renaissance as well as with Renaissance sensibility. The landscapes of this time may present the powerful, the great, and the violent, but these elements are held within a rigidly controlled composition. The wild and irregular may have value, but as contrast, as the frame for a beautiful scene (compare the young Addison's description of the Alps as a setting for God's garden of Italy); or, as in Bernini, the wild and irregular may represent a transport which is *above* the order of nature. For Burnet, two new absolute values have emerged: infinity and irregularity have become desirable in themselves, and have begun to supersede order, symmetry, and the other classical components of beauty as primary aesthetic values.

The reason for the change is to be found in the whole structure of attitudes toward and beliefs about the first things of man's existence: God, reason, nature. The themes which were to be repeated endlessly for generations all appear in Burnet, and we should do well to look at them closely in this early skeletal expression. There is the Longinian note in the phrase "a pleasing kind of stupor and admiration," and in the whole tone of the passage; there is the mind filled and overborne—the implied loss of thought, the complete suspension of the work of the busy understanding in a wise passiveness; and, behind and explaining these experiences, "the shadow and appearance of INFINITE" inspires thoughts of "God and his greatness."

Shaftesbury develops these themes into what in effect is the first of a long line of eighteenth-century "sublime poems" devoted to the evocation of saving nature. Significantly, he begins, as does Thomson in *The Seasons,* with the arctic, a region that had been considered an evidence of the animosity of nature toward man. Nature's curse on man has become nature's blessing. The "vast deserts," the arctic, the Sahara, the seas, have a special value because they represent nature wholly untouched by the artificial works of man.

> All ghastly and hideous as they appear, they want not their peculiar Beautys. The Wildness pleases. We seem to live alone with Nature. We view her in her inmost Recesses, and contemplate her with more Delight in these original Wilds, than in the artificial Labyrinths and feign'd Wildernesses of the Palace. The Objects of the Place, the scaly Serpents, the savage Beasts, and poisonous Insects, how terrible soever, or how contrary to human Nature, are beauteous in themselves . . .[17]

This is a far cry from the traditional scene of beauty. Although the idyllic has its place in Shaftesbury, for him as for succeeding romantic poets the wilderness and the immense take precedence. All the parts of the earth, the great skies, the sun and stars, present an image of Deity:

> . . . . . *Nature* is the glass reflecting God,
> As, by the *sea,* reflected is the *Sun.*[18]

However, before this theory could achieve pragmatic form, with nature assuming its role as saving element, it was necessary to see the human personality as *formed by* sensations. The contribution of Locke's psychology was required. To Burnet the mountains may suggest noble thoughts and improving meditations, which he expresses in a grand style; but he could no more think of the earth itself as an avenue of grace than could Jeremy Taylor. We must, then, understand the means of grace; and so we come to a consideration of the metamorphosis of the imagination.

IV THE IMAGINATION IN THE NEW EPISTEMOLOGY

A revolutionary change in epistemology has its effect on every phase of human thought and activity, but on none, perhaps, more than on ideas of art and the relation of art to the human mind. Poetry deals in images, perceptions, responses in relation to thought; changes in the conception of how the mind perceives and how the sensory experience affects imagining are vital to those whose stock in trade is the significant image. The triumph of Lockian epistemology, occurring so rapidly and so sweepingly, was bound to have an influence on poets and all other artists in a short time. Many aspects of representative eighteenth-century poetry and writing about poetry can be explained by that Lockian picture of the mind which became dominant before the end of the second decade.

In this chapter we shall consider the a priori assumptions that may be deduced from Lockian theory. It is necessary, also, to keep in mind the enthusiasm for nature which arose almost simultaneously with the new epistemology. The latter movement is in many ways alien to the spirit of Locke, and yet fuses with his philosophy to produce many characteristic features of the "romantic."

From the nature of the mind as described by Locke, we could

expect a new poetry to be highly visual in nature, for the faculty of sight came to monopolize the analysis of intellectual activity. Since ideas are images, since even complex ideas are multiple pictures, and since understanding itself is a form of perception, the visual and the intellectual would tend to become amalgamated. Abstraction is only one sense impression isolated from the others, usually intermingled with it; the gap between the impression and the "intellectible," which it had been one function of poetry to fill, would be narrowed to the vanishing point.

The problem of light would be important. Thomas Warton objected to the poetry of Pope, saying that Belinda, the "fated fair"

> Upon the bosom bright of silver Thames,
> Launches in all the lustre of brocade,
> Amid the splendours of the laughing sun.
> The gay description palls upon the sense,
> And coldly strikes the mind with feeble bliss.[1]

The world of sunlight cannot be considered truly "poetic," since the understanding and the imagination deal in different kinds of images. If a poet, like Pope in *An Essay on Man*, addresses himself to the understanding, he runs the risk of being condemned for writing a "species of poetry" that "is not the most excellent one of the art." [2] Poetry of the understanding "coldly strikes the mind," since it is intellectual and not of the imagination. The world of Pope is indeed one of brilliant light, with, mostly, an absence of chiaroscuro, and it is likely that the association of brilliantly illuminated images with the understanding rather than with the imagination helped cause the romantic reaction in favor of the night scene. Certainly, it was not long before the moon became a symbol of the imagination.

Metaphor would be reduced in importance, because, in Lockian epistemology, it is unnecessary for accurate thought and may be confusing. Locke had eliminated the concept of the "intelligible" —apprehensible by the mind only, "mind-stuff" into which physical impressions are transmuted. Metaphor had seemed useful because it was one way of solving a practical problem: it enabled the mind to apprehend, in a limited way at least, pure truth, with the aid of sensory equipment. How can the pure idea, which transcends the impressions, be conveyed to other minds? Yet knowledge must begin with the senses. Thus St. Thomas Aquinas explains that

> Incorporeal things, of which there are no phantasms, are known to us by comparison with sensible bodies of which there are phantasms. Thus we understand truth by considering a thing of which we possess the truth; and God, as Dionysius says, . . . we know as cause, by way of excess and by way of remotion. Other incorporeal substances we know, in the present state of life, only by way of remotion or by some comparison to corporeal things. And, therefore, when we understand something about these things, we need to turn to phantasms of bodies, although there are no phantasms of the things themselves.[3]

Fulke Greville expresses a common but even more extreme view:

> For al the Sunne doth, while his beames descend,
> Lighten the earth, but shaddow every starre:
> So Reason stooping to attend the Sense,
> Darkens the spirits cleare intelligence.[4]

The higher, abstract, purely "rational" principle strains every resource of imagery, so far beyond the "sense" is the spirit's clear intelligence. Greville says of the art of rhetoric,

> Besides this Art, where scarcity of words
> Forc'd her, at first to *Metaphorike* wings
> Because No Language in the Earth affords
> Sufficient Characters to expresse all things: . . .[5]

We cannot get along without metaphor to supplement the inadequacies of language, but we must be sure that the rational purpose dominates. If the metaphor is merely delightful to sense, the lower rules the higher:

> Yet since, she playes the wanton with this need,
> And staines the Matrone with the Harlots weed.

Metaphor can hardly be dispensed with, but the great danger of its abuse leads to such warnings as this.

Locke's system came as a liberation from this necessity. He seemed to obviate the need for the confusing apprehension of abstract ideas by borrowing "metaphorike wings." On the one hand, he showed that—contrary to general, deluded opinion—the most complex and "intellectible" ideas are made directly out of the atoms of everyday experience. Each of these atoms should, ideally, be identified by an exact name or "sign." Vibrations of meaning, associations on the periphery of the central and limited definition of the word, should be eliminated, so as to ensure precision of reasoning. On the other hand, he sets limits to what we can know. It is folly to attempt to strain after cloudy ideas that are above the severely limited capacity of the understanding; and eighteenth-century definitions of pride echo his point. Locke confirmed the growing belief that man should seek to know well only the planet on which he lives and the heavens as far as he can observe them, leaving, perhaps to another life, the ultimate mysteries of metaphysics.

Thus in poetry the common impression, the universal experience, would take on first importance. Presentation of reality would be a primary desideratum. Description for its own sake would be valuable. Variety could be obtained by such devices as using the principle that one simple idea will call up a whole train of ideas. The German philosopher A. G. Baumgarten rather startles us by announcing, apparently as a remarkable discovery, that a "law of the imagination" is that "an idea perceived of a part of a thing recurs as the whole of it. This proposition is also referred to as the association of ideas." [6] Thus, once an idea, a picture, is called up in the mind, others appear in an established sequence to form a complex idea. (This process might be called a "train" and not, as Baumgarten has it, "association" of ideas; the latter, in Locke's terminology, refers to chance and irrational combinations of impressions.) When Thomson writes,

> let Peru
> Deep in her bowels her own ruin breed,
> The yellow traitor that her bliss betrayed,[7]

he exemplifies this principle. The "yellow traitor" sets in motion the whole train of ideas—the gold, the cruel conquerors seeking it—

just as the statement about the southwest wind set in motion the sequence of propositions for the country gentlewoman in Locke's illustration of the inutility of syllogisms.

Most important, all thought now appears as the direct material of sensations; the other great point is that the personality is formed by its sensations. The suspicion which had attached to the imaging faculty, that a purely sensory pleasure betrays its higher function, is reduced. Baumgarten defines a poem as a "perfect sensate discourse"; by this phrase he means that the poem presents imagery as having a perfection of its own. "A sensuous discourse," he adds, "is perfect in proportion as its component parts arouse many sensuous ideas." The "sensuous" has taken on a dignity new to moral philosophy. For, as the concept of a hierarchy of the soul was abandoned, each activity of the mind tended to become the equal of every other activity; and one task of the philosopher was to find what lofty purpose the purely sensuous might serve.

In what sense, then, may it be said that nature speaks to man? The old idea of macrocosm-microcosm became untenable as the new philosophy showed that the universe is not centered in man, and that the cosmos does not parallel the human soul. In the new world of thought, the meaning of nature centers in a subjective effect of impressions upon the mind. A symbol seems to well up from within the mind in response to certain experiences. It is not something the mind beholds and identifies, as the title of a book is identified. A symbol, gestating in depths of mental action beyond the conscious understanding, can only partially and haltingly be expressed in the language of that understanding. To put the matter another way: in the older view, images have a dual nature. They are "sensuous," possessing an attraction in themselves which can be at once a resource and a danger for the artist; but essentially they are also carriers of built-in meaning which must be discerned by the judgment or reason. The artist combines the delight of the lower faculty with the perception of the higher, reason having preëminence. In the newer opinion, the stronger the sense impression, the less immediately obvious its intellectual connections, the deeper it penetrates into the depths of the mind and the more likely it is to evoke a meaning which lies outside the scope of the understanding.

The meaning of the new epistemology for the artist would center in his understanding of the word "imagination." What changes occurred in this area, and what did they signify?

Locke states that imagination is the instrument of perception, and that the understanding itself is a kind of perception. He refers, obviously, to the "imaging" power in the narrow definition of the word. It has been said that the effect of this remark is to make all thought poetic. The effect may, however, be just the opposite. If the mind's activity is centered in the imaging activity, how can we distinguish the beautiful from the true and the useful? In fact, Locke makes no provision for aesthetic values. Just as there is no explanation for the awareness of the conscience in the moral life, so there is none for the sense of the amiable or the sublime. The solution for the conscience was to set up beside the understanding another potentiality of the mind, one which tended to become an autonomous authority, independent of the judgment of reason. The almost inevitable next step, already foreshadowed in Shaftesbury, was to make the imagination a third partner in the enterprise of the mind.

Before considering how this evolution took place, it would be well to look at one of the best statements of the older attitude. Hobbes, who is often thought to have been hostile to the arts, made one of the most eloquent as well as deeply reasoned analyses of the relationship of imagination to the mind and to truth. "Judgment," he wrote in his Answer to Davenant's Dedication of *Gondibert*, "begets the strength and structure, and fancy begets the ornaments of a poem." Taken by itself, as it too often is, the sentence seems to destroy any idea that imagination serves a vital function; but in his subsequent paragraphs Hobbes changes its whole import. The fancy, he tells us, swiftly ranges over the materials of memory—the impressions of decaying sense—forming new combinations which account for the creative activity of the mind. The analogy suggests the "radar" picture of mental operations that some modern physiologists draw. Hobbes commends the "admirable variety and novelty of metaphors and similitudes," since fancy is the means of discovering new truth; thus, where philosophy has failed, as it has, hitherto, in regard to the doctrine of moral virtue, fancy herself must take the "philosopher's part." Far from being ornaments, the creations of fancy may be new apprehensions of truth. The imagination, or fancy, is above all an explorer and discoverer. ". . . in the *senses* there are certain coherences of conceptions, which we may call *ranging;* examples whereof are; a man casteth his *eye* upon the ground, to look about for some small thing lost; the *hounds* casting about at a fault in hunting; and the *ranging* of spaniels . . ." [8] By this "quick ranging of the mind" men discover similitudes in things otherwise unlike (the source of "those grateful similes, metaphors, and other tropes . . ." of orators) or dissimilitudes in things which appear the same.[9] "And this virtue of the mind is that by which men attain to exact and perfect knowledge." The "metaphors and other tropes" are antennae whereby the mind can reach new ideas, which perhaps cannot immediately be reduced to abstract formulation.

Behind these images of the mind is the conception of a unity in mental operation. The difference between fancy and judgment is that between discovery and conservation: the one ranges out in search of new truths to be discovered in new relationships among the mind's remembered impressions, while the other maintains the structure of what is known and restrains the exuberance of the explorer. It is logical that the senior partner, the judgment, should have the final say, but this fact does not detract from the essential importance of the junior. The joint activities of the partners constitute wit, "which seemeth to be a tenuity and agility of spirits, contrary to that restiness of the spirits supposed in those that are dull."

Hobbes's statement has an especially modern ring because in his psychology there is no hierarchy within the mind. The mystical conception of the reason which was universal in his time is, of course, quite incompatible with his conception of thought as a physical process. Accordingly, he was able to escape from the concern for "higher" and "lower," and to see the true relationship of the "faculties" somewhat more clearly than was the average writer on rhetoric or poetry.

Nevertheless, as Miss Rosemond Tuve reminds us, the Renaissance theorist always saw the activities of the mind as constituting a whole:

> Because [the Renaissance man] had conceptions very different from ours of the mind's operations and of its relations to reality, any divisions which, like ours, separate "imagination" from "logical thought," or which separate the judgment-pleasing "cause" of a poem from its aesthetic value, do not really make sense. If we were to intrude such distinctions, we would make it impossible for a Renaissance writer to describe how he thought a poem was written.[10]

Always the reason is the center in which all mental activities should focus. The faculties of the body form a family, and the life of the mind is similar to that of a well-run family—well-run, that is, according to the views of a patriarchal society, with the reason (the father) in communication with and firm control of the group.

> The work of the Imagination or the Fantasy (or of the two together, when distinguished) was to receive, compare and combine impressions of whatever the senses enabled man to perceive, and it was in continual and unbroken co-operation with the Understanding which judged the truth or falsity of things (by logic) and with the Will which (if uninfected) moved man to favorable affections towards the good, and unfavorable towards the evil . . . the main impression one receives in reading of the process of rational activity, in any typical treatise, is an impression of the total mind-act.[11]

It follows, Miss Tuve concludes in an important sentence, that the "emphasis on man's intellective power, like Sidney's emphasis on poetry's concern with universals, is characteristic of this whole period; throughout it, writers unhesitatingly refer man's literary activities to the contemplating intellect which was thought to apprehend the true nature of things . . ."

This was the situation at the beginning of the eighteenth century. Within a few decades, however, the "total mind-act" was being replaced by the separation of imagination from logical thought, with the conclusion that seldom the twain should meet. "Judgment-pleasing" is in the romantic movement distinguished from aesthetic value. This is the gulf that separates the art of the past two centuries or more from all its ancestors; to this difference, truly a "dissociation of sensibility," we can attribute many if not most of the distinctive features of art for generations. This dissociation begins to be evident for the first time in Addison's papers on the "Pleasures of the Imagination."

Yet the same Addison, only a short time before the appearance of these papers, had published a series of essays which illustrate admirably how the older critical theory worked. His critique of Milton is almost a complete exemplification of the old order; it is as if he brought the past to its finale before he sounded the notes of the new symphony.

The essays on *Paradise Lost* belong essentially to the Renaissance tradition that works of literature are products of the craftsman, or "maker," which are designed to imitate nature for the inspection and delight of the reason, and to enlist the imagination in the service of the higher power so as to influence the will. The attempt is to determine how the poet achieved his goal, through analysis of the structure of the fable, the design of the whole, the utilization of images, the manipulations of sounds, and so on. The poet exemplifies the reason at its grandest as he majestically marshals all the faculties of the soul in the service of Truth. The epic, the supreme kind of poem, represents this grand campaign at its most impressive; it was, truly, the "noblest work of the mind of man."

Addison, for the most part, draws on the authorities who had described the tactics in this campaign, especially on Aristotle freely interpreted and expanded, and Le Bossu, with Longinian additions. Nevertheless, he is original in some respects. To devote a long series of papers to one poem, even a poem as important as *Paradise Lost*, was an innovation. True, John Dennis had written a long commentary on Blackmore's *Prince Arthur*, but as a kind of desperately needed sermon to warn epic poets of small caliber. Most of the writers of Arts of Poetry and prefaces talked about a genre as a whole, introducing critiques of the *Iliad, Aeneid,* and other works as examples. To concentrate appreciatively and at length on the effects produced by one poet and one poem marked a change; the discussion of the genre and its characteristics becomes illustrative of the analysis, rather than vice versa. Concentration on an individual work of art suggests a romantic focus on uniqueness of the poem.

But the Milton critique does remain within the tradition of criticism according to objectively stated rules for a genre, which are assumed to be universal and timeless. Episodes are not considered as entities for their own sakes. The great similes are parts of a unity whose soul is the great idea embodied in the fable; as bodies of that soul the elements of the poem have importance. Addison would agree with Dennis

> that Right Reason requires, as well as Aristotle, that a Fable should be the form of an Epick Poem, and an Action the Subject matter of it: That that Action should be one, and at first should be Allegorical and Universal, and should in a manner become afterwards Singular by the imposition of Names; and by the same imposition of Names should likewise become important; and then too, that it should be extended with Episodes, but Episodes which would not corrupt its Unity; in the next place, that it should be entire; that is, that it should have a Beginning, a Middle, and an End . . .[12]

Like Dennis, Addison emphasizes the "great" and the passion of admiration. He would agree, to be sure, that "A poet . . . is oblig'd always to speak to the Heart." Dennis goes far, as does Addison, to emphasize this point; "it is for this reason, that Point and Conceit, and all that they call Wit, is to be for ever banish'd from true Poetry; because he who uses it, speaks to the Head alone." But this is passion galvanizing the formula set forth earlier, and quoted above. The poet must not speak "to the Head alone," but of course he does speak to the head and that is, after all, his great purpose; but he must enlist the will to serve the reason. Thus, as much as "Sir Tremendous Longinus" dwells on the sublime and derogates the strongly intellectual kind of poetry, the sublime effect never becomes an end in itself. Again, although in both Dennis and Addison the "glorious" replaces the "beautiful" as the highest aesthetic effect, the ultimate result is to be dictated and judged by "Right Reason."

Nowhere before Addison's papers on the "Pleasures of the Imagination" is the idea overtly expressed that beauty, goodness, and truth inhabit separate compartments in the mind, and that they represent autonomous and equal functions of the personality. The aesthetic, in Western thought, was ultimately a form of knowledge. When St. Thomas Aquinas says that beauty coincides with but is distinguishable from good, he speaks for philosophers in general. The senses most concerned with beauty are sight and hearing, for they affect apprehension and minister to reason. "Beauty," he concludes, "affords to our faculty of knowledge something ordered, over and above the good." [13] The "something ordered" appears to be the complete union of form and matter, very rarely observed in the actual world; knowledge is illuminated by the rare kind of perfection presented by a beautiful object. Beauty is a perfection of truth, and exists as an objective fact apprehended by reason.

Only six years before Addison's papers on the "Pleasures" appeared, Muratori sweepingly asserted the ancient opinion. Harmony and music, this extremist remarks, are superficial ornaments of verse.

> The beauty which by its sweetness delights and moves the human understanding is nothing else than an illumination or resplendent aspect of the truth. This light, this aspect, whenever it succeeds in illuminating our soul, and by its sweetness driving out ignorance (one of the most grievous penalties bequeathed us by our first father) causes in us a delicious pleasure, a most grateful emotion.[14]

The sensuous cannot be considered as an end in itself, since it cannot be a form of knowledge. In a hierarchical universe, it is a means, not a final cause.

It is true that in the decade preceding Addison's essays, the tendency was to give the sensuous a high value in and of itself. The love of strangeness in beauty, the preoccupation with the great and the terrible, the emphasis on strong emotion as represented in the heroic drama, the rise of interest in landscape painting, all would point to an increasing interest in sensation. Yet the essence of the theory was unchanged. The reaction of the neoclassical orthodoxy against the extremes of wit and high emotion, moreover, tended to reëmphasize the older stress on beauty as knowledge and on art as a rational function.

A note of warning is essential at this point. There is a common but wrong impression of what reason meant to such a critic as Dennis. That faculty is thought of as a dry, syllogistic, specialized activity, suited to the discourse of a lawyer, perhaps, but essentially alien to the creative process. A pathetic picture of the imagination, in a strait jacket imposed by this harsh taskmaster, presents itself.

Probably, however, this impression is the result of our identifying Locke's "understanding" with the older "Right Reason." For the older philosopher, reason was dynamic, unlimited, powerful. Reason had a kind of identification with the divine; it included intuitions of goodness and value, of eternal truth. It was the vital center of all mental activity. Truth might take many forms in the various aspects of life, yet at the center it was one. Leonard Welsted, in his *Dissertation Concerning the Perfection of the English Tongue, and the State of Poetry* (1724), makes clear that mathematical reason is not the same as poetical reason; but reason is the essential at all times. Poetry, he says, depends largely on imagination, "that bright emanation of reason, painting or throwing light upon ideas." The significant word "emanation" recalls John Davies' image of the soul as divided into separate faculties, yet constituting "one Substance indivisible," as there are three persons in the Trinity.

Not so long (as history goes) after Dennis formulated his definition of the great poem centered in and governed by Right Reason, Poe, in his famous essay "The Poetic Principle," expressed a dramatically opposed opinion about the function of poetry. Perhaps there has been no more radical change of attitude in intellectual history. He speaks of the "heresy of *The Didactic*." The sole

BOWLING GREEN STATE UNIVERSITY LIBRARY

arbiter of poetry, he tells us, is taste; "with the Intellect or with the Conscience, it has only collateral relations. Unless incidentally, it has no concern whatever either with Duty or with Truth." The conception of the "total mind-act" has broken down indeed!

Neither Addison nor other pioneers of this view had a conscious revolutionary purpose. It might be said that they were forced into their opinions. The idea of "pure" art was not a "young Turk" revolt against a stuffy and sterile authoritarianism. On the contrary, the evolution of the attitude stated so forthrightly by Poe is logical and almost if not quite inevitable.

Locke thought of the "complex ideas" as essentially definable: indeed, he distinguished between simple and complex ideas by saying that the former are certain and distinct, although they cannot be analyzed or defined; whereas the latter can be defined but are often confused and obscure to sense. Precisely in this way, Baumgarten, in 1735, makes the first distinction between the "aesthetic" and the "understandable." As examples of complex ideas, Locke mentions beauty, a man, theft (*Essay*, II, xii, 5). Not all these words, however, can be reconciled with his criteria of the complex idea. Theft can be defined, as can the word "man"; but Locke's attempted definition of beauty significantly has no substantive: "consisting of a certain composition of colour and figure, causing delight in the beholder." This is the description of a sensation, not a definition. What is beauty? It is a value sensed; it is a response, a very real and definite operation of the mind, which yet cannot be accounted for by Locke's theory of the understanding. We value an object, say a painting, because of its beauty, as we value one deed over another because it "seems right." The sense of a powerful but subjective impression causes Locke's dilemma in accounting for all value judgments; for he never really explains the sense of easiness or of uneasiness which, it appears, is the motivating force of action. Hence Morgann, in the passage quoted in chapter I, says that the "*first principles of character* . . . seem wholly out of the reach of the Understanding." Such responses have something of the immediacy of the "simple ideas," like the impressions of colour; yet in their complexity and associations they suggest rather the combinations made by the understanding. They are, to invent a term, "complex impressions." They represent states of mind rather than knowledge or opinion; but states of mind, by Locke's own admission, are springs of action.

The solution to the problem seems to be that the mind responds in specialized and discrete ways to its environment. One "power," one kind of sensitivity, perceives the true—that is, relationships between simple ideas which seem to accord with the structure of reality. Another sensitivity responds to moral value, and a third recognizes beauty. To put the matter in this way, however, is somewhat inaccurate. It would be more precise to say that the mind is so constituted that it makes certain kinds of responses to certain kinds of impressions. Beauty does not exist as an objective quality in a universe of atomic motions. It, like the understanding, is a function of the organism God has adjusted to the universal order. As Jonathan Edwards remarks, in *A Divine and Supernatural Light:*

> It is out of reason's province to perceive the beauty or loveliness of any thing: such a perception does not belong to that faculty. Reason's work is to perceive truth and not excellency. It is not ratiocination that gives men the perception of the beauty and amiableness of a countenance, though it may be many ways indirectly an advantage to it; yet it is no more reason that immediately perceives it, than it is reason that perceives the sweetness of honey: it depends on the sense of the heart. Reason may determine that a countenance is beautiful to others, it may determine that honey is sweet to others; but it will never give me a perception of its sweetness.

To a certain extent, this statement is a repetition of what has always been obvious; only the senses react to immediate physical stimuli, as to sweetness. The radical note is sounded by the implied elimination of reason from the work of judging. Beauty has been removed from the reality of truth or knowledge, and has ceased to be an objective quality inhering in things—points which the older conceptions of aesthetics took for granted. Poe, then, says nothing really new, but merely sums up the developing attitude: "When, indeed, men speak of Beauty, they mean, precisely, not a quality, as is supposed, but an effect—they refer, in short, just to that intense and pure elevation of *soul*—*not* of intellect, or of heart— . . . which is experienced in consequence of contemplating 'the beautiful' " (*The Philosophy of Composition*).

Another kind of experience seemingly left out of the Lockian understanding is represented by the word "grace." If supranatural influences on the mind are excluded, if sensations constitute all that can happen to the soul, how can divine assistance be accounted for? The age of Locke was truly religious and earnestly desired to retain a feeling of the immediacy of the divine; the emphasis on immensity is a manifestation of that desire. Yet, if there is to be divine influence on the soul, a Lockian must explain that influence as part of the operation of nature. It proved surprisingly easy—deceptively easy—to fill old molds of thought with new content. Jonathan Edwards, an early convert to Locke's epistemology, did not for that reason abandon his faith in foreordination.

> Hence Edwards' thought cohered firmly about the basic certainty that God does not impart ideas or obligations outside sense experience. He does not rend the fabric of nature or break the connection between experience and behavior. The universe is all of a piece, and in it God works upon man through the daily shock of sensation, which "is such an impression or motion made in some part of the body, as produces some perception in the understanding." [15]

Faith that the universe is divinely planned and perfectly operating makes this adjustment easier. If natural law embodies the will of God, no event happens accidentally. It follows the the sensations which a human being receives from nature produce certain foreordained effects upon his consciousness. The avenue whereby impressions produce spiritual effects might, given the complex of ideas I have discussed, very well be the imagination. The secondary qualities of matter—impressions of color, odor, and the others, which, it seems, are purely subjective effects with no real counterparts in nature—present the problem of the fictitious. If God has so constructed our mental equipment that we seem to perceive qualities in matter that are not really there, what purpose may He have had for the "gay delusion"? Beauty itself raises this question once it is found to be an effect, a subjective impression only. Perhaps these appearances without substance are means of grace. We now can see why Poe gives the effect of beauty a locus—"soul"—above that of any other faculty. Beauty retained its traditional position as a supernal quality, having a divine purpose; but the means changed altogether when the Platonic gave way to the Lockian.

Beauty as a means of grace served, moreover, to rescue art from a grave danger. The purpose of the understanding in the great scheme of things is easy enough to explain. It must exist to provide men with a workable cognition of the external world, the knowledge, the opinion, the analytical distinctions necessary as the basis of action and ultimately of salvation, since it reveals the need for revelation. When we ask, however, why the color, shape, and scent of a rose affect us, we raise puzzling questions. Perhaps, indeed, the awareness is the *raison d'être* of the whole activity. If man is strictly and solely an experiencing being, if his personality is composed of his impressions, if consciousness is the ground of his mental life, we might even reach the conclusion that, as Pater intimates, he does not have impressions in order to think, but thinks in order to appreciate impressions. This possibility is given a terrifying force when beauty is no longer regarded as an objective fact or an idea self-existent and transcending nature.

To say, then, that response to beauty is a means of apprehending perfection is now out of the question. Not without reason does Walter Pater appear as a descendant of Lockian philosophy, in the 1873 conclusion to *Studies in the History of the Renaissance:*

> At first sight experience seems to bury us under a flood of external objects, pressing upon us with a sharp importunate reality, calling us out of ourselves in a thousand forms of action. But when reflection begins to act upon those objects they are dissipated under its influence; the cohesive force is suspended like a trick of magic; each object is loosed into a group of impressions,—colour, odour, texture,—in the mind of the observer . . . the whole scope of observation is dwarfed to the narrow chamber of the individual mind.

Although Locke would be uneasy about the tenor of this statement, he could not really object to the use of the word "reflection," or to the image of the mind located in its "narrow chamber," recalling his own description. But note Pater's conclusion: the solidity of the objects about which we talk dissolves, when we look within our own minds, into a stream of "impressions, unstable, flickering, inconsistent, which burn and are extinguished with our consciousness of them." All, therefore, we can be sure of is the impression itself—"a single, sharp impression," to which "what is *real* in our life fines itself down." Pater has realized how infinitesimal, how difficult to catch is the "simple idea" which Locke had assumed to be so clear-cut and sure; and yet it is still the only ultimate reality available. Quite consistently, then, does the awareness of this impression, its effect in terms of pleasure and pain, appear to be the final purpose as it is the final reality in life. Pater, it would seem, is not merely voicing a mood of decadent weariness or irresponsible hedonism; he is pursuing to a conclusion a conception of reality as existing within the consciousness.

At no time has so radical a conclusion proved permanently satisfying for most people. There must be something beyond mere sensation for the sake of awareness if life itself is not to be ultimately inexplicable and our existence an anomaly. The new philosophy of sensation, then, set a strange and yet essential problem to critic and poet alike. All these dilemmas centered in the questions, What is the imagination, and why should a presumably rational creature have it at all? The questions were old, but the terms in which they must be answered, after the beginning of the eighteenth century, were new indeed.

Two other conditions of imagination as the term was to be redefined should be mentioned. A certain *passivity* of the experiencing mind and an enhancement of the importance of extrarational mental activities are characteristic of the new attitudes toward art, from the very beginnings of romanticism. There are good reasons for these tendencies.

Hobbes's picture of the fancy is one of great activity, involving a sense of exploration, the excitement of new discoveries about to be made. The mind, acting with one of its powers, searches constantly in its storehouse of ideas. The work of the "ranging spaniel" is very much like that which Luis de la Puente describes as meditation, which "runneth from one thing to another, seeking out hidden verities." [16] Call it fancy or meditative reflection or what you will: the work of "invention" is the key to higher mental action.[17]

Opposed dramatically to Hobbes's central figure of the fancy as explorer is Locke's of the understanding as "considerer." In every visualization of the mental process he sees the understanding as a static observer; the ideas rather than the power of the mind seem to be mobile. Hobbes envisions the impressions as static ("the decaying sense") and the mind as moving and searching—like the agitated hounds "at a fault in hunting." Thus Locke's static immovable understanding looks rather like the judgment without her dynamic junior partner in the enterprise of wit. Locke's picture of the mind recalls Hobbes's phrase "restiness of the spirits"—which he identified with dullness! Locke stresses the accurate observation of what comes into the mind: the understanding is a judge and not an explorer of the memory; the emphasis is on the respectful disposition, "according to their true natures," of the ideas derived from the senses. Locke follows the Baconian principle that mankind needs more and more facts, which, considered carefully by the understanding, will inevitably fall into true patterns. It is not wit, the new inventions and strange combinations of ideas, that is needed so much as more information. Such an attitude fell in with an extreme distrust of hypotheses. A rigid conception of the scientific method which was triumphant in the nineteenth century held that the investigator must keep his mind completely open until he has painstakingly gathered all his data. Presumably, then, the evidence will almost of itself constitute the truth.

It comes as no surprise that "metaphor and allusion" are, for Locke, not antennae of the mind. The understanding, with its love of combining ideas, may be tempted into frivolous mental games under the impression that it is discovering truth. Locke suggests that there is a natural love of intellectual play, to which the "frisking" ideas he describes in *The Conduct of the Understanding* may appeal. Locke, to be sure, is not alone responsible for the distrust of wit; his importance is rather that he gives further impetus to a movement that had been under way for a long time.

The decline of wit in the sense of the conceit was hastened. Addison frankly disparages novelty and "invention" in poetry; the greatest poets—the writers of epics—"endeavor rather to fill the mind with great conceptions than to divert it with such as are new and surprising," and consequently have "seldom anything in them that can be called wit." To "fill the mind" is taken quite literally by many eighteenth-century theorists. Overpowering effect rather than discovery comes to be the desideratum. Or novelty and variety of images—new experience, not new insight—may be desired. And the "metaphysical" shudder is replaced by the "gothic *frisson*," the exploitation of magic and wonder taking the place, in part, of the intellectual image.

The genius, it was said in the eighteenth century, is like a polished mirror. He receives with great accuracy and special sensibility the impressions from nature. Added to this figure is that of the magnet: the impressions move of themselves, without conscious volition or even awareness, into creative groupings. Impressions sink so deeply into the mind that they find a level far below the awareness of the understanding, doing their work with a fine automatism.

John Livingston Lowes's theory of the "hooked atoms" descends from such ideas. His attitude toward the creative process represents a remarkable compromise between those old opposites in Locke's theory, conscious understanding and unconscious associations. Impressions, entering during "conscious intellectual activity," descend into the "deep well of unconscious cerebration," where "images and impressions converge and blend even in the sleepy drench of our forgetful pools." This is an aspect of genius, which "owes its secret virtue at least in part to the enhanced and almost incredible facility with which in the wonder working depths of the unconscious the fragments which sink incessantly below the surface fuse and assimilate and coalesce." [18] Such sentences hark back more directly to Lockian sources than to the Coleridgean theory of the imagination: the very figure of the "hooked atoms" suggests the persistent integrity of each impression and the basic atomic theory of the seventeenth century rather than the transformation performed by the creative secondary imagination. It is not easy to see how the atoms can "fuse," since Lowes's comparison implies fully retained identity of each unity. Finally, "it is again conscious energy, now of another and loftier type, which later drags the deeps for their submerged treasure, and moulds the bewildering chaos into unity. But interposed between consciousness and consciousness is the well." Throughout, the conscious mind is relatively static. Its fishing activities in the subconscious must make use only of what has been produced beyond its control. The materials it uses, the associations (which Hobbes would have represented as having been made by a direct activity of the mind aware of its own purposes), now become the work of impressions moving of themselves "with enhanced and almost incredible facility." The hooked atoms, like the gangs of ideas in the area outside the understanding, lead their own lives.

Beyond these points, Lowes's assumptions about the nature of poetry reflect eighteenth-century influences. The whole of *The Road to Xanadu* is concerned with showing how what Locke would call "agreeable pictures, and pleasant visions" originate—for, Lowes clearly intimates, Coleridge's greatest poems are the apotheosis of purely "beautiful" art. The artistic imagination, in this view, is removed from concern with intellectual meanings and insights to be discovered within the corpus of experience. The imagination exists in its own realm and is its own excuse for being. It presents no truths, nor is it intended to, and the "didactic heresy" is ruled out of court. Between the extremes represented, on the one hand, by the neoclassical interpretation of *utile dulci,* and by such opinions as that of Lowes, on the other hand, there is a revolution in thinking about the imagination. To understand it, we must study Addison's papers on this subject; his essays are the gateway to the age of the aesthetic.

V "THE PLEASURES OF THE IMAGINATION"

Early in the year 1712, Addison put forth the first of two major bids for lasting reputation as a critic. The papers on *Paradise Lost* were published in the *Spectator* at weekly intervals, beginning in January and ending with the issue of May 3. Only seven weeks later, on June 21, another series began, entitled "The Pleasures of the Imagination." As would be expected, there are many connections between the two series: elements of thought, echoes of phrases, even outlines of propositions. Yet deeper study will show that to go from the Miltonic appreciation to the theory of the imagination and its influences on the psyche is to go from the world of late baroque and neoclassical, from the milieu of Dryden and the young Pope, to the anteroom of Wordsworth, Ruskin, and even the twentieth-century poets. The difference may be epitomized in part by the statement that "The Pleasures of the Imagination" is the first work ever written on aesthetics as a wholly autonomous subject.

Addison has usually been undervalued, and so has the *Spectator* as a whole. Its "demure" style, which seems only to summarize, clearly and succinctly, what every thoughtful man believes, camouflages many revolutionary speculations on science, religion, and art.

These speculations, however, are far from being unique products of genius. Rather, they owe their importance to the fact that they are masterly syntheses and statements of ideas and themes which were emerging but had not yet been explicitly formulated. In the mind of Addison, the intellectual elements of the time came together in new and vastly significant relationships. Ideas were projected in profoundly influential images which we encounter again and again for decades to come. In the "Pleasures" series, the themes combine in a striking and highly important theory: so we can say, literally, that there are few works on the nature of literature written since the early part of the eighteenth century that do not reflect it.

True, neither Addison nor his contemporaries realized how revolutionary was that synthesis. Addison himself remained a theoretical neoclassicist and exemplified his formal theory in his own drama. (An interesting parallel is Shaftesbury, who, although setting forth a concept of "pure" nature as ideal, nevertheless retained strict neoclassical principles of form in judging literature.) It was only when Addison considered the imagination as a thing in itself that he was led into new paths.

I have discussed the dilemmas arising from a new epistemology: the problem of values in general, the necessity of finding new channels for old and valued experiences, and of reconstructing on new foundations the dignity of the soul. These were the underlying issues Addison set out to deal with in treating the nature of imagination; for the dilemmas came, as if by intellectual gravity, to rest there.

Addison began by granting, and without qualification, that many experiences seem to happen without an immediately evident final cause; to put it another way, much of sensation does serve the final purpose of giving pleasure. He significantly used the word in the title he assigned the series, and thereby inaugurated a fashion for "Pleasure" works, usually in verse. From Akenside on, "Pleasures" appear frequently in English literature—"Pleasures of Melancholy," "Pleasures of Hope," and so on.

At first glance, this tendency would indicate a trivialization of life, or perhaps the rise of a pure hedonism which reduces even serious occupations to mere diversions. The point, however, is that Addison had given "pleasure" a new and truly ontological meaning. Nowhere do we find the traditional and hitherto inescapable warnings that imagination must remain the faithful servant of reason. Nowhere does Addison assert that the pleasure obtained from imagination must be used in the service of truth. Nowhere does he make the compromise that, although poetry exists primarily for the sake of giving pleasure, the pleasure must disguise a rationally justifiable purpose.

On the contrary. The very absence of rational activity becomes a virtue of the imagination (*Spect.* 411).

> Besides, the pleasures of the imagination have this advantage, above those of the understanding, that they are more obvious, and more easy to be acquired. It is but opening the eye, and the scene enters. The colours paint themselves on the fancy, with very little attention of thought or application of mind in the beholder. We are struck, we know not how, with the symmetry of any thing we see, and immediately assent to the beauty of an object, without enquiring into the particular causes and occasions of it.

Viewed in isolation, such statements would seem to lead to aestheticism, whatever Addison intended; indeed, they ultimately did. But Addison allayed the fear of such a result. The pleasure, he says, has a final purpose. It is in the final purpose that he is most interested, and this is the real theme of the papers. He does not really abandon the moral criterion, but sets it up according to the new rules of the mind. The pleasure the imagination thus passively experiences is evidence, not of a perilous sensuousness, but of a spiritually improving effect. In *Spectator* 580 he exclaims, "A spirit cannot but be transported after an ineffable manner, with the sight of those objects, which were made to affect him by that Being who knows the inward frame of a soul, and how to please and ravish it in all its most secret powers and faculties." This is to occur in the future life; the sentence appears in one of a series of papers dealing with the mystique of space and divine omnipresence. The glory of heaven will consist in the heightening and intensifying of sensuous impressions: "I have only considered this glorious place with regard to the sight and imagination, though it is highly probable that our other senses may here likewise enjoy their highest gratification." By the pleasures of the imagination we are raised by progressive stages to a perfect state of perception.

> The senses are faculties of the human soul, though they cannot be employed, during this our vital union, without proper instruments in the body. Why therefore should we exclude the satisfaction of these faculties, which we find by experience are inlets of great pleasure to the soul, from among those entertainments which are to make up our happiness hereafter?

According to Pauline doctrine, the soul will have a glorified body after the Resurrection; but Addison is transporting into the next life something very much like pure aesthetic experience in this. These meditations begin, moreover (*Spect.* 565), with a reverie in a night landscape of the type that was soon to become familiar in romantic poems. Over it presides that potent symbol of imagination, the moon, which "opened to the eye a new picture of nature, which was more finely shaded and disposed among softer lights, than that which the sun had before discovered to us." The sun of understanding, the moon of the imagination—Addison's message is that each reveals a picture, each a true picture in its kind, of divine nature.

Aesthetic experience is identified as a means of grace, in the sense that one area of sensuous experience is designed to produce, directly, a spiritual effect. Addison's exaltation of pleasure takes place in a very different atmosphere from that of Pater's remarks on the sensuous.

It is important to understand, first, what Addison means by imagination. Why did the romantics employ a word that was, in so many ways, ill-suited to their meanings? Conservatism of vocabulary may be one answer. It is frustrating to attempt to talk of "imagination" in the Renaissance and "imagination" in the nineteenth century in common terms. The word "aesthetic," which I have used above, might have served Addison's purposes more precisely, but it had not yet been invented; terminology is slow to follow changes in thought.

But there was another reason for Addison to use the ancient and time-honored word. The *Spectator* is revolutionary without appearing to be so. Addison begins this series of papers by seeming merely to clear up a confusion that has long bothered writers; and indeed, "Imagination" has always been "employed in a . . . loose and uncircumscribed sense." "I therefore thought it necessary to fix and determine the meaning of these two words . . . [fancy and imagination]" (*Spect.* 411). But in the end he slips away, and we have nothing but the shadow of a definition. We learn that, as earlier writers had said, imagination lies between the senses and the reason. It is arbitrarily limited to visual experience: "by the pleasures of the imagination, I mean only such pleasures as arise originally from sight." Locke's influence is apparent. But we are left to wonder whether the imagination is a special "power," like the understanding, an entity that exists and whose functions can be described, even though its essence is unreachable. Or is it merely a name for a group of neurological processes, as the later mechanistic, associationist psychologists were to maintain? Addison clearly leans to, but does not specifically state, the first of these views. When he tries to explain the mechanism of trains of ideas (his only real attempt to grapple with the "efficient causes," which, he says, do not interest him), he suggests, but with a kind of smile, a somewhat Cartesian operation of body in relation to mind. But by 1712 Cartesianism had long been out of date. The most we can assume is that the response of the mind even to nonrational sensations does not consist only of physical modifications of the organism.

Many eighteenth-century theorists tried to make good Addison's failure to define specifically. Their efforts proved the wisdom of Addison's vagueness on the subject; he, like his mentor Locke, produced a much greater effect by concentrating on function, which could be discussed intelligently, and leaving open ultimate physiological questions, which were far beyond the capacities of current natural philosophy.

The conception of the imagination shows the inspiration of Locke everywhere. Not only does Addison frequently quote from the *Essay Concerning the Human Understanding,* but, even more important, the vocabulary, the counters of thought, constantly recall that work. The imagination occupies the gap between the immediate sense impressions and the understanding. It is not, however, as in older epistemologies, a transmitter and first organizer of impressions later to be organized and evaluated by the authoritative reason; it is a terminus in itself. Yet it shares qualities of both sense and understanding, for it functions both as a sensitivity to immediate sensations and as an independent organizing power capable of grouping impressions to produce certain effects. "We cannot indeed have a single image in the fancy that did not make its first entrance through the sight; but we have the power of retaining, altering and compounding those images, which we have once received, into all the varieties of picture and vision that are most agreeable to the imagination . . ." The placing of imagination between sense and understanding refers to its mixed functions rather than to its position in a scale of values. The revolution represented by the statement that the imagination has over reason the advantage of being purely sensuous and requiring no intellectual effort sets the tone for the discussion. What are its specific functions in the divinely planned order of the psyche?

The imagination, for Addison, serves as a means of reconciling man, with his spiritual needs and his desire to belong to a living universe of purpose and values, with a cosmos that begins to appear alien, impersonal, remote, and menacing. It is in this sense of reconciliation that I employ the word "grace." Orthodox theology interpreted man's need for finding life and purpose in his world as the need for reconciliation of a sinful and rebellious being with a merciful yet righteous God; it involved the relationship, immediately, of one personality with another. The new philosophy, however, raised the problem of reconciliation with what might very well seem a mere machine, an order of atoms moving according to inexorable law.

Addison's point is that the mind of man is so constituted that, living in a mechanistic world, he still is brought into contact with value and purpose; he is "at home" because of sensations he derives from that cosmos itself.

The process is one of intensified identification with the natural order, resulting in a sense of harmony. The words "complacency," "cheerfulness," and the like frequently appear. A divine unrest certainly is not what imagination produces. Speaking of beauty, he uses the very word which was to play so large a part in romantic literature: "the very first discovery of it strikes the mind with an inward joy." Ascent above nature is replaced by a yearning for stretching out one's arms to comprehend, to bring nature into one's soul. The new faith is well expressed in James Beattie's *The Minstrel* (Book I):

> O how canst thou renounce the boundless store
> Of charms which Nature to her votary yields!
> The warbling woodland, the resounding shore,
> The pomp of groves, and garniture of fields;
>
> . . . .
>
> These charms shall work thy soul's eternal health,
> And love, and gentleness, and joy, impart.

In two respects this represents a reversal. First, although Spenser and Milton and Dryden describe nature and are as aware of its beauty as any romantic poet could be, I doubt that this mysticism of groves and fields, this attribution to the setting of life of the power to "work thy soul's eternal health," is to be found elsewhere. And the second point of difference is the reason for the first. No matter how important the "book of nature" may have been for, say, Hooker, it had to be *read*. What Quarles called the "hieroglyphicks" and "emblems" of God's glory had, as the names indicate, to be riddled out by conscious thought. The noteworthy fact about Beattie's lines, as well as Addison's statements, is that they make the process passive on the part of the beholder. Nature is automatically exalting (perhaps a better word for the eighteenth century is "expanding") and will impart virtues to the soul. "It is but opening the eye, and the scene enters."

Man must realize, as Shaftesbury asserted, that he is made for nature, and not nature for him. What a shock could be involved here! Is man to lose his dignity, his intimations of immortality, his sense of kinship with the ultimate ground of being? If made for nature, is he to be regarded as only a member of the "natural" kingdom of the animals? And, moreover, imprisoned, it now seems, in the narrow cabinet of his impressions, denied the conviction of immediate contact with the divine, he must find within that suddenly narrowed space the security which had been symbolized by the "candle of the Lord."

What might have seemed an insuperable handicap could, however, give the needed support and assurance. If personality is constituted of experiences, may those experiences, in a harmonious universe, be the very means of grace? But we must look outside the reason for that means. The understanding may tell us how the universe operates, but it cannot place us in touch with value and meaning. We may proceed to the conclusion that, as George Santayana says, "Aesthetic and moral judgments are accordingly to be classed together in contrast to judgments intellectual; they are both judgments of values, while intellectual judgments are judgments of fact. If the latter have any value, it is only derivative, and our whole intellectual life has its only justification in its connexion with our pleasures and pains." [1]

A nebulous feeling that aesthetic response may convey a sense of purpose and values in the universe existed before Addison; it is the inspiration for Shaftesbury's nature hymn. But a convincing and apparently factual analysis of just how nature could serve as a means of grace was needed. Addison's great contribution was to provide just such an analysis; and, when we read the nature poetry of succeeding decades, we should be aware of the often unspoken conviction that the rhapsodies are supported by a valid psychological theory.

Addison set out, in good eighteenth-century style, to systematize his conclusions about sensation. He neatly classified the effects of imagination, reducing them to the convenient and mystical number three, distinguished according to their "final causes." This division exerted an almost hypnotic effect on eighteenth-century philosophers, even though Addison himself described aesthetic phenomena of great importance which he did not file under any of the three main heads. In a short time after the series appeared, it began to be evident that the three aesthetic classifications were frequently taking the place of the older genres in characterizing kinds of poetry. Certain poems began to be "great" or "sublime" rather than epics or georgics or pastorals. Effects on the imagination rather than subject matter and themes became the criteria of classification.

Addison's types of pleasures of the imagination seem to have been suggested by a sentence of Longinus' *On the Sublime*, about which he had been thinking much as he wrote the Milton essays. "Look at life," it reads, "from all sides and see how in all things the extraordinary, the great, the beautiful stand supreme, and you will soon realize the object of our creation." [2] Each of these words, however, undergoes a sea change in Addison's discussion.

The preëminent category is the "great." To it Addison gives the content of a developed mystique of space, culminating in the magic of "immensity" and finding its symbolic projection in mountains and oceans (see chap. iii). He formulates this mystique and image in *Spectator* 413:

One of the final causes of our delight, in anything that is great, may be this. The Supreme Author of our being has so formed the soul of man, that nothing but Himself can be its last, adequate, and proper happiness. Because, therefore, a great part of our happiness must arise from the contemplation of His Being, that he might give our souls a just relish of such a contemplation, He has made them naturally delight in the apprehension of what is great or unlimited. Our admiration, which is a very pleasing motion of the mind, immediately rises at the consideration of any object that takes up a great deal of room in the fancy and, by consequence, will improve into the highest pitch of astonishment and devotion when we contemplate His nature, that is neither circumscribed by time nor place, nor to be comprehended by the largest capacity of a created being.

A major objection to Locke's *Essay Concerning the Human Understanding* was the elimination of the innate idea of God from the mind. True, "by thought and meditation" men may attain the "truest and best notions" of God (*Essay*, I, iii, 16); but, it might well be concluded, the constructions of reason give nothing of the support that an intuitive knowledge, interwoven with our very being, would provide. "Indeed it is urged, that it is suitable to the goodness of God to imprint upon the minds of men, characters and notions of himself, and not to leave them in the dark and doubt in so grand a concernment" (*Essay*, I, iii, 12). This is a pallid reflection of the passionate conviction of a More or a Norris.

Addison attempts to show that God does indeed provide some intuitive knowledge of and assurance about his being, not innately, but by a natural process as certain and inescapable as perception of the very simple ideas. In a later issue of the *Spectator* than the "Pleasures" series, he speaks of a stormy sea, which is the biggest object a person sailing on it can perceive: "Such an object naturally raises in my thoughts the idea of an Almighty Being, and convinces me of His existence as much as a metaphysical demonstration" (*Spect.* 489). Here is a kind of parallel with the movement of the conscience to the level of immediate impression; and again the locale of important spiritual and moral experience moves from the rational to a nonrational part of the mind. The line which leads from More through Burnet ends here.

It is not surprising that Addison should follow in paths the Master of the Charterhouse had pioneered. Both Steele and Addison had been Charterhouse scholars. Addison wrote an impressive Latin ode on the *Sacred Theory*, and Steele paid a moving tribute to Burnet (at a time when the Theorist was in bad odor with the orthodox) in *Spectator* 143 and 146. The links between Shaftesbury, Locke, and Addison are equally understandable. There is something of "cosmic Whiggery" about this stirring in England, and the third Earl of Shaftesbury, Addison and Steele, Hutcheson, and Thomson are all members of an unorganized but recognizable party in literature as well as in politics.

How Addison's theory of the "great" passed over the line from the earlier concern for magnificence and sublimity may be realized from a look at a popular writer on landscape, William Sanderson, whose *Graphice* was published in 1658. The background of Locke's and Addison's emphasis on vision to the point of monopoly of mental activity may be observed in Sanderson's dictum that sight "is the form, and perfection of man: by it, we draw near to the *divine* Nature, seeming that we are *born, only to see.*" He describes noble and splendidly diversified landscapes, in which the infinite perspective is a great feature: "proud *Hills,* covered with whitenesse of *Snow,* which the Sunbeams exprest, like *Silver Towrs,* that reached up to the next *Region,*" are represented as extending "so farre, untill your sight is lost, into the *Edge* and *Circle* of an *Horison,* where *Heaven* and *Earth,* beget a wonder . . ." [3] The observation of nature in such scenes has great value for the soul, and explains why we draw near the divine through the visual. The traveler, having turned his back to meditate upon what he has seen, with all its "contrarieties in *Nature* and *Affection,*" its "beautifull *Objects,* and *Ornaments* of *delight,*" considers how the universe was created for man's use and shows forth, as does the human microcosm, the glory and might of the Maker.

The traveler turns his back to consider; he realizes that the universe exhibits a great moral lesson, but he must reason to derive that lesson. Addison's innovation consists in the omission of turning one's back, of conscious reflection. The effect as Addison describes it is indeed not finally a lesson at all, for it is a state of mind. The analogy is with those powerful impressions which, as Locke observed, influence our moods and actions even though they lie outside conscious awareness.

The emphasis of Addison is on the single, great, "stupor"-producing impression. Size, quantity of response caused by quantity of stimulus, takes on unprecedented importance. At this point we see how Addison, and the romantic tradition he did so much to inaugurate, departed from the true Longinian spirit; and part of the puzzling relationship of *Peri Hupsous* to the "natural sublime" may be cleared up.[4]

Sanderson's treatise shows why *Peri Hupsous* was especially congenial to an age that built St. Paul's Cathedral and appreciated the paintings of Salvator Rosa. The landscapes of Sanderson are compositions of the noblest objects, where human and natural grandeur meet: a picturesquely ruined stone bridge, ruined classical buildings, a river flowing between orchards of palms and sycamores, stately cities, famous towers, spiring steeples. The great and glorious objects of nature, such as Vesuvius in eruption, a "blazing flash to frighten *Heaven*," are scenes intended to exhibit magnificent contrast and variety, light and dark in "glaring" opposition.

The word "illustrious" epitomizes this appeal. Man, like his mind, is a creature of two worlds. Subject to the unending cycle of birth, growth, and decay, the prey of petty accidents and relatively tiny in size, he is limited and inglorious; but he possesses a love of the glorious and a potentiality of glory for himself. The spirit of *Peri Hupsous* is expressed in Ptolemy's explanation of his motive for studying astronomy: "I know that I am mortal, a creature of a day; but when I search into the multitudinous revolving spirals of the stars, my feet no longer rest on the earth, but, standing by Zeus himself, I take my fill of ambrosia, the food of the Gods." [5] The elevation of man to this lofty state is the purpose of the "sublime" rhetorical style. It calls forth the potential human kinship with what is most glorious in the hierarchy of the universe.

What shall we say then was the reason that prompted these great Souls to overlook nicer Elegancies, and to aim only at Sublimity in their writings? Among many other things there is this perhaps to be said for it: Nature did not yet regard Man as a Creature of a low and mean Condition; but sent him into life and this World, as into a vast Amphitheatre, to be a spectator of all that pass'd she enter'd him, I say, in those lists, as a valiant Candidate, who was to breath nothing but Glory; and therefore inspir'd his Soul with a strong and invincible Passion for everything that was most great and divine.[6]

This translation, published in the same year as Addison's papers on the imagination, is a culmination of the late seventeenth-century sensibility. Significant is the mistranslation of the first sentence quoted: in the original text it lists the three categories of artistic effect, including *to kalòn,* the beautiful, and the extraordinary; Welsted has made sublimity the whole show.

Size, in this description of the sublime, is certainly one element; but only because size, as in the example of great rivers, makes the objects illustrious and conspicuous. The great for Longinus is the counterpart in nature of the supreme reason in the mind of man. The great river rather than the small one appeals to us because of the loftiness in the human being, which waits to be evoked. Longinus, unlike Addison, emphasizes the elevation of the writer's own soul.

Addison certainly possessed Longinus' feeling for greatness as glory; witness the constant emphasis on this quality in the Milton papers and the use of the word "great" for the name of a category of aesthetic effect. But a subtle yet crucially important change from Longinus' meaning occurred by the time Addison wrote the "Pleasures." The change, I think, is essentially this: in the Longinian tradition of the sublime, the great in nature *calls out* the great, which is already there, in man; in the newer version, the great in nature *produces* greatness in man. Ultimately, this is why physical size, quantity, and so on are of first importance in Addison's papers, as they never are in Longinus, and why the word "illustrious" does not really correspond to Addison's "great" as a pleasure of the imagination.

Sanderson always reminds us that we are created to see a universe designed for our use and enjoyment, in which we live as the spiritually most noble objects (of those belonging to earth proper). To see the universe in its true glory is of greatest importance, and the sublime landscapes painted by artists, as well as great descriptions in poetry, serve to open our eyes.

The romantic, on the other hand, is concerned with the effect which the scene produces in a relatively passive consciousness. The concern is with "enlargement" rather than with elevation of the mind. Our admiration, Addison writes, "immediately rises at the consideration of any object that takes up a great deal of room in the fancy." Admiration, as in Longinus, is still the characteristic and vehement emotion of the supreme aesthetic experience, but spaciousness replaces the criterion of intrinsic nobility. The image of "an object that takes up a great deal of room in the fancy" is not entirely metaphorical. According to eighteenth-century theories of imagination, the contemplation of a physically vast object, or one suggesting vastness, somehow increases the physical extent of the mind, and such enlargement is a means of making the mind godlike. Awareness, it would seem, occupies a room whose walls can be pushed back. Behind the concept lies a spatial image of the mind, for Lockian descriptions of the perceptive process are in terms of physical locations: the original physical impressions brought to the understanding seated in its "cabinet," the observation in the camera obscura, the watching of the "puppets," and others.

This room of the mind is narrow. A restriction of the mentality, or at least of its scope, is apparent everywhere in Locke's epistemology. No longer is man like an angel in apprehension, for the operation of reason is confined to specialized functions dealing with restricted bodies of data. Although most men of the age agreed with Locke in suspecting those wingy speculations which seemed to encourage superstition and fruitless theorizing, yet the limited mind hardly fitted into vast spaces and immensity as astronomy had revealed it. The physical enlargement of the mind from the narrow limits of its cabinet therefore became desirable. By that enlargement the mind would take on something of the "vastness" which had been an attribute of divinity.

The category of the "great," moreover, is a means of implementing the ideal of the horizontal comprehension of nature. "Such wide and undetermined prospects are as pleasing to the fancy,"

Addison writes, "as the speculations of eternity and infinitude are to the understanding." This suggests a doctrine of correspondence between the faculties.

Philosophical theory moves into aesthetics. In the last number of the *Spectator*, Grove describes the universe as an "immense theatre" within which man has been placed as spectator; but the spectacle is not for his benefit alone, as in Sanderson. Spiritual ascent consists in increased capacity to grasp the grandeur of the scene and to understand the "hidden springs of Nature's operation." He adds: "In eternity a great deal may be done of this kind" (*Spect.* 635). In the beatific vision, which contrasts instructively with the vision of God at the climax of Dante's *Paradiso*, "how shall I fall prostrate and adoring, my body swallowed up in the immensity of matter, my mind in the infinitude of His perfections." The spiritualization of "matter" in "immensity" is evident. Thus comprehension of wider and wider circles of knowledge, rather than spiritual ascent in the strict sense of the phrase, is the vision of the heavenly life; and the "wide and undetermined prospects" of nature serve to give us an experience of this kind here on earth.

Thus, although Addison and his successors use Longinus freely and by no means entirely lose the feeling for the true "sublime," they add to and transform it. Addison himself never spoke of this category as the sublime. For him, sublimity proper never ceased to be primarily the characteristic of a rhetorical or poetical style rather than the name for a source of an effect. Only when effects rather than genres become the criteria for differentiation of poetry does "sublime" become the name for what causes the experience.[7]

The other two categories suggested by Longinus' statement—the beautiful and the extraordinary translated as "new"—reveal important changes from their original in both content and purpose. Beauty as a value of art shows a marked decline in importance as the great emerges to occupy its own place in aesthetics. The beautiful had for the Renaissance been a supreme idea, representing an ultimate perfection toward which the created universe aspires; it is an objective and yet supernal fact; it is imperfectly to be seen *in* objects, and is to be recognized by a high, nonphysical faculty. The mind, said More, has "cogenite" ideas of beautiful form. Beauty, an integral part of the soul, recognizes its counterparts in the physical world. Even in its lowest levels, beauty never lost this touch of divinity and majesty.

For Addison, however, beauty comes dangerously close to being merely the pretty. Something of the rococo spirit is evident. The final causes for the appearance, the illusion, of beauty are twofold: to encourage propagation of the species, and "to render the whole creation more gay and delightful." The second cause explains the mystery of why "secondary" qualities appear. The aesthetic response is characteristic of God's great spectacle (*Spect.* 413):

> We are every where entertained with pleasing shows and apparitions; we discover imaginary glories in the heavens, and in the earth, and see some of this visionary beauty poured out upon the whole creation; but what a rough unsightly sketch of nature should we be entertained with, did all her colouring disappear, and the several distinctions of light and shade vanish?

However lovable we may find beauty to be, nevertheless it is a deceit, and the great—based on perceptions of the real—is necessarily given the place of honor. And the great consists of "wide and undetermined" prospects; it is necessarily without form and symmetry. Thus are the primary objective realities of the universe, as they seemed to the classical and Renaissance worlds, reduced to second rank and transferred to the subjective consciousness (*Spect.* 412).

> There is not perhaps any real beauty or deformity more in one piece of matter than another, because we might have been so made, that whatsoever now appears loathsome to us might have shown itself agreeable; but we find, by experience, that there are several modifications of matter which the mind, without any previous consideration, pronounces at first sight beautiful or deformed.

Beauty, now an illusion rather than a kind of knowledge, serves to arouse delight and to reconcile us to living in the universe (in itself a dull place) rather than to rouse us to ideal aspirations. "The very first discovery of it strikes the mind with an inward joy." Saint-Just, the utopian and apologist of the French Revolution, once remarked that "happiness is an idea new to Europe." As an ideal to be attained in this life, joy was a relatively new conception. The word "pleasure," used in the title of the series, is a touchstone. The tendency had formerly been to contrast the temporal "pleasure" with the true and eternal "joy." Thus Donne: "To be able to compare the joyes of heaven, and the pleasures of this world, and the gaine of the one, with the losse of the other, this is the way to this cleanenesse of the heart . . ." [8] In Addison's usage, "pleasure" has taken on a spiritual value and "joy" arises from a purely sensuous delight God Himself has prepared for us. Another idea has found aesthetic projection. Harmony with nature accounts for the puzzling illusions of the senses; they keep us in what later would be called "mental health," although, significantly, there was no term for the idea in the eighteenth century.

The idea of beauty finds its imaginative symbol in the famous figure of the romantic hero:

> In short, our souls are at present delightfully lost and bewildered in a pleasing delusion, and we walk about like the enchanted hero of a romance, who sees beautiful castles, woods, and meadows, and at the same time hears the warbling of birds and the purling of streams; but, upon the finishing of some secret spell, the fantastic scene breaks up, and the disconsolate knight finds himself on a barren heath or in a solitary desert.

The discovery of the distinction between primary and secondary qualities, Addison seems to think, is an achievement of the moderns, and he cites Locke's *Essay Concerning the Human Understanding*. He is quite complacent about the situation, but the image of the enchanted hero has an almost premonitory force. Suggesting the medieval romances, it has the feeling of the illusionary scene which is seldom absent from the romanticists' attitude toward the Middle Ages. Again, the awakening on the heath is ominous (in Keats's "La Belle Dame sans Merci" it happens in earnest), as if the spell of nature which would last for a century were to break up eventually. Addison's almost miraculously chosen words are an omen of what was to occur: "lost and bewildered in a pleasing delusion . . ."

What if nature as spiritual support for man in his newly discovered universe turns out to be a deception after all? And not a deception planned by a beneficent Creator? Again, is there not, unconsciously expressed, a suspicion that a subjective art cannot in the long run be substantial and true? However pleased Addison may seem to be by the modern discoveries, the sense of imprisonment in a world of subjective phenomena brings on a deep restlessness. We desire, in Keats's phrase, "fellowship with essence"—that essence which, Locke sternly informed the world, is forever unknowable, the essence of a pebble, or ourselves, no less than that of God. We want to have contact with what is real and true beyond our little selves. Romantic irony is implicit in the awakening of the enchanted hero.

The third category of aesthetic impressions is the "new," which, I believe, is suggested by Longinus' word "extraordinary." The influence of the new philosophy is to be seen in Addison's treatment of this aesthetic quality. For Longinus, the word would include mainly the marvelous, the prodigies and fearful events that arouse wonder. Addison's "fairy way of writing," of which more later, might in part be included here. But the word Addison uses is the "new," with no suggestion of the admiration belonging to the sublime. "We are indeed so often conversant with one set of objects, and tired out with so many repeated shows of the same things, that whatever is new or uncommon contributes a little to vary human life . . ." (*Spect.* 412). The "new" does not mean new combinations of ideas, the novelties of wit, so much as simply new sensations and unfamiliar scenes. We think of the conventional tourist.

On a higher level, the desire for the "new" encourages us "in the pursuit after knowledge," and furthers the search "into the wonders of [God's] creation." Here is the sign of the Baconian theory of scientific investigation. The advancement of learning requires the collecting of as many facts from as broad a range as possible, to be presented to an unprejudiced understanding for classification. Scientific endeavor of this kind could take the distorted form of gathering great numbers of curios in the manner of Shadwell's Virtuoso. Behind such grotesqueries lay the conviction that an unbiased, alert intelligence provided with an adequate method will automatically be capable of ordering the facts. Extending the boundaries of the known in terms of *quantity* of experience is more important than "invention" within the area of what is already known. One function of poetry, accordingly, is to bring new pictures before our imaginations. Even Dr. Johnson remarks that a merit of the poet is that he describes "new images." These are not metaphors or other media of intellection but, literally, new experiences. Description for its own sake is a function of the poem.

The final cause, the encouragement of the pursuit after knowledge, is rather at variance with Addison's phrase "tired out with so many repeated shows of the same things . . ." The suggestion of a need for novelties to cure ennui has a familiar, modern ring. Ennui as a problem had appeared in the drama, but had been treated satirically in the comedy of manners. Addison takes it seriously, however, as a continuing and expected part of common experience. Indeed, boredom is an oblique result of regarding the universe itself as an entertainment.

A new terminology was needed to express a new kind of thinking about art. When, in 1735, A. G. Baumgarten applied to the "science of perception" the word *aesthetá*, he signalized a change that had in fact occurred. The influence of such English writers as Shaftesbury and Addison was felt early and strongly in Germany, and Baumgarten could hardly have failed to know the *Spectator* essays on a subject that deeply interested him.[9] He sharply separates the mental activities into things known by the reason (*noetà*) and those perceived (*aesthetá*). The latter class constitutes a material of knowledge separate from and parallel to that of reason; the objects of aesthetic are not merely raw material for a higher faculty, but have a "perfection" of their own.[10] Sensations of the latter kind are vivid but confused—that is, not analyzed and organized (by the reason or understanding); the materials of the *noetà*, in contrast, are analyzed but not individualized. The qualities of the *aesthetá*, then, constitute a "perfection" as they would not for an earlier philosophy, and logical clarity and precision tend to become alienated from the poetic effect. All this was merely a systematization of new ways of thinking that had already developed. One result of the differentiation in a philosophical system of the "aesthetic" was that a new, separate branch of philosophy was established. Before Kant, no major philosopher devoted a large and distinct part of his work to the theory of art and its effects; after Kant, few major philosophers failed to do this.[11]

In the establishment of "aesthetic," Addison, I believe, played a great part. He wrote perhaps the first real treatise on aesthetics. Yet his essential contribution was not the recognition that the new epistemology led to the specialization, horizontally, of mental faculties; others had anticipated him here. Nor was the recognition that the new epistemology had elevated the simple idea to new dignity and significance peculiarly Addison's; Baumgarten's distinction could and no doubt would eventually have been made. Addison's peculiar contribution was to establish a moral and ideal justification for giving to the purely sensuous an unprecedented dignity and value. With his final causes, he did much to allay the distrust of the "lower" and perilous sense impression. With this change, he indicated a new course for the arts to follow.

So many later developments of art, especially of poetry, in the eighteenth century and even beyond are adumbrated in Addison's papers on the imagination that we can consider only the most striking.

The difference between the great and the literary sublime may be illustrated by contrasting two descriptions. In one of the *Paradise Lost* essays (*Spect.* 315), Addison describes an episode from that epic:

Satan, after having long wandered upon the surface, or outmost wall of the universe, discovers at last a wide gap in it, which led to the creating . . . His sitting upon the brink of this passage, and taking a survey of the whole face of nature that appeared to him new and fresh in all its beauties, with the simile illustrating this circumstance, fills the mind of the reader with as surprising and glorious an idea as any that arises in the whole poem. He looks down into that vast hollow of the universe with the eye, or (as Milton calls it in his first book) with the kenn of an angel. He surveys all the wonders in this immense emphitheatre that lie between both the poles of heaven, and takes in at one view the whole round of the creation.

The scene is sublime and "immense," but not in the romantic manner. It is part of a great episode, which creates the setting for the "surprising and glorious" idea. The scene is not its own end, nor yet is it properly the infinite. The "vast hollow of the universe" of Milton is not Space deified. Satan's view recalls the great landscape painting, which is to be reflected upon; it is not an effect on a passive imagination. Sublimity, in short, is still a means. The aesthetic and the rational dwell in one house. The controlling idea is a thought and not an impression.

The scene, however, takes on a new rationale within a few decades. Young, in *Night Thoughts*, IX, thus describes it:

> Something, like magic, strikes from this blue vault;
> . . . . We feel
> A sudden succour, unimplor'd, unthought;
> *Nature* herself does half the work of *man*.
> Seas, rivers, mountains, forests, deserts, rocks,
> The promontory's height, the depth profound
> Of subterranean, excavated grots,
> Black grow'd, and vaulted high, and yawning wide
> From *Nature's* structure, or the scoop of *Time*,
> If ample of dimension, vast of size,—
> E'en these an aggrandizing impulse give; . . .

The magic of nature does "half the work of man." The effect is "unthought." The magic effect is quantitative; the grot produces its ineffable effect, if "ample of dimension"; the result is an "aggrandizing impulse." The feeling for glory has been transformed into unrelieved vastness.

The principles underlying the effusions of Young would be obscure to Milton. We can understand them if we look at their statement in Addison. The pleasures of the imagination, he tells us, derive from two sources: immediate experience of sensations, especially from nature and from artistic creations, above all those of architecture; and secondary pleasures "which flow from the ideas of visible objects, when the objects are not actually before the eye, but are called up into our memories or formed into agreeable visions of things that are either absent or fictitious" (*Spect.* 411).

Supreme among the arts that evoke the secondary pleasures is poetry. The poet can "get the better of nature," for "words, when well chosen, have so great a force in them, that a description often gives us more lively ideas than the sight of things themselves" (*Spect.* 416). This remark appears to be inconsistent with Addison's expressed preference for nature over art. An illusory quality of the imagination would seem to conflict with the faith in the spiritual influence of pristine scenes of nature presented as accurately as possible. The conflict bothers writers in the eighteenth century. Some prefer the straightforward description; Mrs. Montagu went so far in this direction that she could obtain the proper effect from descriptive poetry only when she sat, book in hand, beside the actual scene described. Others, as Lessing in the *Laocoön,* stressed the effect, even divorced from reference to any reality. Yet there is also a certain consistency between Addison's views, and to understand it involves an understanding of his conception of the imagination.

The world presents "visionary" beauty and would make but a poor impression did we see it in its stark truth. God the Artist therefore has endowed us with the gift of seeing colors, of smelling odors, which are nothing but colorless and scentless atoms. Through the secondary imagination we can behold visionary scenes far more entrancing than any that can "be found in the whole compass of nature." In using our imaginations independently to create our own fantasies, or at least our heightened impressions of reality, we are merely coöperating with the divine art. The criterion throughout is not the constitution of reality but subjective response.

For the imagination has laws of its own, and they are different from the principles of knowledge. Addison associates symmetry and the like with beauty, which is of lesser importance than the great in his scale of aesthetic values. Succeeding writers go beyond him, associating a subordinate art with the analytical understanding, which arranges images in balanced patterns, and which thus could be thought of as the power that most appreciates symmetry and proportion; but, according to this opinion, the higher imagination almost per contra avoids ordered perfection of form. The popularity of the "natural" or "English" garden was already evident when Addison was writing.

Addison, then, feels that the artist is a "second maker under Jove," but not in the sense that Renaissance writers used this image. The artist does not complete and exemplify an objective ideal design which imperfect matter can only partially realize in nature. He is the skillful manipulator of pictures, the master of the sensations, who like a magician may call up more wonderful scenes than any we can observe with our own eyes (*Spect.* 416).

> The reader finds a scene drawn in stronger colours, and painted more to the life in his imagination, by the help of words, than by an actual survey of the scene which they describe. In this case the poet seems to get the better of nature: he takes, indeed, the landscape after her, but gives it more vigorous touches, heightens its beauty, and so enlivens the whole piece, that the images which flow from the objects themselves appear weak and faint, in comparison of those that come from the expressions.

The procedure of the poet, as Addison describes it, shows how he adapts Locke's epistemology: "As we look on any object, our idea of it is, perhaps, made up of two or three simple ideas; but when the poet represents it, he may either give us a more complex idea of it, or only raise in us such ideas as are most apt to affect the imagination." The simple idea, the single impression, as Pater says, is the firm reality. The sentence is remarkably parallel to another in the last paragraph of the last paper in the series (*Spect.* 421), where Addison makes God Himself the great Artist of the soul. Thus he describes heaven and hell in terms of the effects on the imagination:

We have already seen the influence that one man has over the fancy of another, and with what ease he conveys into it a variety of imagery; how great a power then may we suppose in him, who knows all the ways of affecting the imagination, who can infuse what ideas he pleases, and fill those ideas with terrour and delight to what degree he thinks fit? . . . In short, he can so exquisitely ravish or torture the soul through this single faculty, as might suffice to make the whole heaven or hell of any finite being.

We return, then, to the conflict between art as representation and art as magical impression. In one essay (421) he says that a "noble metaphor," to please the imagination, should exhibit a likeness to its object "very exact, or very agreeable, as we love to see a picture where the resemblance is just, or the posture and air graceful." This is to destroy the principal function of metaphor. Earlier (414) he says of the picture in a camera obscura that the "chief reason" for the delight it gives the imagination is "its near resemblance to nature," which is heightened by the "motion of the things it represents." Yet in the same essay (414), where he extols exact resemblance, he commends the poem of imagination that "bestows a kind of existence, and draws up to the reader's view several objects which are not to be found in being. It makes additions to nature, and gives a greater variety to God's works." The paradox appears complete in one sentence: "But tho' there are several of these wild scenes, that are more delightful than any artificial shows; yet we find the works of nature still more pleasant, the more they resemble those of art" (*Spect.* 414).

Which is superior, art or nature? Addison seems to resolve the ancient question by answering: both. The explanation is not, I think, merely a genial but illogical syncretism; rather, the imagination is both a means of receiving, in all their integrity, the impressions of a nature that is an unfoldment of divinity, and, also, a creator of illusion shows after the manner of the divine art. We are pleased to observe the precise representation of the wild scenes that, as Beattie says, can work our souls' eternal health; we are pleased with what "seems to get the better of nature" and we rejoice in our enchanted garden.

What of the artist himself? Addison has little to say on this subject. The implication is, however, clear: the poet, especially, is a conscious manipulator of images, is in control of his material at all times, and works according to real, if not consciously apprehended, aesthetic principles to produce precisely foreseen effects on the psyche of the reader. The comparison with God the Artist of heaven and hell is decisive. It is possible, however, to see the artist very differently. Perhaps he is primarily a receiver and transmitter of impressions, even to the point of exercising no conscious control. Perhaps the impressions work on him, forming their own combinations in the nonconscious depths of the mind, and he merely records his visions and dreams. What leads to such a conclusion is an inconsistency in the idea of the imagination. Addison emphasizes that the imagination is a power of passive response and that it is quite unlike the understanding. Yet the imagination is also a faculty of creation, even of calculated planning to produce evaluated responses. Does the poet, then, work by instinct? Or, as Addison almost suggests, does the understanding itself move into the aesthetic, working on the imagination for its own purposes?

Another final cause for the pleasures of the imagination, one not included in the primary triad, is our delight "in those accidental landskips of trees, clouds and cities, that are sometimes found in veins of marble; in the curious fret-work of rocks and grottos; and, in a word, in any thing that hath such a variety of regularity as may seem the effect of design in what we call the works of chance" (*Spect.* 414). Again, it must be emphasized that this pleasure is immediate and unreasoned; we do not reflect that it suggests design. The Boyle Lectures were designed to appeal to the understanding. But, as the effect of the great creates in us, without ratiocination, the idea of the divine, so the "accidental landskips" create, also without mediation of thought, the impression that the universe is no mere fortuitous concourse of atoms. This sentence illustrates, moreover, the complexity of relationship between the words "design" and "nature." On the one hand, the eighteenth century sought the wild and irregular, which was no product of the artificial, and therefore false, mind of man; on the other hand, it delighted in manifestations of regularity in the natural, considering that they demonstrate a great Artist at work. So Addison says that "we find the works of nature still more pleasant, the more they resemble those of art." A compromise is seen in such phenomena as the "artful irregularity" of garden designs which "Capability" Brown created.

The last six papers of the series present what is, in all probability, the first system of aesthetics recognizable as such. Again, elementary and crude in some respects though it is, the system traces out the forms of a new kind of art in a new kind of society. In Addison's rapid survey of the arts, the criterion is always the effect produced upon the psyche. The division of arts is between those that produce direct response, that seem to present to the eye the very images that produce the pleasures, and those that raise ideas by using the "signs of things." Within these groups, the preference among arts in the first class is for the most literally representative; that in the second classification, for the art that is least literal, that most strikingly "gets the better of nature."

Since Addison's preference is for the second of the two groups, I have discussed poetry first. Within the first classification, the arts producing direct responses to images, architecture and gardening—little natures—and statuary as imitative are most important. The statue, Addison says, "shows us something *likest* the object that is represented" (*Spect.* 416). Such a sentence reveals how far he is drifting from the classical idea of ideal imitation. Painting is in an anomalous position, as it is generally in eighteenth-century aesthetic theory; it seems to be like reality, yet it is two-dimensional, and much of the representation available to statuary is lost; but it does not possess the capabilities for new creation that language does.

Architecture produces the effect of the great both by its bulk and by its "greatness of manner" (*Spect.* 415). This art is a favorite with Addison, for it can provide a single vast idea, and the effect of the great is enhanced if it is produced not by a complex of impressions but seemingly by one limitless simple idea. So concave and convex figures in buildings have a "greater air" than any others. These figures are preferable because in them "we generally see more of the body, than in those of other kinds." This principle recurs in critical discussions of the "natural sublime." The eye must take in all the expanse at once, avoiding the danger that if "the sight must split upon several angles, it does not take in one uniform idea, but several ideas of the same kind."

The pleasures derived from seeing buildings can in theory be divided among the triad, but in practice the great takes preëminence to the virtual exclusion of the other. Perhaps never before had so much emphasis been placed on the artistic value of *mass*. Addison cites a long passage (based on Evelyn's translation) from Fréart's *Parallel of the Ancient and Modern Architecture*. But, while the French writer, also, stresses the need for few divisions of buildings, his reason is different. Fréart is concerned to avoid any impression of the "little and mean." We must, he says, achieve "grandeur of manner." The key words are the opposed adjectives "magnificent" and "mean." Fréart is concerned that a structure reflect the nobility, the exaltation, in a hierarchy of society, of its owners. Hence, the recurrent term "mean" as signifying all that is to be avoided. He wrote in the age of Louis XIV, when the principle of glory was fully exemplified by the king's builders. The building should be grand because the imagination delights in grandeur.

Addison, on the contrary, is confident that the vast impression produces a spiritual expansion, since, as Young expressed it (*Night Thoughts*, IX),

> . . . vast surveys, and the sublime of things
> The soul assimilate, and make her great.

Fréart is interested in the opinion, the artistic judgment, passed upon a building; Addison is attempting to describe an irresistible effect. Vast temples have been built, Addison explains, in order "that such stupendous works might . . . open the mind to vast conceptions, and fit it to converse with the divinity of the place."

"Everything that is majestic imprints an awfulness and reverence on the mind of the beholder, and strikes in with the natural greatness of the soul." The sentiment is Longinian, but the passiveness of "imprints" is incongruous with the spirit of *Peri Hupsous*; "arouses" might have been more appropriate. Although Addison discusses "greatness of manner," it is resolved, finally, into the illusion of bigness only. "Magnificence" in the true sense of the word has no real place in his discussion. "Stupendousness" is all, for it is a spiritual quality.

Poetry is, after all, the queen of the arts in Addison's discussion, and, since his influence is largely literary, we shall consider in more detail his analysis of the poetic imagination at work. If architecture, representing one extreme, overpowers us with the direct apprehension of the literally great idea, the poem, representing the opposite pole, has its own merit of a very different kind. When we view an object, "our idea of it is, perhaps, made up of two or three simple ideas; but when the poet represents it, he may either give us a more complex idea of it, or only raise in us such ideas as are most apt to affect the imagination." This statement is worth repeating, for it implies two points of great importance for the evolving romantic movement in literature.

First, poetry increases apprehension, gives us more images than our own sensations and memories do. The simple ideas are to be worked together and added up in a quantitative manner. And, second, poetry selectively filters impressions, picking out those "most apt to affect the imagination." The implication is that the powers and senses of the mind respond in specialized ways to the simple ideas that impinge on consciousness. Certain impressions are peculiarly adapted to one power rather than another, as we do not hear green or see the sounds of a flute. The division of impressions among the three powers is not so absolute as that of the senses, and yet some groups of images seem to be adapted in a special way to the faculty of knowledge, others to the imagination, and so forth. (The adaptation, to be strictly accurate, is the other way round.) Among those "most apt to affect the imagination" are the secondary qualities of matter—indeed, many of them seem to have no other purpose—and the large, undistinguished impressions. The detailed, especially the distinguished and classified, appeals naturally to the understanding. The powers are mutually exclusive. The poet should, as much as possible, use imaginative words as opposed to words with exact and limited meanings. Addison suggests that the process may be more complex than an immediate response would be. ". . . raise in us such ideas as are most apt to affect the imagination" would imply that certain ideas may be a starting point, evoking clusters of associations peculiar to the workings of the imagination.

We can see now why Addison repeats none of the warnings, invariable before his time, about imagination getting the better of judgment and about how Right Reason must always assess the pleasures of the imagination. It is true that there can never be a complete separation of powers, although in such later movements as surrealism there was a desperate attempt to make a complete break of nonrational from rational in the creative process. Nor does he go to the extreme of Poe, who asserts that "he must be theory-mad beyond redemption who, in spite of these differences [between the mental faculties] shall still persist in attempting to reconcile the obstinate oils and waters of Poetry and Truth" (*The Poetic Principle*).

Yet Addison has made the understanding and the imagination seem very much like oil and water. Apparently he envisions a mutually occupied territory between the understanding and the imagination. They can meet, since, the world of nature being the great object of imagination, students of nature in their studies can, as a kind of by-product, provide pleasure for the imaginative sensitivity. "But among this set of writers, there are none who more gratify and enlarge the imagination, than the authors of the new philosophy, whether we consider their theories of the earth or heavens, the discoveries they have made by glasses, or any other of their contemplations on nature" (*Spect.* 420). "This set of writers" refers to those who are obliged to follow nature exactly, as historians, geographers, and scientists. The response of the imagination to their writings is, however, sharply to be distinguished from the delight the understanding derives from learning. While the understanding can "open an infinite space on every side of us," the imagination cannot follow all the way; she finds "her self swallowed up in the immensity of the void that surrounds it." The imagination, therefore, does not serve to make vivid the abstractions of science. Her pleasures are quite discrete from those of the understanding; while the sober sister is engaged in measuring, analyzing, hypothesizing, the other is rapt in a "pleasing astonishment." There is a suggestion, in eighteenth-century poetry, of borrowing by one power from the other. The auras of ideas are exploited; the poet tends rather to describe the law of gravitation than to state it by way of increasing the reader's knowledge. He aims at wonder and a kind of awful mystery.

Some of the aversion to the "philosophical poem" may arise from this separation of powers. The point is not that the conceptions of reason have no place in poetry, but that they must, so to speak, be naturalized and subordinated in the land of the poetic muse. The mind enjoys a multiplicity of pleasures. In *Spectator* 421, Addison reflects the common eighteenth-century fear of thinking that gets very far from immediate sensory experience.

> The pleasures of the imagination are not wholly confined to such particular authors as are conversant in material objects, but are often to be met with among the polite masters of morality, criticism, and other speculations abstracted from matter, who, tho' they do not directly treat of the visible parts of nature, often draw from them their similitudes, metaphors, and allegories. By these allusions a truth in the understanding is as it were reflected by the imagination; we are able to see something like colour and shape in a notion, and to discover a scheme of thoughts traced out upon matter.

Addison does not assert that the imagination, reflecting the truth in the understanding or serving as a means of exploring ideas, supplements the inadequacy of language to express "intellectuals." An allusion may be useful to illustrate and explain, but there is no hint that "metaphorike wings" may carry us where the language of reason is helpless.

The next sentence makes the point clear: "And here the mind receives a great deal of satisfaction, and has two of its faculties gratified at the same time, while the fancy is busy in copying after the understanding, and transcribing ideas out of the intellectual world into the material." Two faculties are gratified at the same time. As far as instruction goes, the understanding does the job alone; the imagination follows after, rather than precedes, as Hobbes's discussion would suggest. But it is desirable that the abstract ideas be brought back to common sensory impressions, and that those ideas appear in images providing entrancing objects for the imagination to contemplate. The statement, considered in its entirety, is not very different in tenor from Poe's forthright assertion that "with the Intellect or with the Conscience, [poetry] has only collateral relations" (*The Poetic Principle*).

When, later in the century, Bishop Lowth states that the purpose of poetry is a unity of "advantage and pleasure," and proposes "utility as its ultimate object, and pleasure as the means by which that end may be effectually accomplished," we recognize a voice that already belongs to the past.[12] For Addison nowhere suggests that the mind is won to belief or galvanized to action by the imagination. The passiveness of the process is remarkable. This kind of poem, or this kind of writing whether in poetry or prose technically (the epic being considered didactic), Addison discusses briefly, almost as an afterthought, at the end of the "Pleasures" series.

Metaphor and similitude, then, although they illustrate ideas for the intellect, serve primarily to give pleasure to the imagination. In doing so, they should appeal to the distinctive threefold categories of the imagination, and should present precise resemblances.

> A noble metaphor, when it is placed to an advantage, casts a kind of glory round it, and darts a lustre through a whole sentence; these different kinds of allusion are but so many different manners of similitude, and, that they may please the imagination, the likeness ought to

be very exact, or very agreeable, as we love to see a picture where the resemblance is just, or the posture and air agreeable.

This is as complete a statement of the antithesis to the "organic metaphor" as may be readily found. The metaphor becomes a thing in itself, to be contemplated for its own sake.

Here, perhaps, begins a "dissociation of sensibility." The specialization of the mind was bound to produce consequences of great importance. The assumption that there is a peculiar vocabulary of imagination leads to a warning that the poet should avoid similes based on instances that are "too mean and familiar," however appropriate those instances may be for the subject. One of Addison's achievements was to help convince poets that there is a single truly poetic diction. Allusions to chess or tennis or trade, he tells us, are per se excluded from this enchanted world. The result was to blur the distinctions between levels of poetry according to genre. There is only one genre—the poetic—and it comes to be identified with the sublime; even the beautiful serves as a means of enhancing the great effect. It is especially ironic that Pope should have been blamed for legislating poetic diction when, with his adaptation of style to genre, with his use of familiar language that would be excluded under Addison's test, he belongs to the older tradition.

It is instructive to compare Addison's attitude with that of another writer, Joseph Trapp, whose *Praelectiones Poeticae* were composed at about this time. He states as a matter of course that "the style of Poetry is extremely various; because every Species of this divine Art has a diction proper to itself." [13] Trapp in some ways is close to Addison, usually preferring an elevated, grand style and, for metaphors, descriptions of nature; but he does grant that a beautiful and sublime thought may, by choice, be expressed by "plain and simple" words—a point in harmony with the true Longinian spirit. Various kinds of poetry are adapted for various utilitarian purposes. He frequently repeats the old saws that poetry "observes certain Laws and rules," and that it "is brought to the test of right Reason" (*Lect.* II). We are emphatically reminded that "Profit may be the chief End of Poetry, and ought to be so; but for that very Reason

Pleasure should be joined to it, and accompany it, as a Handmaid, to minister to its Occasions" (*Lect.* III). As Addison's title indicates, however, the handmaid is in process of becoming co-mistress in the house of the mind; in the near distance looms the idea that effect is everything.

The reduction of the poetic principle to pure effect is well illustrated by what may be Addison's single most startling innovation. In *Spectator* 419 he discusses what "Mr. Dryden calls the fairy way of writing . . . wherein the poet quite loses sight of nature, and entertains his reader's imagination with the characters and actions of such persons as have many of them no existence, but what he bestows on them." The mention of Dryden indicates that Addison is referring to the great debate that had raged, in earlier decades, over whether supernatural "machinery" may properly be introduced into the heroic poem. Dryden, in *An Essay of Heroic Plays*, stoutly defends "the enthusiastic parts of poetry," instancing the ghost of Polydorus in Virgil, Tasso's "Enchanted Wood," and Spenser's Bower of Bliss.

> And if any man object the improbabilities of a spirit appearing, or of a palace raised by magic; I boldly answer him, that an heroic poet is not tied to a bare representation of what is true, or exceeding probable; but that he may let himself loose to visionary objects, and to the representation of such things as depending not on sense, and therefore not to be comprehended by knowledge, may give him a freer scope for imagination. 'Tis enough that, in all ages and religions, the greatest part of mankind have believed the power of magic . . . [14]

Dryden is always concerned with the *decorum* of use of the supernatural: Is it justified by truth, by "nature," even if it is outside visible nature? He attempts to show that the representing of apparitions is based on probability. Thus, in the *Apology for Heroic Poetry and Poetic Licence*, he remarks that imaginary creatures may be "founded on the conjunction of two natures, which have a real separate being"; Biblical authorization is cited; and the basic argument, in both essays, is that men have commonly believed in effects of magic and the like, so " 'tis still an imitation, though of other men's fancies."

All this is rooted in Neo-Aristotelian doctrines of imitation as tested by truth to nature. Addison himself, in earlier *Spectators* (70 and 74), defended "Chevy-Chase" in the spirit of Dryden, since it is a miniature epic according to the rules of the "greatest modern critics" for the heroic poem, and passes the Longinian test for sublimity; and he defends the use of the marvelous in terms reminiscent of Dryden.

We are surprised, then, to see, in *Spectator* 419, a departure from this kind of argument. The new line of justification is based on subjective effects primarily. Addison in fact redefines "the fairy way of writing" to mean a source of vivid impressions on the imagination rather than an imitation of nature.

His definition of the supernatural is very different from that of Dryden and the French critics who debated about the appropriate "machinery" for the epic. Dryden's examples are classical, and have an allegorical character (at least as they were interpreted in the Renaissance). The marvels of Ovid's *Metamorphoses*, the shade of Patroclus in the *Iliad*, the kingdom of the dead in the *Aeneid* —these Dryden speaks of. Such episodes, even though they are derived, ultimately, from folklore and primitive religion, have become "classical"; they have undergone the metamorphosis of a long tradition of high art and, to apply here the praise given Dryden's own style, what was brick the poets have made marble.

But Addison uncompromisingly speaks of Märchen, the raw material, so to speak, out of which such epic scenes as Aeneas' descent into the underworld were made. The poet who indulges in this kind of poetry, Addison believes, should "be very well versed in legends and fables, antiquated romances, and the traditions of nurses and old women, that he may fall in with our natural prejudices, and humor those notions which we have imbibed in our infancy." It is certainly not the traditions of nurses and old women, legends and fables, that Dryden defends; a primary goal of Renaissance literary theory was to exclude such crude and irrational material from the charmed circle of serious literature. All this looks back into the dark experience of infancy and childhood, of the race as well as of individuals. It recalls Locke's example of the nurse's tales of goblins in the dark, which the philosopher took (as no doubt Dryden would also) to be dangerous "notions" and "prejudices" that should be exposed by reason. Addison is deliberately defending as legitimate material for poetry that which cannot pass the tests of right reason, truth to nature, and good sense.

What happened here is, in fact, a prototype of what happened to the word "romantick" itself. It had been a synonym for the wild and extravagant, for imagination run wild. But in time the word became defiantly a term of commendation, as the peripheral in culture became central. Even so, what had been outside the pale of the rational perversely took on a peculiar value—the locus of conscience, for example, being transferred to the lower faculties. Addison is "romantick" when he justifies this poetry of the wild and false by the very arguments that the "Right Reason" critic would have used to condemn it. "[Such stories] bring up into our memory the stories we have heard in childhood, and favour those secret terrors and apprehensions to which the mind of man is naturally subject." Should the "secret terrors and apprehensions" be "favored"? Should they not rather be exposed to the clear light of the understanding? If, recognizing the importance of superstition in life, the artist represents it, should he not do so with a serious and rational end in mind? Yet Addison justifies reveling in the secret terrors and apprehensions, for these "descriptions raise a pleasing kind of horror in the mind of the reader, and amuse his imagination with the strangeness and novelty of the persons who are represented in them."

This is the rationale of Gregory Lewis' *Tales of Horror*, with their preposterous *frissons*, of the thrilling Gothic romances, and, in part, of the ballad revival. The association of ideas, which worried Locke, has been taken into respectability, for, as he himself said, we are all subject to irrational ideas. Like storms and frozen seas, superstition itself has been given usefulness in a universe where whatever is, is right. A consequence is a kind of divided-self conflict later in the century. "Monk" Lewis is an interesting example. He could compose horrific imitation ballads, which play upon the secret terrors and apprehensions of human nature, and he could then parody his own creations in cruelly rationalistic satire. A divided soul, he seems to do penance for deserting his own standard as a man of wit and reason.

Addison intimates a reason for the strange delight in wonder and horror, which he calmly accepts as a universal trait of human nature. The imagination by this means may form an idea of the "many intellectual beings in the world besides our selves" who doubtless exist and "who are subject to different laws and economies from those of mankind." This justification is the one closest to Dryden's, and, like Dryden, Addison says that these beings should be represented "naturally," that is, according to what we reason to be a priori rules for their behavior. (There is an interesting joining of ideas here. Addison's statements on this point are suggested by a passage in Thomas Burnet's *Archaeologiae Philosophicae* which Coleridge later added as the epigraph to *The Rime of the Ancient Mariner.*)

Yet this argument in Addison's essay seems "tacked on," and is not quite consistent with the main premises. The atmosphere of the supernatural had changed. Belief in the physical appearance of angels and other spirits, as well as of ghosts, had been regarded by religious philosophers as necessary to preserve religious faith against the insidious menace of Sadduceeism. Newton, Boyle, Burnet, and many others recognized this problem. More, Glanvill, and Cotton Mather collected tales about sightings of apparitions and operations of witches. Yet these men were all enthusiasts for the new philosophy. Glanvill wrote a defense of scientific method and was a spokesman of the Royal Society, and Cotton Mather's intelligent labors as a Fellow of that body are well known. Mather was, moreover, a Newtonian from the first, and almost became a martyr to his belief in the value of smallpox inoculations.

Not the new physics so much as the new psychology precipitated a crisis over the real experience of the supernatural. Locke stated that "angels of all sorts are naturally beyond our discovery; and all those intelligences, whereof it is likely there are more orders than of corporeal substances, are things whereof our natural faculties give us no certain account at all" (*Essay*, IV, iii, 27). For "our senses not being able to discover them, we want the means of knowing their particular existences" (*Essay*, IV, xi, 12). The mere fact that the mind can form ideas of these beings no more proves their existence than does the fact that we can imagine a centaur prove that creature's reality. Locke's conception of the mind, furthermore, destroys any notion of a ghost hovering about. Who could be haunted by a disembodied understanding? His implication that God may have given matter the power of sensing and reflecting had an uneasy effect. Locke's own belief in immortality was undoubtedly sincere, but it would have to be a different kind of immortality. A gulf, greater than any men had known before, had opened between the mind and any supernatural world that might exist. Addison's point is that we want to believe in the existence of spirits; we can never really know anything about them; and a pleasing delusion, not unlike that of color, is justified.

> . . . when we see, therefore, any of these [spirits] represented naturally, we cannot look upon the representation as altogether impossible; nay, many are prepossest with such false opinions, as dispose them to believe these particular delusions; at least, we have all heard so many pleasing relations in favour of them, that we do not care for seeing through the falshood, and willingly give our selves up to so agreeable an imposture.

Thus an ambivalence of a new kind is inescapable. These poems do, Addison admits, describe delusions; and even Shakespeare, who excelled in this noble extravagance, touches a "weak superstitious part of his reader's imagination." Yet this irrationality is Shakespeare's strength. Here the powers of the mind come into conflict. The understanding correctly terms legends "weak superstitious," but the imagination responds with delight. Addison is actually pleased that the "English are naturally fanciful, and very often disposed by that gloominess and melancholy of temper, which is so frequent in our nation, to many wild notions and visions, to which others are not so liable." Is it possible that a taste for wild notions is a positive advantage to the poetic sensibility? Nor is this the noble madness, the possession by a god or daimon, which had been attributed to poetic genius from Plato on; the poet's eye is not in a fine frenzy rolling. Addison concentrates on the reader, not on the poet; he describes a manipulation of sensibility in an area particularly susceptible of such manipulation. Nowhere else does Addison come so close to pure aestheticism. A justification of wonders is simply the fact that they do please the imagination; their very remoteness from truth and good sense gives them an especially imaginative quality. Nothing could better indicate how resolutely the imagination had struck out to make its own laws and follow its own ends.

The final cause, nevertheless is, as we might expect, not entirely absent. We learn that "almost the whole substance of [this kind of poetry] owes its original to the darkness and superstition of later ages [than the classical period] when pious frauds were made use of to amuse mankind, and frighten them into a sense of their duty." Here, by implication, the "Gothick" period, which for centuries had been considered an age of darkness and barbarism happily terminated by the rebirth of ancient culture, is rehabilitated and even exalted. How can such a reversal be justified? Addison explains that one virtue of the superstitions of the dark ages is that "our forefathers looked upon nature with more reverence and horror before the world was enlightened by learning and philosophy." The implication is that, in ages of superstition, men, in spite of and partly because of intellectual darkness, live closer to saving nature than they do in times of enlightenment. A reason for the romantic attempt to re-create the atmosphere, or supposed atmosphere, of folk literature is the effort to regain the reverence for nature, the simplicity and immediacy of feeling, attributed to the uneducated, pious man.

As we read this *Spectator*, a cold wind for a moment seems to blow across the page: perhaps there is an inveterate enmity between the understanding and the imagination. When Addison speaks of "men of cold fancies, and philosophical dispositions" who "object to this kind of poetry, that it has not probability enough to affect the imagination," our thoughts go forward to this kind of phrase, used by writers at the end of the century, who said that an age of philosophy cannot be an age of poetry. We think of Macaulay, saying that poetry, like the magic lantern in a dark room, shines best in a dark age. Can an age of imagination, which seemingly must precede full civilization, be reconciled with the progress of the human mind? The possibility that imagination, far from being an ideal ally of reason, is its inveterate rival and antagonist, now emerges into the open.

One passage from this series reveals, as though unconsciously, the real significance of Addison's theory more strikingly than does any overt statement. Describing the effects of the imagination, he characterizes the three most admired masterpieces of classical art in terms of the great, the beautiful, and the new. In each instance, subjective effect is divorced from theme and content in a way that is new in criticism. Thus the *Iliad* "strikes the imagination wonderfully with what is great": "Reading the Iliad is like travelling through a country uninhabited, where the fancy is entertained with a thousand savage prospects of vast deserts, wide uncultivated marshes, huge forests, misshapen rocks and precipices." How divorced from "Right Reason" is this formlessness, this absence of humanity! The *Iliad* has indeed become a "romantic" poem, though Pope's translation of Homer was yet to be published, with its representation of the *Iliad* as a noble, heroic poem of a noble society. Only when the subjective impressions derived from a poem were completely dissociated from its content could such a passage be written.

Students of the history of romanticism have observed that, as Albert Gérard says, "En sapant le primat de la raison, le dix-huitième siècle prépare la voie à la théorie de l'imagination." He adds, however, the common impression that "En tout état de cause, l'abolition du primat de la raison devait être l'œuvre des philosophes," and hence, "les critiques n'ont ni la puissance de raisonnement abstrait ni l'autorité nécessaire pour imposer leurs intuitions." [15]

This view, it seems to me, contains a mixture of truth and error. On the one hand, the primacy of reason had been abolished long before the end of the eighteenth century, so far as aesthetics was concerned. Its abolition took place in no vacuum, nor was it the rediscovery of a great truth that a narrow and rigid conservatism had obscured. Rather, it was a consequence of great cultural changes, bringing about new cultural needs—and that is the theme of this book. We do not understand high romanticism, I think, unless we realize that the essentials existed long before the birth of Wordsworth, long before Rousseau. On the other hand, dilemmas and problems of great complexity and importance did emerge from the early, relatively crude concepts of the romanticists. These were dilemmas that philosophy was called upon to resolve, but the full story of the attempts at solutions lies beyond the scope of this book. I shall complete the story by surveying several of the most interesting and important theorists of the eighteenth century after Addison, and by showing what the concept of the imagination had become before the time of Wordsworth and Coleridge.

VI THE IMAGINATION AS A MEANS OF GRACE

The eighteenth was the century when the aesthetician came into his own, although he was hardly aware that he was theorizing specifically about aesthetics. Like Baumgarten, in the *Reflections on Poetry*, he may have intended only to elucidate the real meaning of an ancient authority; like Addison, he may have seemed only to be clearing up the meaning of ambiguous words; like Hutcheson, he may have been a moral philosopher, fitting each "power" of the mind into a grand system that would relate it to the whole of nature.

Important and thorough studies of these systems have been made, and it would be useless to cover ground that has been covered already.[1] In reviewing certain aspects of the aesthetic theories that sprang up in this century, I make no claim to completeness. My purpose is to concentrate on the *place* of imagination, how it was seen in the context of the new attitudes toward man, human nature, and the relations to external nature which I have described in the preceding chapters.

Before the details of systems can be fully understood, their rationale must be appreciated. The key to the problem is the word "imagination." If the mind is fragmented, if understanding, imagination, and moral sense represent specialized responses to varying kinds of impressions, there may follow certain kinds of solutions to the problem of why we have imagination at all, and what functions it should perform. The common belief is that, by means of imagination, a supernal influence, capable of elevating and transforming the soul, flows into the mind. This conviction, defined by Addison, became the theme on which many variations were composed. The theorists were interested in filling in the gaps which remained after Addison's papers appeared. What forms does the divine power assume? What are the mechanisms whereby immediate sense impressions from physical nature may work their beneficent effects? In the present chapter, I am more concerned to keep ultimate purposes in mind and to sketch *kinds* of answers to the problems than to review the entire history of aesthetic speculation.

A new and revolutionary image of the human mind had come into being after the publication of Locke's *Essay*. Ideas had been contributed, and there existed, as yet inchoate, a new system of mental and moral philosophy. Yet, at the end of the first quarter of the century, no systematic exposition of the new conceptions had been made. For an age that intensely desired to see order and method in the maze of experience, the situation was intolerable; and it might have been predicted, by the 1720's, that the systematizing philosopher would soon appear.

The philosopher was Francis Hutcheson, founder of the Scottish school for the study of man. In systematization rather than in original contributions lies his greatest importance. He provided, in *An Inquiry into the Original of Our Ideas of Beauty and Virtue* (1726), the textbook of a new moral philosophy. It is significant that he began with an effort to reconcile the two sources of the new morality—Shaftesbury and Addison. The dominant influence of Shaftesbury is unmistakable, from the language and structure of Hutcheson's concepts as well as from his eulogy of that writer in the preface to the fourth edition of the *Inquiry*. Molesworth, who is also eulogized, was a kind of transmission agent for Shaftesbury's ideas, and to him especially is due the Shaftesburian influence on the radical and republican philosophers of the later decades. And Hutcheson, like all the members of the Scottish philosophy-of-man school, owed his psychology ultimately to Locke.[2] The Addisonian note will appear in the subsequent discussion.

Hutcheson carries to the very extreme Locke's point that all mental activity is a species of perception. These perceptions are actions of sense. The mind operates through its powers of sensitivity to sensations. "Inner senses," finer than the basic external ones, provide for a perfect adjustment of the personality to all the exigencies and problems of life, whether material, moral, or philosophical. Faith in the natural harmoniousness of man's being is the soul of Hutcheson's philosophy. The natural, almost instinctive response to the environment—if the personality is in order—serves as conscience and reason both; and the moral sense plays the part that "attraction" plays in holding the universe together in a perfect system. No longer do we think of reason as a kind of schoolmaster in the soul, governing the many violent impulses of our passions and wills; rather, the immediate responses fall into their right relationships, impelling the mind to the right activities.

> Without a distinct consideration of this moral faculty, a species endued with such a variety of senses, and of desires frequently interfering, must appear a complex confused fabrick, without any order or regular consistent design. By means of it, all is capable of harmony, and all its powers may conspire in one direction, and be consistent with each other. . . .[3]

Where selfish and public interests (both are quite natural) conflict, the moral sense "recommends the generous part by an immediate undefinable perception." Its authority being that of immediate response, it has the undefinable character of pure sensation. The word "undefinable" runs like a leitmotiv through moral philosophy. The impression now is that what can be clearly stated, precisely limited, cannot have great moral validity, and indeed may be contrary to those generous impulses with which God has endowed our natures.

Yet Hutcheson does talk at length about reason. This power has two functions. On a lower plane, it is merely instrumental, just as Shaftesbury implies. Concerned with details and means to ends, reason in this aspect is no trustworthy guide to ultimate purposes and principles. The tendency is for mere instrumental reason to promote the narrow, selfish desires of the individual. On a higher level, however, is "reflection"—meaning, here, a capacity of the mind to rise to the loftiest heights, to survey the inner senses, and to determine what each does and why. Surveying the mind from this eminence, we come to our senses, in a literal meaning of the word. Then the superiority of the moral sense becomes apparent, and we yield to its promptings. The mental life, like a fine watch, may get out of adjustment, a common cause being the false customs of society. When selfish principles of action gain the upper hand, we should exercise

> our powers of reasoning and comparing the several enjoyments which our nature is capable of, that we may discover which of them are of greatest consequence to our happiness; our capacity, by reasoning, of arriving to the knowledge of a *Governing Mind* presiding in this world, and of a moral administration, are of the highest consequence and necessity to preserve our affections in a just order, and to corroborate our *moral faculty*.[4]

It seemed to Hutcheson, as it did to the traditional philosopher and the theologian, that the end of life is beatitude; but, unlike the others, he believed in beatitude in this life and in this world; and so "pleasure" and "delight" and "joy" are the key words. The large, general, emotive kind of reason, then, establishes a state of mind which permits the various inner senses to perform their work in their due relationships. The higher reason is a kind of super-sense, a "calm, settled" perception of the Whole. To further this grand perception was a primary aim of the reflective-descriptive poets of the Thomson school.

The imagination, as one of the noble inner senses, Hutcheson defines in a way that obviously goes back to Addison, whom he cites as authority.[5] This faculty, as the title of the *Inquiry* hints, is a kind of counterpart for the moral sense. Hutcheson assumes that the pleasures of the imagination have a final cause, which he defines in Addisonian terms; indeed, in the *System of Moral Philosophy*, he refers the reader to *Spectator* 412 for the ultimate purpose of "grandeur," which is Addison's "the great."

The finer senses, since they *are* senses, all imply a passivity in the subject. They contemplate the ideas which the external senses convey to the mind. Just as some men naturally have an acute sense of colors, while others are blind even to the primary ones, so do some perceive the distinctions between, say, proportion and imbalance of objects, while others have no aesthetic awareness. The "greater capacity of receiving such pleasant ideas we commonly call a fine genius or taste." [6] Aesthetics thus has gone far toward becoming mechanical, as the idea of the genius has also. He now appears to have an exceptionally delicate and receptive sensibility; and he may be able to transmit to others, through images and words, the special quality and range of his perception.

The change in values is illustrated by one remark. The moralist usually had considered it a matter of course that the "rational" is superior to and served by the merely sensual; in the universe the ideal is the high and perhaps the only true reality. Hutcheson, in the first preface to his *Inquiry*, objects to this attitude.

> We shall generally find in our modern philosophick Writings, nothing further on this Head, than some bare Division of them into *Sensible*, and *Rational*, and some trite Common-place Arguments to prove the *latter* more valuable than the former. Our *sensible Pleasures* are slightly pass'd over, and explain'd only by some Instances in *Taste*, *Smells*, *Sounds*, or such like, which Men of any tolerable Reflection generally look upon as very trifling satisfaction.

When "sensible" pleasures—to be sure, of the finer kind—take on their own intrinsic value and rival the "rational," then for the first time we are within sight of an independent aesthetic theory.

That much of Hutcheson's work, like that of other authors I have discussed, is intended to fill deficiencies in Locke is indicated by this statement: "our late Inquirys have been very much employ'd about our *Understanding* . . . We generally acknowledge, that the Importance of any Truth is nothing else than its Moment, or Efficacy to make Men happy, or to give them the greatest and most lasting Pleasure; and *Wisdom* denotes only a Capacity of pursuing this End by the best Means." What purpose does this instrument of knowing and thinking serve? Locke had ignored this question, like an unwanted guest. Hutcheson considers it central. In the last clause of the passage, he faces the facts that, given the psychology of sensations, even the understanding serves a subordinate purpose, and that pleasure is indeed the real end of existence. To exist harmoniously in a harmonious universe, in the joy of being, is the supreme desideratum.

Thus Hutcheson established what might be called the "naïve" aesthetics of romanticism. The harmonious and beautiful universe really does have the qualities of beauty and majesty and order that we sense in our best moments, when our highest faculties are well employed. Harmonious mind, harmonious universe—all is clear, simple, and bright. Subjective and objective merge. We need not worry about whether truth or beauty or moral excellence exists without or within us; they are in both places simultaneously, perfectly corresponding. "As, in approving a beautiful form, we refer the beauty to the object; we do not say that it is beautiful because we reap some little pleasure in viewing it, but we are pleased in viewing it because it is antecedently beautiful" (*System*, I, iv, 12). Thus the ancient questions, which had so long plagued thinkers, about the reality and value of mind, of nature, of sensations, of qualities, seemed resolved: no longer need we look outside either nature or ourselves for the highest truths and values. The mists that had obscured the truth had blown away. It was a magical moment. If there was a "peace of the Augustans," perhaps it was here.

But, on closer examination, the answers seemed not so convincing, the old dilemmas, in new dress, appeared again; the shock on awakening from the spell was severe, and part of the "romantic agony" of later generations may be traced to that awakening. Without the optimism there might not have been some of the depression of Leopardi or of Hardy, or of certain writers in our own time.

Two opinions about the imagination and its place, one substantially traditional and the other relatively new, are dramatically confronted in Sir Joshua Reynolds' Seventh Discourse to the Royal Academy, and Blake's celebrated marginalia thereto. Thus Reynolds:

> To speak of genius and taste as in any way connected with reason or common sense, would be, in the opinion of some towering talkers, to speak like a man who possessed neither; who had never felt that enthusiasm, or, to use their own inflated language, was never warmed by that Promethean fire which animates the canvas and vivifies the marble.

Reynolds is not saying that imagination and emotion are to be excluded from art; quite the reverse. He is merely reasserting the ancient principle that the arts, though sensuous and passionate, are, if they fulfill their proper functions, the instruments—as is everything else in human life—of the central reason which guides and interprets life. He is not asserting a narrow and rigid dogma of rules; on that point there was already clear and general agreement. He is asserting the unity and the integrity, in the strict sense of the word, of the mind in all its actions. "It is the very same taste which relishes a demonstration in geometry, that is pleased with the resemblance of a picture to an original and touched with the harmony of music."

Blake's comment on this passage expresses the doctrine of the independence and supernal worth of the imagination. "Demonstration, Similitude, and Harmony are Objects of Reasoning Invention. Identity and Melody are Objects of Intuition." Only through the faculties of intuition can humanity achieve the salvation it so urgently needs; the rational faculty has brought us to our divided and imprisoned condition. We must free the imagination to perform its gracious work. So Blake would naturally object to such a statement as this: "In the midst of the highest flights of fancy or imagination, reason ought to preside from first to last, though I admit her more powerful operation is upon reflection." Blake retorts to

Reynolds: "If this is True, it is a devilish Foolish Thing to be an Artist." For, Blake exclaims, "all that is Valuable in Knowledge is Superior to Demonstrative Science, such as is Weighed and Measured"; and all who agree with Reynolds think "Mind and Imagination not to be above the Mortal and Perishing Nature."

When Locke narrowed the understanding to an efficient organ for knowing facts and forming accurate opinions from sense impressions, he thought he was eliminating those misty and unfruitful fancies about the higher reaches of the mind, which More had called the *mens*, the power of transcendent knowledge. Locke thought he was establishing common sense on its throne; but in fact he simply drove the *mens* elsewhere, to a nonrational area of the mentality.

Samuel Johnson, the most formidable and solid critic of the century, was of Reynolds' way of thinking about imagination. "The noblest beauties of art," he asserted in the *Life of West*, "are those of which the effect is co-extended with rational nature, or at least with the whole circle of polished life; what is less than this can be only pretty, the plaything of fashion, and the amusement of a day."

The controversy continued even into the period of the triumph of romanticism. Keats, Jeffrey says in his review of August, 1820, might as to subject matter be compared with Johnson, Theocritus, and Milton, but the comparison as to treatment is pejorative for Keats.

> The great distinction, however, between him and these divine authors, is, that imagination in them is subordinate to reason and judgment, while, with him, it is paramount and supreme—that their ornaments and images are employed to embellish and recommend just sentiments, engaging incidents, and natural characters, while his are poured out without measure or restraint, and with no apparent design but to unburden the breast of the author, and give vent to the overflowing vein of his fancy.

This is the crux of the matter; Jeffrey could also remark that "any one who, on this account, would represent the whole poem as despicable, must either have no notion of poetry, or no regard to truth." Not poetical insensitivity but a profound concern for the issue of greatest importance in the aesthetic revolution produced Jeffrey's censure. Jeffrey's comment is the epitome of the whole change I have been describing: the impression becomes the end in itself rather than a means of vitalizing a central idea. The result is that the genius "unburdens" his breast, the exhibition of his sensibility being the substance of his art.

These critics were, however, decidedly outnumbered, and the position of which they disapproved was to exert the dominant influence for generations. A survey of a few outstanding writers after Hutcheson will show that, although Blake's remarks have a peculiar vehemence because of his own faith and insight, his attitude, in important respects, was far from unique.

Mark Akenside's *The Pleasures of Imagination* (first version, 1744) shows in its title the source of the poet's inspiration. "The Design," a prose composition prefixed to the first edition, is an exceptionally interesting critical document. Not that it is wholly new; rather it is one of the most useful, and truest in the sense of representing the faith of practicing poets, statements of the faith that the imagination had inspired.

Addison had remarked that the imagination is "between" the senses and the understanding. Akenside brings this up to date, placing the power between the senses and the moral sense, which now occupies the place of honor in the mind: "There are certain powers in human nature which seem to hold a middle place between the organs of bodily sense and the faculties of moral perceptions: they have been called by a very general name, the Powers of Imagination." The idea of a collection of powers under one name owes something to Hutcheson's practice of breaking down the mental life into many different powers. The word "perception" is used here in the manner of Hume's *Treatise of Human Nature* (III, i, 1):

It has been observ'd, that nothing is ever present to the mind but its perceptions; and that all the actions of seeing, hearing, judging, loving, hating and thinking, fall under this denomination. The mind can never exert itself in any action, which we may not comprehend under the term of *perception;* and consequently that term is no less applicable to those judgments, by which we distinguish moral good and evil, than to every other operation of the mind. To approve of one character, to condemn another, are only so many different perceptions.

We need not postulate direct influence from Hume, however, for this idea (which should be recalled in considering the contemporary vogue for personification in poetry and rhetoric) merely summarizes what was implicit in Locke's remarks about thinking as seeing, as these remarks were extended by Shaftesbury and by Hutcheson. It is evident that the imagination, being the most immediately perceptual of the "intellectual senses," will be most closely in sympathy with the moral power.

Next, Akenside specifically says what Addison had implied: the "objects of sense" may be classified according to the special mental powers to which they are adapted. The grouping of sense impressions is mutually exclusive: each of the faculties has, so to speak, its own raw material. In this poem, Akenside says, he will "characterize those original forms or properties of being, about which [the imagination] is conversant, and which are by Nature adapted to it as light is to the eyes, or truth to the understanding."

Akenside takes over from Addison the ubiquitous triad of pleasures, but each, in the division of the faculty, becomes virtually a "power" in its own right. From Addison, too, comes the "amalgamating" principle: that various pleasures from various powers may be combined in a quantitative manner to produce a greater total delight. Thus the pleasures of imagination, the only ones proper to poetry strictly speaking, may yet be increased by "a *similar* exhibition of properties quite *foreign* to the imagination, insomuch that in every line of the most applauded poems, we meet with either ideas drawn from the external senses, or truths discovered to the understanding, or illustrations of contrivance and final causes, or above all the rest, with circumstances proper to awaken and engage the passions." Such a statement in effect reverses the traditional plan of a serious poem. Imagination, as Jeffrey asserts, is always "subordinate to reason and judgment" in the great poets;

but, in Akenside's remark—which is almost an apology for including in his poem material extraneous to the true pleasures of imagination—there is the assumption that, instead of imagination contributing to vitalize the process of reason, the reason may serve to enhance the imagination.

The full force of Jeffrey's censure does not, however, come down on Akenside and the poets of his persuasion because, in the eighteenth century, theory usually outran practice. *The Pleasures of Imagination,* like most of the "sublime" poems around it, has a core of versified philosophizing and didacticism. Akenside sets forth specifically how all the pleasures of imagination, whether derived from primary or from secondary sources, "might be deducible from one or other of those principles in the human mind, which are here established and explained." This is clear theorizing, even though embellished and ornamented by an intricate style; the idea is a central thread on which the images are strung.

Even so, Akenside thought of his didactic purpose in a way different from that of earlier philosophical poets. "The author's aim was not so much to give formal precepts, or enter into the way of direct argumentation, as, by exhibiting the most engaging prospects of Nature, to enlarge and harmonize the imagination, and by that means insensibly dispose the minds of men to a similar taste and habit of thinking in religion, morals, and civil life." This sentence recalls Hutcheson's description of the work of the higher reason: to set the powers each in its due place by demonstrating the grand scheme of a harmonious universe, and to encourage each power to perform its work on the psyche as God has intended. Being harmonious, the imagination, we may conclude, will be universally valid; mere subjective, unique impression will be minimized. Thus Akenside can dwell on the spiritually elevating function of this power:

> It is on this account that [the author] is so careful to point out the benevolent intention of the Author of Nature in every principle of the human constitution here insisted on; and also to unite the moral excellencies of life in the same point of view with the more external objects

of good taste; thus recommending them in common to our natural propensity for admiring what is beautiful and lovely.

This is what I have called the naïve aesthetic of romanticism. In the poem, Akenside (Book III, 11, 281 ff., 308 ff., 1744 version) expresses the faith without reservation:

> O! teach me to reveal the grateful charm
> That searchless Nature o'er the sense of man
> Diffuses, to behold, in lifeless things,
> The inexpressive semblance of himself,
> Of thought and passion.

Does this effect spring from

> that mystic tone
> To which the new-born mind's harmonious powers
> At first were strung? Or rather from the links
> Which artful custom twines around her frame?

The poem antedates Hartley's associationist theory, but the alternatives are here: Is the influence of nature due to inborn "harmonious powers" of sensation or to association derived from custom? However important the problem was to become in psychology and aesthetics, it made little difference at this time, at least so far as the final-cause doctrine was concerned. Whatever the means, the ultimates remained constant.

There is, however, a serious questioning of the doctrine (I, 526 ff.).

> For what are all
> The forms which brute, unconscious matter wears,
> Greatness of bulk, or symmetry of parts?
> Not reaching to the heart, soon feeble grows
> The superficial impulse; dull their charms,
> And satiate soon, and pall the languid eye.
> Not so the moral species, nor the powers
> Of genius and design; the ambitious mind
> There sees herself: by these congenial forms
> Touch'd and awaken'd, with intenser act
> She bends each nerve, and meditates well-pleased
> Her features in the mirror.

Akenside's poem is vibrant with the conviction that "brute, unconscious matter," embodying God's design and reflecting His omnipresence, is truly sublime and beautiful, and that mind is adapted to perceive its grandeur and beauty. But an apprehension momentarily appears. Does the scene *automatically* produce its spiritual effect? Can mere matter work our "souls' eternal health"? Perhaps real beauty is in mind alone.

Thomas Reid, in a letter of 1790 to Alison, said that the Platonic school, Shaftesbury, and Akenside "believed intellectual beauties to be the highest order, compared with which the terrestrial hardly deserve the name." [7] I share Hipple's skepticism about the sweeping application of this statement: "I doubt, however, that any of these authors, classical or modern, would subscribe to the opinion as Reid has developed it." [8] Yet disturbed Akenside was. He had caught a glimpse of a new dilemma of the arts. How can it be assumed that mere greatness of bulk or symmetry of parts is a means of grace? By Akenside's time, there had developed an almost religious faith in the saving influence of nature, as transmitted through sense impressions and the imagination. "Nature" had become a prop to the psyche. The locale of reality, however, had been transferred to the inner being. If this is so, what guaranty have we that the harmony and the elevation of spirit we attribute to natural impressions do not exist in our minds alone, and are not the product of unpredictable moods? What if the images, apparently derived from the world about us, have no real significance apart from our expectations, our own inner happiness, our desires, projected into the images? And if the individual creates the values out of himself, may he not lose the capacity to receive the grace of nature?

Akenside's doubt appears to be resolved by the comfortable reflection that, as Addison suggested, the harmony in nature and the powers of the mind are wonderfully adjusted to each other, and the poem eloquently affirms the faith (I, 109 ff.):

> For as old Memnon's image, long renown'd
> By fabling Nilus, to the quivering touch
> Of Titan's ray, with each repulsive string

Consenting, sounded through the warbling air
Unbidden strains; even so did Nature's hand
To certain species of external things,
Attune the finer organs of the mind:
So the glad impulse of congenial powers,
Or of sweet sounds, or Fair proportion'd form,
The grace of motion, or the bloom of light,
Thrills through Imagination's tender frame,
From nerve to nerve: . . .

Memnon's image, and later the Aeolian lyre, become symbols of the religion of the imagination. Akenside was the true disciple of Shaftesbury as well as of Addison, inheriting the former's belief in the moral quality and ideality of the physical universe. Like Shaftesbury, Akenside makes use of Platonic terms; but, like Shaftesbury, he gives that philosophy the peculiar form which was to characterize much of romanticism. The ideal is absorbed into the material. Where the Platonist ascends a ladder from images to idea, the romanticist perceives, in the images of sense, the full spiritual reality which corruption and bigotry, delusion and superstition, rather than the veil of the material, have long hidden from mankind. We can hardly say that such thinking is this-worldly, as opposed to other-worldly. Rather, the terms lose significance, for this attitude attempts to be *both:* it sees in this world all that had been perceived in both. The imagination is a means of reconciliation, for through it mere sense is infused with ideal meaning. Through the imagination is nature supernaturalized.

That decade of change, the 1740's, saw the publication of a most useful little treatise which gives us, better than more pretentious aesthetic and critical performances, an insight into the state of mind of the common reader. John Baillie's *An Essay on the Sublime* (1747) was published some years after it had been written, and in fact antedates *The Pleasures of Imagination.* Baillie, a physician and amateur playwright, was an enthusiastic reader of and, we suspect, talker about literature. He put together in a literary epistle the ideas and attitudes which he found exciting; his enthusiasm evidently became too strong to resist expression. The result is a revealing exposition of what readers of Thomson, of Akenside, of Young, of the Wartons, believed about the imagination and nature.

The epistle grows out of the problem of the sublime. Longinus, it seems, although laying down rules for writing in the sublime style, had failed to explain what the sublime itself is. Baillie supplies the lack: "But as the *Sublime* in *Writing* is no more than a Description of the *Sublime* in *Nature,* and as it were painting to the *Imagination* what *Nature* herself offers to the *Senses,* I shall begin with an Inquiry into the *Sublime* of *Natural Objects,* which I shall afterwards apply to *Writing.*" [9] Through the enthusiastic italics runs the essence of the naïve aesthetic: poetry paints to the senses what is in nature to begin with. How different this emphasis on quantity, literal description, and reflex-response is from Longinus' true spirit is a point that needs no elaboration. The "great" of Addison has been transmuted into the "sublime"; but the likeness between the two is evident. "Every Person upon seeing a grand Object is affected with something which as it were extends his very Being, and expands it to a kind of *Immensity.*" The title of John Langhorne's poem *The Enlargement of the Mind* literally characterizes this notion. The soul does "soar," but not from lower to higher levels of being; it soars to enable it to see more, to take in "larger Scenes and more extended Prospects," as it "darts from *Planet* to *Planet,* and takes in Worlds at one View!"

Baillie's transformation of the famous Section 35 of *Peri Hupsous* is illuminating. Longinus associates man's preference for great rivers over small ones with the fact that he is a "competitor for honor" in the universe and therefore seeks out the noblest, the grandest, objects in his world. Baillie renders the idea thus: "but to fill the Soul, and raise it to the *Sublime* Sensations, the earth must rise into an *Alp,* or *Pyrrhenean,* and *Mountains* piled upon *Mountains,* reach to the very *Heavens*—" This supercolossal piling up of vast sensations, in sublime disregard of the warning about Pelion on Ossa, produces a mechanistic response: ". . . when a *Flood* of Light bursts in, and the vast *Heavens* are on every side widely *extended* to the Eye, it is then the Soul inlarges . . ." "Vast" appears in every other line. Size and quantity actually "fill" and expand the soul. By contemplating the vast, the soul takes on a likeness of the infinite. How much "greater an Existence must the Soul imagine herself, when contemplating the *Heavens* she takes in the mighty *Orbs* of the *Planets*" than when "shrunk into the narrow Space of a Room"! The image is not metaphorical. In a latter part of the essay, Baillie remarks in all seriousness, "If a great Croud of *Ideas* can be distinctly conveyed into a small *Portion* of the Mind, something of the *Pride* of the *Sublime* will be raised in her; for if she can take in so great a *Variety*, and yet have room for so much more, she certainly must feel something exalted."

Quantity, moreover, can take the form of intensity; this point should be remembered in explaining how the emotions of terror came to be ranked under the "sublime," even though Baillie is traditional in excluding the terrible from the "grand Sensation." Baillie describes a principle that governs much sublime descriptive poetry; it is a variation of Addison's addition of impressions. ". . . may not two or three different Pleasures existing in the Mind at the same time, by a kind of *reverberating* on each other, increase the Intenseness of each, as a Parcel of Diamonds, when artfully set, by a reciprocal *Reflection* of their *Rays*, strike the Eye with redoubled *Lustre?*" Accordingly, he defines poetry in a way that vividly shows what this kind of aesthetic was likely to produce. "What, indeed, is *Poetry*, but the Art of throwing a Number of agreeable *Images* together, whence each of them yields a greater *Delight* than they possibly could separately. . . ." In sum, the function of art has become something new.

A mechanistic process is certain to produce a mechanistic result. The intellectual content has been reduced in importance to the point of being eliminated. The sublime fills "the *Mind* with one vast and uniform *Idea*"; and the soul "becomes, as it were, one simple grand Sensation." Satan in *Paradise Lost* does not interest Baillie as a character or as a symbol of evil; the whole emphasis is on the image, the appearance, the shudder, producing an intense emotion on an elemental level, suggestive of the horror movies of our day. When, as was inevitable, the "final cause" dropped away from the enthusiasm for the "grand Sensation," only a cult of the spectacular and the awful remained. There was left only an unexplained impression that what is bigger must also be better.

Alexander Gerard, who (as he acknowledged) was influenced by Baillie, wrote in *An Essay on Taste* (1756) a good example of the aesthetic theorizing of the mid-century. Most of the theorizers were moral philosophers who employed a new and often pseudoscientific terminology in attempting to set up systems that would explain, with adequate mechanism, the nature and supernal functions of a faculty of "imagination." Gerard I discuss as a good sample rather than as an original thinker.

The word "imagination" had become overworked. It was necessary to make distinctions in order to reconcile the numerous and contradictory activities which it was used to name. At about this time a separation of "fancy" from imagination proper was made, to set off the lofty faculty of redemptive power from the more insignificant recreation of the mind. Again, the imagination, after Addison, indicated both the faculty whereby the mind was impressed, passively, with the forms of the fair and the great, and the creative power that shaped works of art. There was also the problem of distinguishing between the imagination as potentiality and the faculty as cultivated and brought to the highest pitch of sensitivity. The word "taste" came to be employed for a subdivision of the imagination.

Gerard follows the school of Hutcheson in regarding taste as an inner sense. It is "a power which receives its perception *immediately* as soon as its object is exhibited, previous to any reasoning concerning the qualities of the object, or the causes of the perception. It is a power which exerts itself *independent of volition;* so that, while we remain in proper circumstances, we cannot, by any act of the will, prevent our receiving certain sensations, nor alter them at pleasure." [10]

The emphasis on immediacy, on the unwilled, on independence from the reason, presents great problems when we ask why we take pleasure in reading a long, complex poem. Like Baillie, Gerard tries to derive every explanation from magnitude and intensity. Thus when Homer "would convey a sublime Idea of DISCORD, he gives greatness of quantity to this imaginary person, assigning her such prodigious stature, that, while she walks upon the earth, her head reaches to the heavens." [11] From such a description, we feel, the *idea* of discord has gone; she might as well be Famine, or Death. She has become a personified impression. For the sublime object "always implies astonishment, occupies the whole soul, and suspends all its motions." A startling passage attributes the sublimity of heroism, even that, to quantity: "What wonder that we esteem heroism grand, when, in order to imagine it, we suppose a mighty conqueror, in opposition to the most formidable dangers, acquiring power over *multitudes* of nations, subjecting to his dominion wide *extended* countries, and purchasing renown, which reaches to the extremities of the world, and shall continue through *all the ages* of futurity?" [12] Subordination of plot to strong sensations may have had much to do with the beginning of the Gothic novel, and with the substitution of spectacle for drama on the stage toward the end of the century.

A problem that arises from the ambiguous elements in the conception of the "inner sense" involves the nature of the artist. If the aesthetic reaction is exclusively passive, the artist could be envisioned in one of two very different ways. He could be a magician of the sensibility, cunningly manipulating the "perceptive power" to produce calculated effects—exactly the process Valéry later described, when he stressed the artist's calculation of the total effect—the total nonrational effect—a poem is to produce, and when he denied that the artist has anything to do with enthusiasm. At the opposite extreme, the artist could himself be a passive sensibility, an exceptionally delicate and passionate instrument on which nature plays through the imagination. Artistic creation in the latter case would, as Akenside believed, arise from the desire of "men of warm and sensible tempers" to "recall the delightful perceptions" they have had, "independent of the object which originally produced them." Writing a poem might retain something of the immediacy, even of the unwilled character, of the process of aesthetic appreciation. Not surprisingly, Gerard makes the genius a kind of glorified automaton:

In a man of genius, the uniting principles are so vigorous and quick, that, when ever any idea is present to the mind, they bring into view at once all others that have the least connexion with it. As the magnet selects, from a quantity of matter, the ferruginous particles which happen to be scattered through it, without making an impression on other substances; so imagination, by a similar sympathy, equally inexplicable, draws out from the whole compass of nature such ideas as we have occasion for, without attending to any others . . .[13]

Gerard's image of the act of creative imagination provides an instructive contrast with Hobbes's and Dryden's figure of the ranging spaniel. Conscious direction, far from being necessary, may be a hindrance. The independence of the ideas, or rather of their associative principle, reminds us of Locke's "gang" of associated impressions. The process suggests the image of the deep well of unconscious cerebration.

As John Armstrong remarked, genius "may be said to consist of a perfect polish of soul, which receives and reflects the images that fall upon it, without warping or distortion." [14] The artist genius is the ultimate sensibility, whose inner senses are exceptionally keen and in perfect harmony.

And as different minds happen to be more or less exquisite, the more or less sensibly do they perceive the various degrees of good and bad, and are the more or less susceptible of being charmed with what is right or beautiful . . . It is chiefly this sensibility that constitutes genius; to which a sound head and a good heart are as essential as a lively imagination. And a man of true genius must necessarily have as exquisite a feeling of the moral beauties, as of whatever is great or beautiful in the works of nature; or masterly in the arts which imitate nature, in poetry, painting, statuary, and music.

Critical maxims about the superiority of poetic genius to the rules, about nature's children, certainly do not account for a revolution of this magnitude; we cannot look for the cause simply in a revolt against the "neoclassical strait jacket." Behind the change were new conceptions both of the mind and of art. Proof may be found in such discussions as that of William Duff, who placed the essence of poetic genius in an exceptional ability to receive "vivid ideas," in the imagination, from nature. The mechanism is delicately adjusted and is easily disturbed, especially by an overactive understanding. Ideally, the poet should live in "early and uncultivated periods of society," before there is a culturally developed but corrupt society to interfere with the workings of the imagination. Since, as Armstrong says, the poet must receive and reflect without distortion the images of nature, it follows that the poet is most at home in a world like the one which the fabled Ossian was supposed to have inhabited. Duff explains why:

> In the early periods of society, the objects which most powerfully and universally strike the imagination are the various appearances of wild and uncultivated nature; the vicissitudes of seasons, and the more obvious revolutions of the heavenly bodies. Rocks and mountains, woods and valleys, storms and tempests, thunder and lightning, rains and sunshine, a cloudy atmosphere and a serene sky, lakes and fountains, rivers and seas, . . . generally form the sphere of imagery, beyond which poetic Genius will seldom range.[15]

The wording calls to mind Wordsworth's statement, in the 1800 preface to *Lyrical Ballads,* that the poet is concerned "with the operations of the elements, and the appearances of the visible universe; with storm and sunshine, with the revolutions of the seasons, with cold and heat . . ." This kind of nature has supplanted the rational system of things which, for the classicist, was the poet's concern. It is well to remember also, as Wordsworth implies, that the genius, even if unique in the degree of his sensibility, is nevertheless not really *sui generis,* but is in fact the perfect realization of the self which exists potentially within us all; his heightened sensations, transmitted through his imagination in his poems, raise and harmonize our own senses.

Duff informs us that only three "complete geniuses" have appeared in the world so far: Homer, Shakespeare, and Ossian.[16] Virgil, who would certainly have appeared on any such list a few decades earlier, has been replaced by the shadowy Ossian. Shakespeare had the advantage of living in an age not adorned by "false taste." In the critical opinion of the seventeenth century, Shakespeare's supposed lack of formal training was compensated for by his natural understanding. Duff, however, asserts that "I am persuaded, that had Shakespeare's learning been greater, his merit as a poet had been less." "Warbling his native wood notes wild" takes on a very different meaning from the one originally intended, and there has been much confusion over this kind of phrase. Duff implies not merely that the rules may be transcended by a great poet, but that the tradition of culture is a positive handicap to the genius. The poet is thwarted by the artificiality and limitations of reason.

The notion of the imagination as passive affects Gerard's theory in every way. It might be supposed that the reading of a reflective poem would require some intellectual activity, but Gerard explains the process by a "reflex sense."

> . . . the sublime is attained chiefly by the artist's exciting *ideas* of sublime objects. . . . Thought is a less intense energy than sense: yet *ideas,* especially when lively, never fail to be contemplated with some degree of the same emotion which attends their original *sensations;* and often yield almost equal pleasure to the reflex senses, when impressed upon the mind by a skilful imitation.[17]

The reader does not so much follow the poet's train of thought as contemplate those thoughts as he would contemplate a grand scene.

How fully Gerard subordinates intellectual content may be seen in another point. Ideas, he recalls, may be either compounded (as in Locke's complex ideas) or associated, without purposeful arrangement. Either way, the combined ideas "communicate, by the closeness of their relation, their qualities to one another." The principle refers only to the state of easiness or uneasiness in the mind; it operates on a level below true metaphor. Thus "a perception, by being connected with another that is strong, or pleasant, or painful, becomes itself vigorous, agreeable or disagreeable." Obvious as this seems to us, the emphasis upon a passive reflection of images as the substance of all poetry tends to define literature as something approaching impressionism. When (as in Morgann) the states of easiness or uneasiness, produced by these associations, become the true causes of character, however, these relationships assume a clear importance.

No discussion of the aesthetic theories that descend from Addison's *Pleasures of the Imagination* could omit Lord Kames's *Elements of Criticism* (1762), which was to be the textbook of aesthetic theory for some time. In the course of his complete Bacon-like studies of human nature, this member of the Scottish school came to the subject of imagination. His system provides an admirable synthesis of the developing doctrine—the more useful since the author can hardly be accused of extremism or faddism.

Lord Kames classifies and analyzes the various arts so far as they appeal to the imagination. In his discussion of poetry, he attempts to demonstrate, with many examples drawn from ancient and modern poets, how and why certain images and poetic practices succeed in stirring the imagination, and which ones fail. The analysis is an elaboration of Addison's principles. The same kind of distinction is made between understanding and imagination, the same assumption that the appeals to the two faculties must be kept separate even when both appear in the same work, the same kind of belief in the spiritually elevating potentialities of imaginative response.

An axiom is that the imagination responds to the particular—needless to say, one of the fundamentals of romanticism. It follows from the fact that the imagination is the power adapted to take pleasure in the immediate, unorganized sensation. Abstract terms serve the ends of poetry only imperfectly.

> But images, which are the life of poetry, cannot be raised in any perfection, otherwise than by introducing particular objects. General terms,

that comprehend a number of individuals, must be excepted from this rule. Our kindred, our clan, our country, and words of the like import, though they scarce raise any image, have notwithstanding a wonderful power over our passions. The greatness of the complex idea overbalances the obscurity of the image.[18]

The absence of a feeling for symbol is notable. The Lockian atomistic psychology is literally applied. The individual impression is the stuff of poetry, but a general term composed of individuals may be admissible where a feeling of great quantity is present.

Addison's distinction between understanding and imagination becomes very literal; classification of similes is absolute. "Comparisons . . . serve two different purposes. When addressed to the understanding, their purpose is to instruct; when to the heart, their purpose is to give pleasure." [19] How mechanistic is the comparison addressed to the "heart," the following set of precise formulas will show: ". . . a comparison may be employ'd to produce various pleasures by different means, First, by suggesting some unusual resemblance or contrast: second, by setting an object in the strongest light: third, by associating an object with others that are agreeable: fourth, by elevating an object: and, fifth, by depressing it."

The automatic action of the images is so great that the feeling for symbolism disappears. Lord Kames cites *Richard II*, Act V, scene 1, where the Queen upbraids Richard for weakness:

> The lion, dying, thrusteth forth his paw,
> And wounds the earth, if nothing else, with rage
> To be o'erpower'd: and wilt thou, pupil-like,
> Take thy correction mildly, kiss the rod,
> And fawn on rage with base humility?

Lord Kames remarks: "This comparison has scarce any force. A man and a lion are of different species; and there is no such resemblance betwixt them in general, as to produce any strong effect by contrasting particular attributes or circumstances." [20] This curious remark cannot be accounted for, I think, simply on the score of ignorance or poetic insensitivity. Lord Kames was a formidably learned man, and was well aware of the heraldic symbolism of the lion; but his doctrine forbade considering this "comparison" legitimate. His statement indicates how much has been lost. For one thing, there is no longer any sense that the human and the natural world are closely related by parallels, and that, as in nature the lion is king of beasts, he in a manner not only represents but is the king in society. For Lord Kames, experience has become sharply and inescapably divided. Sensibility is rigidly circumscribed, and the only complexity remaining is the accidental fusion of immediate sensations.

For much the same reason, he asserts that an image disagreeable in itself should not be used, however strong may be the resemblance to the idea expressed. Verbal comparisons of chastity to an icicle are bad because "chastity is cold in a metaphorical sense, and an icicle is cold in a proper sense." [21] *An Essay on Man* (II, 145 ff.) contains some objectionable comparisons, as in the following description of the ruling passion:

> Nature its mother, Habit is its nurse;
> Wit, Spirit, Faculties, but make it worse;
> Reason itself but gives it edge and pow'r;
> As Heav'n's blest beam turns vinegar more sour; . . .

The vinegar simile is "unpoetical." He has picked out for censure images with some quality of wit, in a poem not in general highly witty; it is interesting that, with a few exceptions, he approves of *An Essay on Man.* Of wit, he says that it is "appropriate to such thoughts and expressions as are ludicrous, and also occasion some degree of surprise by their singularity," for only "ludicrous combinations of things that have little or no natural relation" are properly witty.[22] A sense of adaptation of style to subject has been lost.

The poet can, to be sure, take certain liberties. He may extend the properties of one object to another—"giddy brink," "daring wound," and so on. But the transference of attributes must arise from a personal, immediate, nonrational experience, somewhat like the Lockian association of ideas. The mind, "in ideas, passeth easily and sweetly along a train of connected objects; and, where the objects are intimately connected, . . . it is disposed to carry along the good or bad properties of one to another; especially where it is in any degree inflamed with these properties." [23] The justification is that the language must express "whatever passes in the mind." Since whatever passes—not just whatever happens, in the sense of a definite and describable event—includes wholly nonrational activities, the writer must find means other than rational language to express those activities. This point was not really appreciated (Sterne is a notable exception) until our own century. If Morgann and Whiter caught a glimpse of it, they were not creative artists.

Lord Kames's theory of poetic diction represents the type of doctrine that Wordsworth was to rebel against. The villains of poetic diction, far more than Pope and his school whom Wordsworth blamed, were the early romantic, "sublime" poets, who held that the imagination has its own distinctive vocabulary, and that the lofty is the only true poetic style. Lord Kames believes, for instance, that the figure periphrasis

> hath a happy effect in preventing the familiarity of proper names. The familiarity of a proper name, is communicated to the thing it signifies by means of their intimate connection; and the thing is thereby brought down in our feeling. This bad effect is prevented by using a figurative word instead of one that is proper; as, . . . when we express the sky by terming it *the blue vault of heaven.*[24]

Thus "imperious ocean" is better than "stormy ocean," the former being more "elevated" than the latter. Poetry should "aggrandize" the object. Elevation produces an effect pleasing to the special faculty of imagination, and to produce this effect is the special work of metaphor. We see that the pleasure of imaginative response cannot be evoked by words and images derived from the world of practical and logical thinking; yet the imagination is not attracted by the illogical, either. Lord Kames demonstrates a certain conservatism in practice. His admiration, even if qualified, for *An Essay on Man* is at variance with the tendency of romantic critics to downgrade Pope to a poet of the fancy rather than of the imagination.

Lord Kames was too much the eighteenth-century moral philosopher to write a long book on the imagination without expressing a conviction that the faculty serves an important function. Man, he observes, is "obviously fitted for contemplating the works of God," and the imagination is the instrument of that contemplation.[25] He repeats the now conventional opinion that the sublime is the highest manifestation of the imagination, and through it the noble work of the faculty is most fully performed. Like Burke, he sees that this vast word had come to include two different meanings: one derived from the Longinian, which was reduced to simple "loftiness"; and the mystique of great extension. Kames, in his customary literal fashion, distinguishes them as physical height and physical greatness.

> The elevation of an object affects us not less than its magnitude. A high place is chosen for the statue of a deity or hero . . . In some objects, greatness and elevation concur to make a complicated impression. The Alps and the peaks of Teneriff are proper examples; with the following difference, that in the former greatness seems to prevail, elevation in the latter.[26]

Kames's theory, however, gives first place to the extension of the mind which other writers described. The emotions raised by a quantitatively huge object dilate the breast and make the spectator endeavor to "enlarge his bulk." Grandeur is productive of an emotion "in every circumstance pleasant," for magnitude is a real property of bodies, "not less than figure, and more than colour." Magnitude in a body "swells the heart and dilates the mind." Again we hear the voice of Addison.

It would be easy to cite many more examples of this kind of theorizing. More interesting is the question whether these theories were translated into deeply grounded attitudes and sensibilities. Were they all on the surface, or did they penetrate the fabric of life? Was there a romantic generation before the last decade of the century?

One answer is found in a series of documents which give us an extraordinarily revealing picture of the beliefs and feelings of common readers in the mid-century and later. Elizabeth Montagu (not to be confused with her kinswoman by marriage, Lady Mary Wortley—whom she hated), the original bluestocking, sometime friend of Dr. Johnson and author of a popular essay of romantic criticism of Shakespeare, was the center of a group that conducted an extensive correspondence from the early 1730's to the beginning of the next century. Her correspondents included many important people in learning, society, politics, and literature—the most faithful being the accomplished Elizabeth Carter, whom Johnson complimented as the best Greek scholar in the kingdom. The reputation of Mrs. Montagu and her circle has suffered from the prejudice against learned women. In fact they were, if sometimes naïvely pedantic, neither poseurs nor *précieuses*. They had their share of common sense and practicality. Mrs. Montagu successfully managed a large and increasing estate which included coal mines, and was a pioneer in enlightened labor relations. The group, while greatly interested in new ideas and books, tended to maintain a cautious reserve about accepting what was not tested and proved in general opinion.

Throughout this great collection of letters, which covered several decades, the imagination is a dominant theme. Mrs. Montagu and Mrs. Carter, as well as others to whom and from whom they received many letters, were firm Addisonians; indeed, the very style of *The Spectator* appears frequently as they record their responses to natural scenes, to literary works, to Gothic ruins. Like Addison, they were preoccupied with the final causes of the aesthetic experience, and these causes they adapted—often with speculations of their own along the approved lines—from the "Pleasures" papers.

These final causes are the elements of a vague but real natural religion. The following extract from a letter of Mrs. Carter, 1785, is typical: "It is true, that the philosopher who examines the wonderful internal construction of natural objects, must discern the *power* and *wisdom* of the Supreme Being; but the superficial spectator who, with a refined imagination, and a sensible heart, surveys the external beauties of the universe, feels his *goodness*." [27]

Seventeen years before, Mrs. Montagu wrote of the ocean that

"It is a noble chapter of the attributes of the supreme being. Its sublime aspect gives the mind a religious awe, a more particular consideration of it leads us to the first good, first perfect and first fair." [28] The combination of Shaftesburian and Addisonian phrases is typical. Although she was a conventional communicant of the Church of England, Mrs. Montagu could remark that "the sea is to me a sermon and prayers, and at once doctrine and devotion." [29]

In a long letter on the question whether the age of chivalry was more inspiring to the poet than was that of Homer (she had read Warton's *Observations on the Faerie Queene*), Mrs. Montagu shows how distinctive characteristics of romanticism had emerged from the doctrine of imagination. "I am sure it is a great advantage to a Poet to have the belief and prejudices of the nursery to assist his fictions; they have a sacred horror which is one of the great sources of the sublime . . . The things we but half believe, and but half understand, are fine ingredients in poetry." [30] The ultimate descent of this from Addison's paper on the "fairy way of writing" is clear, but the whole passage is a fusion of attitudes which we need not attempt to trace to individual authors. In the same letter she observes that an uncertain outline, a twilight atmosphere, as in "Il Penseroso," is best for poetry. One recommendation of the Squire's Tale is that "it was *half* told"; the story "without being unfolded raises great and undefined ideas, and is more sublime in its chaos than in its perfection, as far as it goes in Chaucer." Perhaps there was a deep-lying reason why Coleridge left unfinished "Kubla Khan" and "Christabel."

The preference for this type of literature derives from the peculiar pleasures of imagination: the love of the limitless, the suggestive, the unanalyzed. Imagination works its saving effects because it is the opposite of the clear and reasoned. A distrust of the scientific, the precisely understood, the measured, is a recurring theme. We cannot, Mrs. Carter suggests in the letter quoted above, be made *better* by the philosopher or the man of facts.

A contradiction runs through this correspondence, as it does throughout the early period of romanticism, and we cannot understand the period unless we try to understand the paradox. Mrs. Montagu and her friends held two seemingly incompatible beliefs. First, reason and social progress are most valuable, and the present age is superior to earlier ones because of advances in science, technology, and the administration of government. Thus, even while she admires the sublime gloom of Kenilworth Castle, Mrs. Montagu reflects how good it is to know that in modern times public buildings are courts of justice instead of citadels. But, second, the nonrational side is of indispensable value in life, and the experience of seeing Gothic ruins, of immersing oneself in legend and poetry from "superstitious" ages should be sought. We must, it seems, both cultivate and reject the understanding. Literature is of vital importance precisely because it fulfills a nonrational function. Of romance she says, "I am glad Pegasus like the Hippogriffe of Ariosto took this flight out of the bounds of nature and truth, into the land of bold fiction and airy region of fancy." [31] How can we account for simultaneous confidence in and rejection of intellectual achievement?

The answer lies in the temper of the eighteenth century, its desire to include rather than exclude, to reconcile rather than challenge. On the one hand, as Mrs. Carter remarks, "scientific scrutiny" is productive of many useful discoveries to society; on the other hand, it is self-limiting and falsifying. Left to himself, man becomes ever narrower, absorbed in his immediate desires, his material well-being. Not that practicality is wrong, or that self-interest in moderation is to be condemned; they are part of nature, and whatever is, is right. But, to balance their limitations, a constant stream of inspiration proceeds from the senses. The reason is analytical, defining, practical; the imagination is the opposite. Widening out from self-interest, imagination arouses the moral sense; it enables us to apprehend, in feeling, the wholeness of the universe; it obliterates logical boundaries, producing a single effect from many impressions. All these results are implied in the statement that it "enlarges" the mind. To accomplish its effect, however, imagination must, by definition, be sharply distinguished and separated from whatever the reason would dominate.

Before our eyes we have at all times symbols of the two poles of our nature. The day, with its clear but hard light, is the realm of the understanding, but the imagination reigns under the moon. Mrs. Montagu tells Lord Bath that "the grand jubilee of day is not so delightful to me as the majestick solemnity of the silent Night. One seems then . . . conversing with intellectual beings, nothing marks the hour or place, and one belongs to eternity and infinity." [32]

Elizabeth Carter, the author of a much admired translation of Epictetus, was the most philosophical of the group, and it was appropriate that she should have been the one to set forth most clearly the rationale of these attitudes. In 1770 she wrote as follows:

> I think we may be justified in our taste for the solemn concert of howling winds and dashing waves. The rude and boisterous elements are certainly of as real use in the general system as those of a more gentle and placid temper; and besides the wise purposes which they answer with regard to inanimate creation, it is certainly a subject of high admiration and gratitude to consider in what an unexplicable manner they are adapted to amuse the imagination by various kinds of delight, and to mend the heart by various kinds of feelings. The gracious Author of our being seems, in compassion to our weak and imperfect virtue, to have furnished it with an adventitious and external aid, even from those objects which appear to have no natural connection with it . . . Amidst the gay and smiling scenes of nature our minds are engaged in an attention to our own enjoyments; amidst the unrelenting storm and desolating torrent, our hearts are awed and softened to a tender sensibility of the wants and distresses of others.[33]

Here we see how the romanticists were able to utilize what had previously been regarded as repellent and indicative of a curse on mankind. The emphasis on sympathy and benevolence, furthermore, illustrates the growing concern for humanizing the imaginative response by tracing a connection between imagination and moral sense. A great hope of the later eighteenth century was that the instinct of benevolence, encouraged and if necessary restored by imagination, could solve the practical problems of human welfare.

Mrs. Carter, in a letter of 1777, speculates that, although the transports of imagination occur in solitary reverie, nevertheless the "pleasures of solitude have almost always a reference to society." [34] This apparent paradox arises because the "views of nature aid us in this ideal commerce, as they then strike us only with universal objects, and general participation, and exclude all the particular and distinguishing circumstances, which separate us from those who so agreeably engage our thoughts." Indeed, as Adam Smith asserted in *The Theory of Moral Sentiments,* only through the imagination can we form a vivid conception of another's sensations and hence distresses. Exercise of the aesthetic imagination might strengthen the moral one, which Hutcheson called the "sympathetick" sense. For this reason Mrs. Carter makes a distinction between imagination and fancy. The latter, she says, is associated with the town, with fashionable life, with a great house. It seems to represent the taste of the artificial world, which self-interest abetted by practical reason tends to create. But "the scenes of rural retirement are the range of *imagination,* whose magic powers should be exerted in such operations as help to lead the mind out of the usual routine of common and popular life." [35]

The faith and enthusiasm attain their ultimate expression in Elizabeth Carter's statement about imagination:

> . . . perhaps there is nothing which so indisputably distinguishes the human race from other animals as that power, which not confined by the appearances that offer themselves to the senses, nor by the deductions of the understanding, ranges through all the regions of possible existence: . . . which sometimes gives to external objects a brighter colouring of joy, and a softer shade of melancholy, and by an inexplicable union connects them with the affections of the heart: at others, magnifies and varies them till they become too vast and too complex for the grasp of the mind, which then most sensibly feels the natural greatness of its aims, and the limits of its present capacity.[36]

Having a good classical education, Mrs. Carter could hardly have failed to realize how revolutionary her statement was: for throughout Western thought had resounded the maxim that *reason* is the distinctive form of the human soul. The reversal was now complete, and the nonrational areas of the psyche had been assigned the highest function.

In the writers surveyed in this chapter we observe, in varying degrees, the basic faith of romanticism: that only the poet sees things in their true, organic harmony, as opposed to the man of reason—whether he is philosopher, scientist, or merchant. When Thoreau remarked that it is not important that the poet should say any particular things, but only that he should "speak in harmony with nature," [37] he epitomized the complex of ideas I have discussed. His distinction is that, like the great figures of "high romanticism" who preceded him, he carried those ideas to the point of overt rejection of society as it is. He did not, like Mrs. Montagu, try to put reason and imagination each in its own apartment, and to domicile both comfortably in the existing order of things.

We know how, in the nineteenth century, many factors—utilitarianism, the industrial revolution, the disillusionment about nature after the development of biological science, and the rest—produced a mood of profound disillusionment in artists generally. The belief that art can be itself only if it remains completely apart from society and philosophy became common. The historical events of the century doubtless exacerbated the original separation of the imagination from the concerns of "real" life, but these events were not entirely responsible for the artist's renunciation of reason. The ideological pattern behind Rimbaud or Valéry or Swinburne existed long before their time. History and theory conspired to produce art for art's sake.

VII THE IMAGINATION: BEGINNINGS OF SYMBOLISM

If the Montagu letters give evidence that an unacknowledged cult of nature and imagination existed, they also demonstrate the unchallenged supremacy of the Lockian epistemology. Personality and character, it is now assumed, are shaped by sense impressions. To these sensations, each a discrete entity in the final analysis, we must look for the spiritual, moral, and intellectual content of the mind.

There are independent and autonomous mental faculties, chief among which—under whatever names and whatever subdivisons they may be classified—are a moral sense, imagination, and understanding, in the order which they often came to assume. The first two may be thought of as inner senses, organs by which a beneficent Providence has enabled man, even though he is completely immersed in the physical world, to attain nobility and spiritual greatness. Through them, human beings may commune with the Deity and are guaranteed the capacity to act in accord with God's intentions for human behavior; they confute the dismal superstition of original sin. It is, moreover, through pleasure—a pleasure of an ineffable kind—that man is lifted to his highest state. Salvation consists in restoring harmonious relationships with the great harmonious Whole. To discover how the adjustments are made and how they may be kept in balance is one task of moral philosophy; to exemplify and strengthen them is the function of art.

As we have seen, however, this faith was involved in several great difficulties, one of which was the problem of subjectivity. A corollary of Lockian psychology is that the locus of reality is the perceiving mind. Hence it was possible that the influences from nature and art might dissolve into a series of private impressions, subject to the vagaries and accidents of individual temperaments and to the fortuitous concourse of individual experiences. Yet, if nature is to be a source of grace, that grace must be common and predictable for all; otherwise a new form of predestination, more distasteful than the old because apparently the result of pure chance, might ensue.

Again, the inner-sense theory was full of problems. How could mere sense impression account for the diversity and richness of art? If the direct apprehension of a beautiful scene exhausts the pleasure of imagination, that pleasure is narrowly limited. The separation of imagination from reason began to have its consequences. If the response to art is only to impressions unrelated to and unguided by conceptual thought, what is to prevent a pure aestheticism, an irresponsible hedonism of the imagination, from invalidating the grace of nature?

The theory of the inner sense, moreover, was contrary to the tendencies of the Newtonian age. In this period men had an almost obsessive desire to explain spiritual and supranatural facts by "second causes," the mechanism of nature. Thus John Wesley, with many other religious men of his time, was persuaded by the attempts of Thomas Burnet, Whiston, and others to explain the flood and the final destruction of the earth by volcanoes, comets, or other purely natural phenomena, thus eliminating the need for special intervention. But the inner senses had an occult and nonnatural aspect. The exact mechanism of psychological action had to be explained; the associationist school attempted to bridge the gap by reducing every action of the mind, however complex, to interconnections of impressions, arising out of everyday experience and governed by no innate, mystic force outside the mechanical arrangement of the mind. The challenges to the faith, the responses to the challenges, and the last phase of the religion of imagination are the subjects of this final chapter.

One of the most important challenges to the now orthodox moral aesthetic came from Edmund Burke. To ardent devotees of the imagination as a means of grace, his theory must have come as a shock. Does the imagination have a final cause at all—or at least any we can possibly understand? May it not simply be a source of pleasures which arise, for no final cause, from the accidents of our psychological and physiological make-up? Santayana states the essence of the problem:

> Such value as belongs to metaphysical derivations of the nature of the beautiful, comes to them not because they explain our primary feelings, which they cannot do, but because they express, and in fact constitute, some of our later appreciations . . . When a man tells you that beauty is the manifestation of God to the senses, you wish you might understand him, you grope for a deep truth in his obscurity, you honour him for his elevation of mind, and your respect may even induce you to assent to what he says as to an intelligible proposition . . . Yet reflection might have shown you that the word of the master held no objective account of the nature and origin of beauty, but was the vague expression of his highly complex emotions.[1]

These two points—that the final causes are ex post facto, and that they are the expressions of a noble but vague mystique rather than conclusions drawn from precise and objective investigation—are the fundamental objections to the type of theorizing we have been surveying.

Precise and objective observation was the aim of the most celebrated work on aesthetics in the century. Paradoxically, it is often taken for the epitome of eighteenth-century romanticism, and yet in vital points it challenged that doctrine. Burke's A *Philosophical*

Inquiry into the Origin of Our Ideas of the Sublime and Beautiful (1757, 1758), seen in the context of its time, appears as perhaps the first substantial effort to construct a system of aesthetics in the strict sense of the word. Burke rejects, although with diplomacy, the whole doctrine of the final cause for pleasures of the imagination. In fact, he reverses Addison's procedure; where the latter specifically disclaimed any attempt to account for the efficient cause, Burke says (Part IV, sec. i):

> I do not pretend that I shall ever be able to explain why certain affections of the body produce such a distinct emotion of the mind, and no other; or why the body is at all affected by the mind, or the mind by the body . . . When we go but one step beyond the immediately sensible qualities of things, we go out of our depth . . . if I were to explain the motion of body falling to the gound, I would say it was caused by gravity, and I would endeavour to show after what manner this power operated, without attempting to show why it operated in this manner. . . .

Thus Burke set out to bring the philosophy of aesthetics up to a level with that of physical science, as is shown by the analogy with gravity (recalling Newton's disclaimer of knowing ultimate causes—even though Newton was not entirely faithful to it). Yet Burke's statement is radically out of harmony with the mood of eighteenth-century philosophizing, which was emotionally committed to finding good, substantial reasons why whatever is, is right. Here Burke showed already, in his youth, the temper that led him to reject the rationalism which defended the French Revolution. There was a strong element of intellectual pride in man's confidence that he could understand all things, and by abstract cogitation arrive at an accurate idea of what is good and bad. This confidence was shown by such people as Godwin, who was certain that he could make a good society. It was already evident in the assurance of Addison that he could understand the reasons for God's making the mind of man as He did, and that man, by pure intuition, can apprehend the absolute.

Burke found that aesthetic sensibility is simply a by-product of the simple sensations; it is merely a form of easiness or uneasiness, arising from "these two heads, *self-preservation* and *society*" (Part I, sec. vi). There is no separate, autonomous faculty of taste. "Since the imagination is only the representative of the senses, it can only be pleased or displeased with the images, from the same principle on which the sense is pleased or displeased with the realities; and consequently there must be just as close an agreement in the imaginations as in the senses of men" (Introduction, "On Taste").

This is in the spirit of Locke, who himself objected to the first efforts to engraft the moral sense onto the mind, alongside the understanding. Subsequent attempts to define the moral and aesthetic faculties by calling them "reflex senses," finer than the physical ones, made nonsense of Locke's distinction between basic sensation and the process of understanding. A mysterious "power" that responds as a sense but has capacities to arrange ideas for conscious purposes is hard to envision; and Locke, remarking that a "power" is not a knowledge, implied that the new notions attempted to smuggle in the old innate ideas, disguised under a new, more respectable theory. The question of the genius—is he a conscious manipulator of others' sensibilities or an Aeolian harp?—illustrates the difficulty.

Burke accounts for aesthetic responses by reducing them to the status of simple feelings which accompany the original sensations: we feel not only heat and cold but the sublime and the beautiful as well. Since the aesthetic is thus physiological, Burke rejects the notion that we can judge artistic excellence by a "species of instinct, by which we are struck naturally, and at the first glance, without any previous reasoning, with the excellencies or the effects of a composition." For, "where disposition, where decorum, where congruity are concerned, in short, wherever the best taste differs from the worst, I am convinced that the understanding operates and nothing else; and its operation is in reality far from being always sudden, or, when it is sudden, it is often far from being right" (Introduction). By "understanding" he means the modest good judgment of the mind, the faculty of practical wisdom, rather than the soaring reason which determines the ultimate purposes of God.

The causes of immediate aesthetic responses are "natural and mechanical." Symmetry and perfection are not elements of beauty. So far does Burke accept the romantic taste in practice if not altogether in theory. His reasons, however, are not romantic; these are qualities the understanding would perceive, and not immediate effects of sensation. As Monk says, "In Burke's essay there is shadowed forth the materialistic implication of twentieth-century psychological investigation, the method that seeks a physical explanation even for art itself." [2] The logical consequence is that the understanding is the only faculty capable of passing judgment. It must exert control over aesthetic responses just as it does over other elemental effects—just as it decides whether a feeling of heat or cold, reported by the neural system, is really important or is trivial and to be ignored. Matters of theme, structure, and the like are wholly within the area of understanding.

Burke, in addition to analyzing away the fine inner sense, proceeded to show that the associationist theory, which superficially seemed to carry the respectable credentials of empiricism, was dubious also. We may believe in transcendent purposes in nature; but science will not support us. "When we got but one step beyond the immediate sensible qualities of things, we go out of our depth" (Part IV, sec. i). Since aesthetic as well as kinetic effects of sensations are irreducible, associationism merely takes us pompously in a circle (Part IV, sec. ii):

> . . . it would be absurd . . . to say that all things affect us by association only; since some things must have been originally and naturally agreeable or disagreeable, from which the others derive their associated powers; and it would be, I fancy, to little purpose to look for the cause of our passions in association, until we fail of it in the natural properties of things.

At this moment, perhaps for the first time in Western culture, the aesthetic event emerges as a thing in itself, divested of ulterior involvement. Paramount for Burke, as for Locke and for Hobbes, is the sense of biological well-being. Our sense of life and health and energy is both the efficient and the final cause of aesthetic response. If Burke does make a tactical concession to the teleological school, granting that the senses of sublimity and beauty probably have some final cause, he immediately asserts that it is unknown to us and always will be unknown. We do, however, know about self-preservation. Thus (Part IV, sec. vii),

> if the pain and terror are so modified as not to be actually noxious; if the pain is not carried to violence, and the terror is not conversant about the present destruction of the person, as these emotions clear the parts, whether fine, or gross, of a dangerous and troublesome incumbrance, they are capable of producing delight; not pleasure, but a sort of delightful horror, a sort of tranquillity tinged with terror; which as it belongs to self-preservation is one of the strongest of all the passions.

This is the sublime, an "exercise of the finer parts of the system," as physical labor is of the "grosser." Nowhere does Burke admit that the sublime elevates or enlarges the mind. The test is the sublime of infinity. Burke strips it of mystery; the "delightful horror" arises from a purely mechanical operation. "Whenever we repeat any idea frequently, the mind by a sort of mechanism repeats it long after the first cause has ceased to operate" (Part II, sec. viii). We never get beyond this mechanism. The idea of God, or of the vastness of the universe, is never suggested. The relation of judgment to aesthetic reactions is indicated, moreover, by the example of the madmen who "remain whole days and nights, sometimes whole years, in the constant repetition of some remark, some complaint or song." Their disorder arises from the failure of the "curb of reason." Thus the understanding sets the mechanism in its place, tells it when to end, and, if the personality is in order, controls the psyche. By such phenomena we are refreshed and strengthened, as by healthful exercise.

We are, it follows, justified in enjoying such irrational compositions as the horrific *Tales of Terror* of Gregory Lewis; but, after our indulgence, good sense must take charge and see that we do not mistake the fancies for truth. It is interesting to recall that Lewis wrote parodies of his own tales of wonder and terror—perhaps a wise counterbalance. Mrs. Radcliffe's romances, after arousing apprehensions with suggestions of the supernatural, end with rational explanations of all that has occurred.

Burke attributes to terror all the effects of sublimity. This seemed a radical innovation, and, for reasons that will soon appear, a challenge to conventional theories. Yet his opinion was new mainly because it was explicitly stated. An element of terror was implicit in the theory of the natural sublime even from the beginning. When we look back to Burnet's early descriptions of the vast and astonishing and massively irregular in the natural world, we find that they have a leitmotiv of fear: mountains represent great "ruins" of the earth, they recall the terrifying episodes of the Flood, they bring up the vision of the final burning of the earth, when they will disappear in a great melting of the stones. The word "stupor," constantly used by writers on the natural sublime, as Burke points out, means both fear and astonishment. (His analysis of a complex word, in Part I, sec. ii, is another modern touch.)

The sublime of storms, of arctic cold, and of summer heat appears in Shaftesbury's *The Moralists*, whose great description of the emotions of the mountain climber amidst the snows and precipices suggests that fear is an element of the experience. Dennis' letter on the Alps interprets the emotion of tragic fear as applied to the experience of the menacing in nature.

Addison's own description of the great was concerned primarily with passive response to overwhelming size alone; yet here, as in many other places, his images suggest more than does the exposition. In *Spectator* 489, he amalgamates the great with the terrible experience, returning to his favorite image, the sea; in a calm it produces a "very pleasing astonishment," but, "when it is worked up in a tempest," "it is impossible to describe the agreeable horror" that it evokes. The *coup de théâtre* of the storm in the spectacle of nature is necessary to raise the "great" to its highest pitch. Fear is implied, also, in the response to the "fairy way of writing." It is easy to see why, despite the fact that Addison never included this kind of writing in the works producing the effect of the "great," it came to be associated with sublimity.

Why, then, did such writers as Baillie deny that terror could be a sublime emotion? Why did they so obsessively emphasize vastness? The reason lies, I suspect, in their preoccupation with final causes. The sublime by definition is the noblest, the most improving, of all the aesthetic effects. It takes us out of ourselves, amalgamates our limited beings with the great system. Thus Gerard observes that we "contemplate objects and ideas with a disposition similar to their nature. When a large object is presented, the mind expands itself to the extent of that object. . . ."

Terror, on the contrary, arising from fear for self, seems to shrink rather than to expand the mind; it intensifies the feeling of separateness rather than expanding to a harmony with the Whole. Burke's theory, then, joined the issue of the meaning and place of the imagination.

In yet another way Burke challenged the teleological aesthetic. He made the distinction, commonplace by 1757, between the pleasures of understanding and those of imagination. His point that what relates to practical needs falls within the former class is also commonplace. His innovation consisted in turning upside down the usual valuation of these pleasures. Warton, for example, relegated Pope to second rank among poets because his poetry appeals to the understanding. But for Burke the understanding and its pleasures take precedence. Since beauty is, in the last analysis, nothing but a simple, though strong, biologically conditioned response to immediate sensation, purely aesthetic pleasure is only a recreation from the business of life. The quality of beauty, he says, "is for the greater part, some quality in bodies acting mechanically upon the human mind by the intervention of the senses"; it is small, usually smooth, delicate, melting, languorous, in short, whatever soothes and caresses us. The feelings akin to awe with which the Renaissance regarded the manifestations of beauty are at an opposite pole from this pleasure of imagination.

The discussion of wit and judgment, in the "Introduction on Taste," carries further the transvaluation of aesthetic values. Burke cites Locke as saying that wit traces resemblances whereas judgment finds differences. Burke is convinced that, contrary to usual opinion, these operations differ so materially that their combination is one of the rarest things in the world. Judgment gives us no pleasurable surprise, for our ordinary experience leads us to expect endless differences between things. Tracing resemblances, however, arouses "a far greater alacrity and satisfaction," for "the most ignorant and barbarous nations have frequently excelled in similitudes, comparisons, metaphors, and allegories, who have been weak and backward in distinguishing and sorting their ideas." Now, the aesthetic sensibility is pleased only by resemblances; "in making distinctions we offer no food at all to the imagination." This is the usual distinction between the separating, classifying understanding, and the unifying imagination. But, where most other writers tended to denigrate the understanding and to exalt the ennobling imagination, Burke regarded the understanding as the only responsible faculty. Differences in taste are merely differences in the *degree* of the biological responses which occur naturally in men who possess normal senses. "But as many of the works of imagination are not confined to the representation of sensible objects, nor to effects upon the passions, but extend themselves to the manners, the characters, the actions, and designs of men, . . . they come within the province of the judgment, which is improved by attention, and by the habit of reasoning."

A final contribution of Burke was his attack on the doctrine that art should represent, in glorified form perhaps, the vistas and prospects of saving nature. The idea that the imagination is a fine sense, designed to receive elevating impressions of untouched nature, encouraged the poet to believe that his function is to describe, in heightened tableaux, the grand and the beautiful in the natural world, with moralizing reflections appropriate to such descriptions; he served as an intermediary, bringing the scenes before the mind's eye.

We may recall Mrs. Montagu, sitting, as she writes in one letter, before a scene made famous by a poet's description, alternately reading the lines and gazing at the prospect: for, as she says, she cannot get the effect by reading the poem alone. Burke demonstrated the error in this sort of verse. The representation, the sketching, of a scene is not and indeed cannot be the proper function of the poet. "The picturesque connexion is not demanded; because no real picture is formed . . . In reality, poetry and rhetoric do not succeed in exact description so well as painting does" (Part V, sec. v).

The real material of the poet is, in Locke's phrase, the "signs" of ideas: "a noble assemblage of words, corresponding to many noble ideas, which are connected by circumstance of time or place, or related to each other as cause and effect or associated in any natural way . . ." They "may be moulded together in any form, and perfectly answer their end." A poem need not have even the pretense of a backbone of logic; the organization may be purely aesthetic, or may correspond to the unguided movements of the mind in reverie. No poet had yet dared go to this extreme. And Burke adds one of the germinal remarks that distinguish the *Inquiry*: poetry and rhetoric should "display rather the effect of things on the mind of the speaker, or of others, than to present a clear idea of the things in themselves." The words need call up no image at all.

In effect, then, the plastic arts, with their immediate sense impressions on the beholder, are the only purely aesthetic arts. The poet can deal only indirectly and at second hand with the impressions that produce effects of beauty. And his business is rather the re-creation of what happens in the mind during the aesthetic experience than the direct occasioning of that experience. By the end of the century, poets had begun to learn this lesson, and were turning from the sublime descriptive poetry of the Thomson school to their own and others' sensibilities for their subject matter. In sum, I think it is fair to call Burke's the first really modern work on aesthetics—modern not only in machinery but in spirit as well.

The influence of opinions like Burke's began to be felt, even if the dominant theory continued for a long time to be teleological.

One example was the painter and writer Fuseli, who rejected the optimism about man and nature and the idealistic views of imagination that were popular in his time, and, as a result of this rejection, formulated many important ideas. After Burke, a period of secular romanticism ensued. To understand the art and literature of the later eighteenth century it is important to recognize this fact, and in what ways the minor movement resembles yet differs from the major one.

Fuseli was the favorite pupil of Bodmer, the "merchant of ideas" who introduced into German culture Addison's ideas about the imagination and Blackwell's speculations about the "primitive" epic. For a time in the 1760's, after Fuseli had come to England from Italy, he was in the center of the romantic enthusiasm, acting as a kind of liaison between British and German writers. A typical example of the "storm and stress" period, he gave every indication of becoming an extreme romantic, advancing even beyond the positions I have discussed in the preceding chapter.

After 1770, however, when Fuseli turned from literature to painting, he deliberately cut himself off from the romantic movement. His change was no reversion to the neoclassicism that temporarily reclaimed Joseph Warton. The choice was not inevitably between old, Renaissance-derived theories of rational imitation and the new "romantic"; another course was open, suggested in part by Burke.

Mason rightly says that Fuseli rejected the phase of the romantic movement which is described by Rivière: "It is only with the advent of Romanticism that the literary act came to be conceived as a sort of raid on the absolute and its result as a revelation." [3]

It is illuminating to read Fuseli's reaction to Count Stolberg's conventional, ecstatic account of the Falls of Schaffhausen on the Rhine (which Wordsworth was to describe in a similar way): "To see the simple object before us unite with immensity overpowers, no doubt, every mind; but why 'the manifest omnipotence of God' should be more perceptible to a philosopher in the thunders and foaming clouds of a cataract than in the whisper of a gentle breeze is not easily discovered." [4] How important such a sentence is, I hope my tracing of the mysticism of "immensity" has shown. It is a rejection, not merely of an idea and of a theme, but of a faith that had modified the process of living. Fuseli has, however, in this commentary preserved the sensibility to the vast, which we find long before romantic ideas, but without the final cause.

Fuseli was aware, as any informed person of recent centuries must be, of the immensity of the post-Copernican universe as the background of life; but he was not overawed, and he saw the fallacy of attempts to make it the subject of art: "If what is finite could grasp infinity, the variety of Nature might be united by individual energy; till then, the attempt to amalgamate her scattered beauties by the imbecility of Art will prove abortive." This challenges the conviction that the imagination, by an ultrarational act, can in a moment grasp the oneness of things, the unity which must forever baffle the pedestrian understanding.

Fuseli recognized the failure of the theory of descriptive poetry. In an *Analytical Review* of June, 1798, he condemned the conventional "elegant rhapsodies" in which "torrents, Alps, lakes have roared, towered, spread, forests have waved and landscapes frowned or smiled in sudden alternatives of spring and winter," leaving the reader in a "chaos of undiscriminated imagery." "It ought to be considered," he says, "whether the impression nature made can be conveyed in words." Homer is understood, "not because he describes objects, but because he shows them." In the last two sentences he advances a step beyond Burke.

In another review, four years earlier, Fuseli had called attention to the confusion of poetry and painting that plagued his time, giving rise to "that deluge of descriptive stuff, which overwhelms by a rhapsody of successive sounds what can only be represented by figure." He comments that Lessing, in the *Laocoën,* did see this problem, though "on a tame principle, and without drawing the inferences that obviously derive from his rules." These inferences, I believe, can be understood in the light of Burke's principles. Painting should be painting; it should be the art producing immediate impression. Like Burke, he makes terror the principal ingredient of the sublime. He condemns the "paltry epitomist of

Nature's immense volume, a juggler, who pretends to mimic the infinite variety of her materials by the vain display of a few fragments of crockery" (Lecture VII).

Fuseli rejects the theory of the inspired artist that is based on the exaltation of imagination. The key word is "invention"; the word means, not contrivance, but "finding," its old sense, as in Dryden. "To find something," he says in Aphorism 47, "presupposes its existence somewhere, implicitly or explicitly, scattered or in a mass." Perhaps the most significant aspect of the statement is the *action* indicated: the artist consciously searches, presumably through memory, to locate what he needs for his previously formed design. We go back, then, to the figure of active mind in imaginative activity, to the ranging spaniel as opposed to the loadstone image that occurs frequently in the period. Fuseli reverts to terms that had become uncommon in critical writing. Thus invention "discovers, selects, combines the *possible*, the *probable*, the *known*, in a mode that strikes with an air of truth and novelty, at once" (Lecture III). Such prescription could have been endorsed by Ben Jonson or by Pope.[5]

Yet it would be a mistake to see in Fuseli a complete reversion to classical ideas. Certainly his own paintings would be puzzling if this were true. He recognizes the importance and validity of the principle that are operates through subjective impressions. Perhaps his attitude can be understood by analyzing his recipe (Lecture IV) for staging a scene from *Macbeth*.

It is not by the accumulation of infernal or magic machinery, distinctly seen, by the introduction of Hecate and a chorus of female demons and witches, by surrounding him with successive apparitions at once, and a range of shadows moving above or before him, that Macbeth can be made an object of terror,—to render him so you must place him on a ridge, his downdashed eye absorbed by the murky abyss; surround the horrid vision with darkness, exclude its limits, and shear its light to glimpses.

The romantic elements are apparent. The desideratum of making Macbeth an "object of terror" takes us far from the ideal of imitating action. The emphasis on allusiveness rather than direct statement is typical. The details have much in common with Burke's criteria of the sublime; the use of darkness recalls Burke's conviction that black is productive of sublimity, and the abyss recalls his belief that height is less grand than depth.

In a broader perspective, the tone of the scene as Fuseli envisions it is romantic, and resembles a setting that might have been staged a century before. It is objective, representational of action and of external events. The audience observes both Macbeth and the apparitions. The witches could be real beings, really tempting the king. The second scene exists, however, only within the consciousness. Behind it is a psychology that locates the supernatural in the fevered mind. It takes us vicariously into the very interior of that mind, and the sublimity comes from the mental state rather than from external and substantial horrors. The consciousness is all. We can assume that the consciousness has created the scene.[6]

In study of the nonrational side of experience, by realizing and exemplifying it in art, Fuseli was a pioneer. This fact raises a question of great interest. I have pointed out, in chapter i, how Locke's analysis of association of ideas makes possible a new conception of the nonrational and unconscious activities in the personality. One might have expected new fields to open up, for the writer especially. Shakespeare criticism did begin to show influences from this way of studying the mind. Yet, with the important exception of Sterne, English creative writers and artists for many years did relatively little with "whatever passes in the mind." Fuseli, however, began, especially in drawings, to explore the world of dream, of the unconscious phenomena which may resemble and may even go over into madness. "The Nightmare" is a famous example.

Why, then, were so few innovations made? Why did such techniques as the "stream of consciousness" appear so much later? No doubt there were several reasons. For one, the teleological theory of imagination interposed an obstacle to the study of the mind, for its own sake, in every aspect of its functionings. The concern to show the goodness of human nature, to find the "natural" hidden under the encrustations left by custom and education, obscured the real problems of the personality. Fuseli, after he rejected Rousseau and the cult of nature, could turn to the study of the inner life unhampered by a priori assumptions.

The very enthusiasm for the sublime of terror may have been a deterrent. The situation is confusing. Does not the rage for Gothic romance, for the "pleasing stupor," for the *frisson* of the macabre, indicate strong interest in the dark and obscure sides of human nature? In a way, yes; but this interest, assuming that the irrational has its uses, is directed toward determining how the awful is justified in the great scheme of things. If once it is determined that delight in superstitions is common, the next concern must be to find the peculiar end that response was made to serve. Addison, to be sure, does refer (*Spect.* 421) to the "disordered imagination," but only once; and in two sentences he concludes, "to quit so disagreeable a subject . . ." The prospect of disorder in the source of spiritual influence through sense impression is too unpleasant to bear examination. The tendency, then, was to exploit rather than explore the strange aspects of imagination.

We can understand more about the temper of the period by considering a curious yet apropos contrast of pictures. Horace Walpole, we are told, was shocked by "The Nightmare," but was rather pleased by Copley's painting "Watson and the Shark." This judgment, I suspect, would have been that of the great majority. James T. Flexner describes the Copley painting thus, in contrast with Fuseli's work:

> We are shown a real harbor—identified as Havana—floating an actual boat in which ordinary people behave as ordinary people would when attempting to avert tragedy. In the foreground, a naked boy is being attacked by a very material shark. Far from being asked to accompany the artist down the ghost-haunted corridors of his own mind, we are made spectators at a frightening accident.[7]

The superficial description is fair enough, although I doubt that "The Nightmare" is as subjective as this statement would indicate. But realism, I suggest, is not the reason for the popularity of Copley's painting, which goes contrary to the romantic taste for the misty and indefinite in landscape painting. The principal reason for the preference is probably that a man of the time would see in "Watson and the Shark" a fine exercise in the sublime imagination. Subject and treatment are calculated to produce a powerful emotion in the spectator—the "controlled" emotion of fear, where the feeling is rendered aesthetic in its effect by our awareness that we are not in immediate danger. The sublime of terror, however, is balanced by the sympathetic imagination: we are apprehensive not for ourselves but for the boy. Thus is averted the narrowing effect of the sublime of terror, and compassion is aroused; the sympathetic imagination, like an organ, may be strengthened by a controlled exertion. But in "The Nightmare" we have left the "sublime" altogether and are in the world of another kind of terror; we are haunted by the specters of our own age.

The impact of the Burkian analysis on the faith in nature and imagination was strong, as evidenced in part by the emergence of the picturesque and by controversies about aesthetic effects that were increasingly assumed to be biological-psychological in nature, and unrelated to final causes. To this challenge two notable responses were made: two important works sought to establish the final causes on firmer foundations. They are, for different reasons, worth considering.

The account of the imagination by the moral philosopher Dugald Stewart is the culmination of the traditional theory as it had taken form before the extreme theories of associationism. In substance, his position is a vindication, with expansion and sensible modification, of the original Addisonian view. One distincton is that he stated, clearly and fully, ideas that until then had been expressed confusedly and often only implied.

Stewart begins with the old assumption that the faculties are autonomous and mutually exclusive. They, moreover, are definite and real "powers"—capacities of the mind, whereby it deals with the raw materials of sensation. We determine the area of the imagination by applying the test of pleasure, which, he says, is the sole end of art; this statement, repeated many times (as, for example, by Wordsworth in the preface to the *Lyrical Ballads*), indicates Stewart's belief in the autonomy and independence of imagination. The following passage is an illuminating statement of the proposition:

> The object of the Philosopher is to inform and enlighten mankind; that of the Orator, to acquire an ascendance over the will of others by bending to his own purposes their judgments, their imaginations, and their passions; but the primary and the distinguishing aim of the Poet, is *to please*; and the principal resource, which he possesses for this purpose, is by addressing the imagination. Sometimes, indeed, he may seem to encroach on the province of the Philosopher or of the Orator; but, in these instances, he only borrows from them the means by which he accomplishes his end. If he attempts to enlighten and to inform, he addresses the understanding only as a vehicle of pleasure . . .[8]

This is an explicit exposition of what Addison had vaguely indicated (*Spect.* 421) in his remarks about the mind having "two of its faculties gratified at the same time." When ideas are to be used in poetry at all, they must be employed simply to delight the imagination. The true poem can hardly be notably philosophical.

The power of imagination, for Addison, included both the process of passive appreciation and response, and the activity of conscious creation. Stewart attempts to bring these seemingly contradictory activities into order. Imagination is, he says, a "complex power." It begins with "conception, or simple apprehension, which enables us to form a notion of those former objects of perception or of knowledge, out of which we are to make a selection." Abstraction is defined in wholly Lockian manner as the process of isolating separate impressions from the others which came with them in experience, and "Judgment or Taste, which selects the materials, and directs their combination."[9] To this judgment a subordinate "habit of association," called "fancy," presents "all the different materials, which are subservient to the efforts of imagination, and which may therefore be considered as forming the ground-work of poetical genius." In the older conception of creation, what Stewart calls "fancy" was the imagination. What he calls "Judgment or Taste" —the identification is most suggestive—would have been "Right Reason." But now reason is out of the creative act altogether; the component parts are within the imagination itself.

Stewart imagines Milton creating his picture of the Garden of Eden. Striking scenes, memories of his experiences (reading plays only a small part, it would appear), rush into his mind, brought by association. He then abstracts the most beautiful features from these scenes; taste, finally, directs him in selecting the best of them to arrange in descriptive language. We never see Milton planning the description with relation to the architectonic requirements of the poem, or considering significance to theme.

With this definition of judgment in mind, we can better understand some mysteries of romantic poetry. What is meant when judgment and inspiration are contrasted? What are judgment and fancy? It is clear that the old conflict between the two is not at issue here. This "judgment" is only the developed ability to decide what images, what sound values, will produce the most pleasing or striking aesthetic effect. The poet, for Stewart, is a technician, skillfully operating, by controlled and estimated devices, on the reader's passive sensibility. He completely rejects the theory of automatism; in fact, he says that imagination is not a gift of nature at all, "but the result of acquired habits, aided by favorable circumstances." Keats seems to try to make the best of both worlds by saying that judgment and inspiration operate simultaneously in his creative work.

Stewart is most concerned to defend the traditional idea that imagination is a refined sensibility, which responds to whole and complex scenes; it is not, as Burke maintained, a by-product of biological needs; and it is universal in nature, as opposed to local, private, and trivial associations of ideas. Stewart repeats the common proposition that the imagination responds to the particular sense impression only; hence he emphasizes again and again the complete separation of the intellectual from the poetic. We are interested in the streaks of the tulip, but we do not number them.

"In poetry, as truths and facts are introduced, not for the purpose of information, but to convey pleasure to the mind, nothing offends more, than those general expressions which form the great instrument of philosophical reasoning."

The works of art are divided into two classes. Some, like gardening, appeal directly and solely to perception; the response is immediate and uncomplicated. Others, of which poetry is chief, appeal to the reflective power. Arising from elemental sensation—color is the first—the taste gradually evolves into a "refined" appreciation to be explained by no one principle, indeed not finally explicable at all—except that it is closely identified with holy nature, which is impressed everywhere with "the signatures of Almighty Power, and of Unfathomable Design." [10]

Thus we come round again to the cult of nature that everywhere vivifies the cult of imagination. In nature,

> we do not look for that obvious uniformity of plan which we expect to find in the productions of beings endowed with the same faculties, and actuated by the same motives as ourselves. A deviation from uniformity, on the contrary, in the grand outlines sketched by *her* hand, appears perfectly suited to that *infinity*, which is associated, in our conceptions, with all her operations.

The appreciation of natural scenery is, then, the highest point of taste; when it is reached, the judgment, which first is formed according to "rules borrowed from the arts of human life," is corrected, and the false notions of society are seen to be "puerile." The associations producing love of nature are "invariably confirmed more and more, in proportion to the advancement of reason, and the enlargement of experience." To analyze the components of this supreme taste may be a "task to which the faculties of man are not completely adequate." The religious character of this theorizing is apparent. It is worth while to observe, also, that Stewart gives an excellent account of the rationale of the earliest poems by Wordsworth and Coleridge.

Stewart shares the enthusiasm for the natural sublime. Again, while restating outlines of the orthodox opinion, he attempts to clear away inconsistencies and to reconcile diverse notions. He resolves the problem whether the sublime arises from terror only, or from a mere impression of magnitude, agreeing with Richard Payne Knight that a sense of power is the root of the emotion; but, again in answer to the challenge of Burke, he must demonstrate that the natural sublime has a religious function. Consequently, it is not only power, but the power of Deity that we feel in the emotion. There is a transference from the object of religious worship to "whatever is calculated to excite the analogous, though comparatively weak, sentiments of admiration and of wonder." [11]

The question of height as an element, or the principal element, of the sublime had been much debated. Stewart grants that height is an important sensation for the sublime, and thus modifies the factor of unrelieved bigness, of physical extent, without, however, denying it. The word "sublime" means, literally, high; elevation must be involved in it. Yet Stewart illustrates admirably how the sense of quantity has replaced the Longinian sense of quality. There is no feeling that by the emotion of the sublime man is elevated, or brought back to his true, lofty rank in a universe of qualitatively distinguished degrees. The effect for Stewart is always measurable. Elevation enables us to contemplate *more*, to assimilate a larger and larger quantity of the infinite universe. (Compare my discussion in chapter v, especially of Grove's paper in the *Spectator*.)

> It will readily occur as an objection to some of the fore-going conclusions, that *horizontal extent*, as well as great *altitude*, is an element of the Sublime. Upon the slightest reflection, however, it must appear obvious, that this extension of the meaning of Sublimity arises entirely from the natural association between elevated position and a commanding prospect of the earth's surface, in all directions. As the most palpable *measure* of elevation is the extent of view which it affords, so, on the other hand, an enlarged horizon recalls impressions connected with great elevation.[12]

Stewart is faithful to the spirit of Locke, even when, as in his objection to Locke's identification of experience with consciousness, he sees that the master needs correction. He accounts for the universality of correct taste as opposed to eccentric individual preferences in the same way that Locke accounts for the validity of the complex ideas formed by the understanding. The operations of universal taste are "trains of ideas" as opposed to the unpredictable associations that may occur in any mind. The accomplished poet will realize this fact, and will avoid giving full and literal descriptions; instead, he will artfully suggest by using a secondary impression which will call up the whole train of ideas. Stewart justly pointed out that much of the weakness of romantic descriptive poetry arose from what he calls its "bombast," its attempts to gain effects by piling image on image, to strain panoramic description to the utmost. Mallarmé put the point more subtly when he said that the mind must have the joy of believing that it is creating. If an object is described just as it is, if we are confronted with the whole object, the delights of suggestion and evocation are eliminated.

Stewart's value as spokesman for the faith of early romanticism is enhanced by his modest and sensible approach. He recognizes and tries to avoid possible absurdities and extremes. He is aware that indulgence in imagination can become a morally dangerous luxury; however splendid the faculty is, it must be related to and restrained by an awareness of the fact that it is only one function of the mind. Thus, although he accepted Adam Smith's point that only through the imagination can we identify ourselves fully with others, he saw —long before William James—that excessive contemplation of imaginary sorrows will make one actually insensible to the real plights of real people.

The natural imagination, furthermore, should always be connected with the social scene. Stewart perceived that communion with nature could turn into a new and barren mysticism; he warned against the solitary excursion, and challenged the usual belief that scenery is most inspiring if one is not distracted by company. Mrs. Montagu and her group came to the conclusion that, although the imagination responds to nature in solitude, one must always make a conscious effort to bring the resulting inspiration back into relationship with society. As Wordsworth suggests in *The Prelude*, the pleasures of imagination, at first purely individual and self-centered, grow into a humanized imaginative sympathy. Stewart goes so far as to distrust the isolated experience altogether.

Stewart's theory is of value chiefly as illuminating a movement which was in its last phase and about to give way to a related, but yet different, and artistically far more valuable one. This new movement is exemplified by another analysis of aesthetic that appeared at almost the same time as Stewart's *Elements*. Archibald Alison's *Essays on the Nature and Principles of Taste* (1790) has never received the full measure of recognition that it deserves. Alison helps us understand and appreciate much of the best poetry (not to speak of painting) of the nineteenth and twentieth centuries far more than does Coleridge.[13] Monk, rightly, has high praise for Alison's work; as he says, it marks the culmination of one aspect of the new aesthetic and the starting point of another.[14]

Alison's purpose was to clear up the many confusions that had piled up in the impressive body of aesthetic speculations. He was aware that the structure of the traditional theory was shaky. One evident crack Stewart also had seen. How can taste be nothing but a "sense, or senses, by which the qualities of beauty and sublimity are perceived and felt, as their proper objects"? [15] Alison shows, with critical insight, the stultifying effect of this dogma on all art. If aesthetic appreciation consists only in the reception, by an inner sense, of a limited group of impressions, and if art is merely the reproduction of these impressions, then indeed the field of the artist is narrow and soon exhausted; "the sense of taste would, of necessity, operate to oppose every new improvement" (Conclusion). The poet would have nothing to do but hunt for ways to ring the changes on descriptions of the same sublime and picturesque scenes. Only those scenes could be used; once a poet had done the job capably, everyone else would be merely an imitator.

This may account for a curious fact about the tradition of the "sublime" poem: contrary to almost universal procedure in art, the best example of the type occurs at the beginning. After Thomson's

The Seasons there is a drift downward, until the nadir is reached, just before the end of the century, with the kind of poetry that Fuseli castigated. Since only a restricted group of forms could, by definition, be beautiful, "the period of their discovery must have been the final period of every art of taste." There was a real possibility, at the time Alison wrote this, that English poetry would develop a rigid formalism, like certain Oriental lyrical traditions, in which the art of the poet would consist in contriving minute variations on a very limited body of materials, in a prescribed style. A poetry confined to descriptions of external nature perhaps inevitably comes to this point.

Alison's contribution lay in squarely facing the fact that, given the new psychology, art must be subjective. Sublimity and beauty, he asserted, do not exist in nature; they are qualities that exist only in mental operations. The doubts that had momentarily beset Akenside about the spirituality of matter, the gnawing suspicion that the noble qualities that had been attributed to the world outside us are merely imaginary—these Alison faced. Yet Alison realized that a form of universality must be preserved if art is to retain validity.

The reluctance to recognize subjectivity arose from the natural suspicion that to do so would result in the conclusion that each person is left alone with his unique experiences. The poet may recreate the adventures of his sensibilities in nature, but how can he reach an audience at all? Are we imprisoned, incommunicado, in the private worlds of our own experiences? Again, if nature is not of itself sublime or beautiful, how can we guarantee the efficacy of the graces of nature?

Alison developed the revolutionary principle of subjectivity in such a way as to satisfy the desires for order and purpose in the universe and in the constitution of the mind of man. He did so by his theory of *symbolism* as the instrument of poetry. The "qualities of matter," he explains, "are not beautiful or sublime in themselves, but as they are, by various means, the signs or expressions of qualities capable of producing emotion" (Introduction). The principle of association is the binding element; we need assume no innate dispositions. Very early in life we form associations between certain sensations and certain qualities which evoke definite emotions. The connection, although very close and very strong, may be broken. The magnitude of the ocean, for example, "is expressive to us of vastness, and when apparently unbounded, of infinity" (Essay II, chap. iv, sec. 1). The aesthetic emotion of sublimity follows upon this train of associations. This example is not new: it takes us back to Addison, and other aesthetic writers had employed it *ad infinitum*.

In what, then, was Alison new? First, in recognizing specifically that the ocean is a symbol, or sign. Addison implied this; the Addisonian theory is an unrecognized one of symbolism. But he could not admit that it was symbolic. He felt that infinity really exists in nature, and that this quality is identical with the aesthetic effect. The mind merely receives and records the external fact. It was necessary to recognize just what the aesthetic element was, and how images are related to it.

Alison's second contribution lay in the concrete analysis of the steps that create the aesthetic effect. The aesthetic reaction consists of a great number of individual and discrete effects, each occasioned by a sense impression which acts, not to produce its effect immediately, but to begin a train of associations that results in a definite aesthetic response. Alison denies that there is any inner sense on which the images of nature make a direct impression; on the other hand, the associationists, trying to account for aesthetic effects without an inner sense, suppose "some *one* known and acknowledged principle or affection of mind, to be the foundation of all the emotions we receive from the objects of taste, and which resolves, therefore, all the various phenomena into some more general law of our intellectual or moral constitution." Examples he gives are Diderot, basing everything on perception of "relation"; Hume, on "utility"; and the "venerable St. Austin, who, with nobler views, a thousand years ago, resolved them into the pleasure which belongs to the perception of order and design, &c." The conception of aesthetic experience could not become viable until it was freed from both of these limitations. Alison asserted in essence that the aesthetic experience is both a unique and a complex kind of experience. It was the combination of these elements that laid the cornerstone for a whole new school of art.

In the third place, Alison began to free aesthetic from the looseness and vagueness of most eighteenth-century writers. A theorist will speak grandly of a certain image causing the response of "the sublime." Apparently, whatever the image, if it is "sublime," the effect is the same. Much of the controversy over whether terror and vastness could both be sublime was a confused recognition of this problem. How could a Turner seascape and "Watson and the Shark" produce the same kind of emotion? Yet respectable theory agreed that they must do so. Alison shows that the aesthetic effects are not reducible to a few categories, but are multiple and indeed as various as the world of experience itself. Each symbol appeals to its own "quality," and, it follows logically, the final effect is its own. To be sure, Alison, as a man of his time, classifies these aesthetic effects under the heads of "beautiful" or "sublime"; but obviously they are different *kinds* of sublimity or beauty; and the categories begin to lose significance. The symbol and its precise effect are the essentials; the "sublime" and the "beautiful" are afterthoughts. It comes as a great liberation when poets begin to concentrate on the image and what it can do, and cease to worry about whether they are evoking sublimity or beauty. The material "sign," Alison finds, sets in motion a train of ideas resulting eventually in "a peculiar exercise of the imagination." The word "peculiar" is the key; it is a revolutionary remark. Thus, he says, magnitude "has different characters of sublimity"; otherwise its sublimity would "have the same degree, and the same character" (Essay I, chap. iv, sec. 1).

Alison's general principle gains much of its practical value from the tables of symbols and their aesthetic effects which he worked out in detail. His examples—the howling of storms, arousing emotions of danger; the tolling of the passing bell, calling up deep melancholy; and the like (his extension of aesthetic from vision alone to include other senses has often been noted)—are conventional and uninspired enough, for Alison was no poet himself. It is the method —the concentration on the roots of the symbol, the associations that formed it, and the precise feeling it evokes, rather than a vague final effect of grandeur—that is important. A corollary of the method is to break down the conviction that certain impressions are aesthetic in effect and that others are automatically excluded by their very nature. Any image is potential material for aesthetic use; the associations are the criteria.

Before the rise of the new cosmology, the macrocosm-microcosm relationship had for centuries been the stuff of poetry. The belief had been that the universe speaks to man in symbols: we read God's book in the sun, the moon, the very stones. The objects we observe have clear, public meanings which can be ascertained by reasoning. Locke's psychological system completed the process of destroying this confidence, a process which the disappearance of a man-centered universe had begun. Poets were left with nothing but the images, in their limited selves, to work upon.[16]

Alison restored to poets a symbolic language. The new language was a system of common symbolism however, in a very different manner from the old. The new symbols have no objective, agreed-upon significance. They arise from the inner life of impressions and moods; they must speak to the imagination alone, for in the last analysis they have nothing to do with facts and logical reasoning.

Yet they are a language. That symbols are subjective does not make them irresponsibly personal, with the poet speaking a language intelligible only to himself. Alison showed that a large common ground of emotional associations exists—he assumed among all mankind, but at least among peoples of similar culture. Experiences in childhood and beyond correspond to some extent; the exact associations vary with each individual, but a community of final effects can be assumed. Moreover, the fact that the "signs or expressions of qualities capable of producing emotion" are both common and individual gives a new dimension to poetry which could produce novel and interesting results. Assiduous study of a poet, too, will extend the reader's own symbolic range, for many of the experiences producing the signs can be shared. Furthermore, the test of success in this kind of poetry is not logical communication, which must avoid ambiguity, but emotion. Its quality, its aesthetic intensity, is the sole test. Thus an exact correspondence of associations between poet and reader is not necessary, and may even be undesirable; the aesthetic experience is not limited and defined, but indefinite and unlimited, like the sublime.

The individual symbols and their associations are not so nebulous, however, as many critics have indicated. Alison showed that the symbol has definiteness, even precision. It cannot, of course, be defined in terms of rational thought, but that fact does not make a successful symbolic poem like a bad watercolor, in which everything is blurred and smeared. Symbolism does not arise from chance combinations of ideas: this assumption was one defect of strict associationism. In aesthetic trains of ideas, "it will be found, that there is always some general principle of connexion which pervades the whole, and gives them some certain and definite character" (Essay I, chap. ii, sec. 1). Aesthetic judgment must be in control; Alison does not specifically say so, but there is the implication that a poet who tries to write from immediate inspiration can never be a good symbolist.

Alison's ideas opened up many new possibilities. The poet could explore the inexhaustible number of associations between experience and emotions. The exploration of childhood experiences was exciting; we think of *The Prelude*. The poet could begin to find the truth in Burke's remark, that the real subject of poetry is one's experience of things. Formulas for exploring that experience were provided.

Alison stated that poetical imagination is first fired by descriptions in ancient poetry, when children "have acquired a new sense, as it were, with which they can behold the face of Nature." The "beautiful forms of ancient mythology" develop associations with natural phenomena. Here, as Caldwell has shown for Keats, was a whole new world of poetic material. The familiar mythology, instilled in any boy with a good standard education, could be exploited in a new way; the standard *allegoria,* the usual center of attention, could be ignored and the accumulated secondary associations—the aura of mythology—could provide new and potent symbols, or even a new kind of allegory could be created. Yeats found somewhat the same resource in Irish mythology.

This theory rested firmly on a doctrine of separation of powers as complete as any we have seen. Aesthetic and practical experience, imagination and reason, are as distinct as oil and water. The "man of business, who has passed his life in studying the means of accumulating wealth," and the "philosopher, whose years have been employed in the investigation of causes," we learn, are almost entirely debarred by their associations from indulging the imagination at all. "A beautiful scene in nature would produce for them no other association than its value, or speculations upon the causes of its beauty." And a notable sentence: "In both, it would thus excite ideas, which could be the foundation of no exercise of imagination, because *they required thought and attention*" (Essay I, chap. i, sec. 2; italics mine).

Presumably the philosopher and the man of business once did have aesthetic associations which could be evoked by the material signs; but long nonimaginative experience will break those bonds in the mind, and leave the philosopher and the scientist desiccated slaves to cold reason. How important, therefore, that the artist retain the simplicity and uncommitted innocence of youth!

Alison agrees with his predecessors that man can attain spiritual insight only through the imaginative experience. Nature, if we allow her to do so, gives us a moral education. His attitude is an expansion of Mrs. Montagu's idea that imagination produces a current of inspiration that flows into and vivifies the mind, which otherwise would become absorbed in self and material pursuits. (This coincidence of opinion is not surprising; Alison married a Miss Gregory, who was a protégé of Elizabeth Montagu, with whom she lived for several years and in whose correspondence she figures. Miss Gregory apparently was absorbed in the common interest of the whole group—justifying the cult of imaginative experience of nature.) Alison writes a hymn to the divine imagination (Essay II, chap. vi, sec. 6):

> . . . I believe there is no man of genuine taste, who has not often felt, in the lone majesty of nature, some unseen spirit to dwell, which in his happier hours, touched, as if with magic hand, all the springs of his moral sensibility, and rekindled in his heart those original conceptions of the moral or intellectual excellence of his nature, which it is the melancholy tendency of the vulgar pursuits of life to diminish, if not altogether to destroy.

Some of the most important romantic poetry dealt with the impairment, restoration, and strengthening of the imagination. Yet, despite Alison's genuine belief in the inspiration of nature, his own theory tended to negate it. Purity of poetry, as evoking uncontaminated aesthetic experience, could easily become a goal in itself; the source of the symbols is not of essential importance, and intensity is the first criterion.

Alison exacerbates a further dilemma of the romantic. It was an old observation that men are more given to writing poems, especially love lyrics, in youth than in age. But it would seem that the classical poet was not afflicted with apprehension that his ability to write heroic poems of great theme would fade away. Milton fears that his energy may fail before he can complete his great poem, but he sees his physical disabilities compensated for by a "celestial light" brighter as the body decays. Wisdom, which is essential for a great poet, replaces mere animal spirits.

In the romantic period the order is turned upside down. Many a romantic poet is haunted by the fear that the delicate adjustment of the nerves, the mechanism of keen emotional response that is the organ of imagination, must, like any other function of the body, begin to lose its vigor when youth is past. A "glory" is destined to pass away as man grows into maturity; thus Alison acknowledges that the aesthetic associations formed in childhood are weakened or obscured by others that arise during adult life. The "visionary power," apparently doomed to early extinction, is also the agency of spiritual illumination. Let the aged, then, go to the child and be wise. Can anything replace that power? Memory, perhaps; in reverie some of the original vividness may be recalled—but not all. Unraveling the skein of early experience revives it in a measure. But it would seem that poets are fated to decline into critics; and critical analysis is fatal to real imaginative response.

Edmund Wilson has called attention to the fact that the symbolist movement of the nineteenth century was nourished from many alien sources, of which the chief was English. The connections of Verlaine, Mallarmé, and Baudelaire with English or American writers are well known.[17] Yet, as Wilson points out, the English, in contrast with the French, write little about literature as such. True; but the distinctive fact about the English and Scottish writers of the eighteenth century was their preoccupation with aesthetics. It might be argued that aesthetic theory rather than true literary criticism is likely to produce revolutions in criticism; at any rate, the cult of the imagination is central in European literature after the early eighteenth century, and the premises I have described underlie that cult.

How constant these premises were, may be demonstrated by a brief look at a theory of poetry that appeared more than a century after the first edition of Alison's work. The earlier poems and plays of William Butler Yeats were, by his own account, "symbolist." In a series of essays written about the turn of the century,[18] Yeats set forth an ideal of art which it is instructive to consider in the light of the history I have described.

Yeats defines the symbolism which is the essence of his poetry:

> All sound, all colours, all forms, either because of their preordained energies or because of long association, evoke indefinable and yet precise emotions, or, as I prefer to think, call down among us certain disembodied powers, whose footsteps over our hearts we call emotions; and when sound, and colour, and form are in a musical relation, a beautiful relation to one another, they become as it were one sound, one colour, one form, and evoke an emotion that is made out of their distinct evocations and yet is one emotion.[19]

This description is not very different from Alison's, in essentials. The symbol, by association, evokes emotions indefinable and yet precise; the components, as in Lockian psychology, are distinct impressions, which remain distinct even though they result in a final unity. There is no suggestion of the creating function of the Coleridgean imagination, in which the impressions are completely fused.

"Their preordained energies" would seem to hint at an innate responsiveness of the mind to aesthetic impressions, without the need for associations—resembling the "inner sense"; but the other statements consistently imply an association recorded in memory. Thus, in "Magic," Yeats accounts for occult phenomena which, he says, he had witnessed, by a symbolic-associational theory: "I discovered that the symbol hardly ever failed to call up its typical scene, its typical event, its typical person . . ." Certain symbols, he feels, are effective through "the great memory" possessed by the race, wherein events of ages past are evoked; but, beneath the mystical are associations, formed by definite events, even though in the distant past. "Whatever the passions of man have gathered about, becomes a symbol in the great memory, and in the hands of him who has the secret, it is a worker of wonders . . ."

Some critics of symbolism have failed to understand the importance of the statement by Yeats that symbolic writing is not truly metaphorical. This point Alison's explicit theory makes clear. One reason is that metaphor implies the yoking of image and abstract idea, but, as Alison and Yeats would agree, the symbol of poetry must be entirely nonintellectual. Yeats distinguishes intellectual from emotional symbols. The former "are the playthings of the allegorist or the pedant, and soon pass away." To experience the emotional symbol it is necessary, as Alison also asserts, to avoid conscious intellectual activity; and Yeats, in "The Symbolism of Poetry," advances the intriguing suggestion that the function of rhythm in poetry may be, "by hushing us with an alluring monotony, while it holds us waking by variety, to keep us in that state of perhaps real trance, in which the mind liberated from the pressure of the will is unfolded in symbols." In "Symbolism in Painting," he surmises that "symbols are the only things free enough from all bonds to speak of perfection." Consequently, "if you liberate a person or a landscape from the bonds of motives and their actions, causes and their effects, and from all bonds but the bonds of your love, it will change under your eyes, and become a symbol of an infinite emotion, a perfected emotion, a part of the Divine Essence . . ."

This raises a question that Alison, not being a poet, could hardly answer: What form will the symbolist poem take? Certainly the whole tenor of his theory is against logical or formal structure: the unity must be one of mood; the movement must not be dictated arbitrarily by pure reverie, and yet it must be determined by associational connections. Yeats says that the symbolist poets "would seek out those wavering, meditative, organic rhythms, which are the embodiment of the imagination, that neither desires nor hates, because it has done with time, and only wishes to gaze upon some reality, some beauty."

Yeats, like the theorists of imagination, locates the spiritual in the imagination. Both feel that the emotions represent the powers that shape our essential selves. The spirit is played upon by symbols that evoke these shaping forces.

> Because an emotion does not exist, or does not become perceptible and active among us, till it has found its expression, in colour or in sound or in form, or in all of these, and because no two modulations or arrangements of these evoke the same emotion, poets and painters and musicians, and in a less degree because their effects are momentary, day and night and cloud and shadow, are continually making and unmaking mankind.

The poet, then, is literally a magician who can exercise a supreme influence on mankind. But he must exercise that power only through the evocations of the symbols. It is interesting to see that Yeats indignantly calls for "a casting out of descriptions of nature for the sake of nature, of the moral law for the sake of the moral law, a casting out of all anecdotes and of that brooding over scientific opinion that so often extinguished the central flames in Tennyson, and of that vehemence that would make us do or not do certain things." Thus Yeats would eliminate, as not true poetry, both the descriptive poems of the earlier romantic movement and the didactic poetry of the classical; I have noted that the same consequence follows from the associationist theories of Alison.

One more point may be elucidated from this comparative study. In the aestheticism of the end of the nineteenth century, certain important distinctions must be made. Yeats has expressed his admiration of and debt to Pater, and in many ways this debt is real. Yet there is an important difference between their attitudes. It is Pater who is, in the pure sense, the aesthete. The conclusion to *The Renaissance* fixes the goal of existence in "a life of constant and eager observation. Every moment some form grows perfect in hand or face; some tone on the hills or the sea is choicer than the rest; some mood of passion or insight or intellectual excitement is irresistibly real and attractive to us—for that moment only. Not the fruit of experience, but experience itself, is the end." This is the culmination of a sensationalist philosophy; the sensation, in and for itself, is what the organism exists to provide. Pater was able to absorb abstract thought, even, into his aesthetic, for "the service of philosophy, of speculative culture, towards the human spirit, is to rouse, to startle it to a life of constant and eager observation."

Now this is true aestheticism. Yeats was, I suspect, never a true aesthete. Always, like the theorists of the previous century, he saw a kind of final cause, a purpose beyond itself in the aesthetic emotion. However nebulous and metaphorical the expressions of his ideas are, I think they amount to a fairly clear point: that character, the true personality, is composed of experiences beyond the reach of, and in some degree antagonistic to, the understanding. The poet, then, should have a spiritual ideal; in an indefinable but real sense he helps make us what we are—spiritual or material, slaves of time or beings within Eternity. We exist, not to appreciate and to sense, but to *be*—to be whole and to be free. It is not surprising that Yeats was an early enthusiast for Blake. Like Blake, he felt that man has become imprisoned in one side of his mind; that only through imagination can he be liberated, can he achieve Unity of Being.

I should say, therefore, that the later change in the poetry of Yeats was not so drastic as it might seem. His ideal of poetry as performing an illuminating and saving function was constant. He came to see—as did many poets after the first decade of the twentieth century—that the arbitrary separation of imagination from the practical problems and rational activities of life was false. Almost exactly two centuries after Addison's "Pleasures of the Imagination," Yeats expressed his intention

> To write for my own race
> And for the reality.

It was not that he had lost faith in the imagination, but that he had attained a larger insight. He saw that the light of the imagination must be shed on all human interests, for imagination is not a means of grace but an instrument for the criticism of life.

Notes

NOTES TO CHAPTER I

[1] Basil Willey, *The Seventeenth Century Background*, chap. xi, sec. 1. The comprehensive study of Lockian influences is by Kenneth MacLean, *John Locke and English Literature of the Eighteenth Century* (New Haven, 1936). I have assumed knowledge of the extensive evidence there presented. The statements about the triumph of Lockian epistemology are based on this study.

[2] Perry Miller, *Errand into the Wilderness* (Boston, 1956), p. 168.

[3] John Smith, *The Immortality of the Soul*, in *The Cambridge Platonists*, ed. Champagnac (Oxford, 1901), chap. iii.

[4] *Bateman uppon Bartholome* . . . (London, 1582), III, vi. A good account of Renaissance psychology is given by Ruth L. Anderson, *Elizabethan Psychology and Shakespeare's Plays*, University of Iowa Humanistic Studies (1927). See also Hardin Craig, *The Enchanted Glass* (New York, 1936).

[5] John Davies, *Mirum in Modum, A Glimpse of Gods Glorie and the Soules Shape* (London, 1602), p. 12 recto.

[6] Henry More, *Enchiridion Ethicum* (London, 1690), p. 15.

[7] *Ibid.*, p. 80.

[8] James Gibson, *Locke's Theory of Knowledge and Its Historical Relations* (Cambridge, 1931), p. 30.

[9] *Descartes' Philosophical Writings*, trans. Norman Kemp Smith (London, 1952), "Meditations on the First Philosophy," Med. II. The Latin phrase clearly shows Descartes' nearness to old ways of thinking about the mind "sed tantum ex eo quod intelligantur." The French should also be given, for its simplicity and directness convey the point better than we find it in either Latin or English translation: "mais seulement de ce que nous les concevons par la pensée."

[10] On the reaction against Cartesianism, see my article, "Swift and the 'World-Makers,'" *Journal of the History of Ideas*, XI (1950), 54 ff.

[11] Joseph Glanvill, *Essays upon Several Important Subjects in Philosophy and Religion* (London, 1676), Essay V.

[12] More, *Enchiridion Ethicum*, p. 80.

[13] *Essay Concerning the Human Understanding*, II, iii, 1. Citations from this work, except as otherwise noted, are from the Fraser edition (Oxford, 1914), and for convenience in reference are given by book, chapter, and section. *The Conduct of the Understanding* has been consulted in *The Works of John Locke*, 12th ed. (London, 1824), Vol. II.

[14] Cassirer, *The Platonic Renaissance in England*, trans. J. P. Pettegrove (Austin, 1953), p. 63.

[15] *Essay Concerning the Human Understanding*, ed. Rand (Cambridge, 1931), p. 119.

[16] John Norris, *Cursory Reflections on the Essay Concerning the Human Understanding* (London, 1728), p. 26. For a full account of the reception of Locke's *Essay*, see John Yolton, *John Locke and the Way of Ideas* (Oxford, 1956).

[17] Erwin Panofsky, *Studies in Iconology* (New York, 1939), p. 229.

[18] *Summa Theologica*, trans. Fathers of the English Dominican Province, Q. 85, Art. 2, Obj. 3.

[19] Joseph Wood Krutch, *"Modernism" in the Modern Drama* (Ithaca, 1953), p. 84.

[20] *Ibid.*

[21] *Coleridge's Shakespearean Criticism*, ed. Raysor (London, 1930), II, 196.

[22] Krutch, *"Modernism"* . . . , p. 85.

[23] Maurice Morgann, *On the Dramatic Character of Sir John Falstaff*, in *Eighteenth Century Essays on Shakespeare*, ed. D. Nichol Smith (Glasgow, 1903), p. 219. Morgann's essay was published in 1777, but written earlier.

[24] Walter Whiter, *A Specimen of a Commentary on Shakspeare* . . . (London, 1794), p. 64.

[25] *Ibid.*, p. 78.

[26] E. S. Dallas, *The Gay Science* (London, 1866), I, 207.

NOTES TO CHAPTER II

[1] R. S. Crane, "Suggestions toward a Genealogy of the 'Man of Feeling,'" *ELH*, I (1934), 207.

[2] *Works of Isaac Barrow*, ed. Tillotson (London, 1696), II, 107.

[3] The Latin version, *Telluris Theoria Sacra*, appeared in 1681–1689; the English, written by Burnet himself, in 1684–1690. For accounts of this book, see Basil Willey, *The Eighteenth Century Background*, chap. ii; and

Tuveson, *Millennium and Utopia* (Berkeley and Los Angeles, 1949), pp. 117–118.

[4] *Remarks upon an Essay Concerning the Human Understanding. In a Letter Address'd to the Author.* This and two subsequent pamphlets on Locke's *Essay* are anonymous, but there is every reason to attribute them to Burnet. See H. O. Christophersen, A *Bibliographical Introduction to the Study of John Locke* (Oslo, 1930), pp. 44–48.

[5] *Remarks* . . . , p. 5.

[6] *Works of John Locke* (London, 1824), III, 187.

[7] Thomas Burnet, *Third Remarks* . . . (London, 1699), p. 8. I have given an account of these pamphlets, and of extensive marginal comments on them in Locke's handwriting, in "The Origins of the 'Moral Sense,'" *Huntington Library Quarterly*, XI (1948), 241 ff.

[8] Wordsworth, *The Prelude* (1850 ed.), I, 340 ff.

[9] Letter to Ainsworth, 1708/09, in *The Life, Unpublished Letters, and Philosophical Regimen of Anthony, Earl of Shaftesbury*, ed. Rand (London and New York, 1900), p. 403.

[10] *Ibid.*

[11] Shaftesbury, *Inquiry Concerning Virtue*, in *Characteristicks* (1st ed., 1711), I, 27.

[12] *Characteristicks* (5th ed., 1732), II, 28.

[13] *The Moralists, ibid.*, II, 214.

[14] *The Prelude*, VIII, 669 ff.

NOTES TO CHAPTER III

[1] Shaftesbury, *The Moralists*, in *Characteristicks*, III, 1.

[2] Henry More, *Democritus Platonissans* (Cambridge, 1646), p. 2.

[3] Nicholas of Cusa, *The Idiot in Four Books* (1650 trans.; reprinted by California State Library, 1940), p. 23.

[4] Shaftesbury, *Characteristicks*, III, 1.

[5] See William Boulting, *Giordano Bruno* (London, 1914), p. 120; Leonardo Olschki, *Giordano Bruno* (Bari, 1927), pp. 36 ff.; A. O. Lovejoy, *The Great Chain of Being* (Baltimore, 1936), pp. 116 ff.; F. R. Johnson and S. V. Larkey, "Thomas Digges, the Copernican System, and the Idea of the Infinity of the Universe in 1576," *Huntington Library Bulletin*, no. 5 (1934), p. 114.

[6] More, *Democritus Platonissans*, stanza 5.

[7] *Ibid.*, stanzas 69–70.

[8] E. A. Burtt, *The Metaphysical Foundations of Modern Physical Science* (New York, 1932), pp. 137 ff.; see also John T. Baker, *An Historical and Critical Examination of English Space Theories from Henry More to Bishop Berkeley* (Bronxville, N. Y.), 1930.

[9] *Œuvres de Descartes*, ed. Cousin (Paris, 1825), X, 161. Letter of December 11, 1648. My translation.

[10] George Berkeley, *Philosophical Commentaries, Generally Called the Common Place Book*, ed. A. A. Luce (London, 1944), note on entry no. 298.

[11] Henry More, Appendix to *The Antidote against Atheism*, in *A Collection of Several Philosophical Writings of Doctor Henry More* (London, 1772), chap. vii.

[12] Samuel Clarke, Boyle Lectures, *A Discourse Concerning the Being and Attributes of God* . . . (5th ed.; London, 1719), pp. 404 ff. This passage occurs in correspondence between Clarke and "a Gentleman in Gloucestershire." On the development of the ideas here described, see the full account in Alexander Koyré, *From the Closed World to the Infinite Universe* (Baltimore, 1957).

[13] *Sir Isaac Newton's Mathematical Principles of Natural Philosophy and His System of the World*, trans. Andrew Motte, ed. Florian Cajori (Berkeley and Los Angeles, 1934). General Scholium to the 1713 ed. of the *Principia.*

[14] C. S. Lewis, "Addison," in *Essays on the Eighteenth Century Presented to D. Nichol Smith* (Oxford, 1945), p. 11.

[15] Thomas Burnet, *Sacred Theory* (English version), I, xi.

[16] *Ibid.*

[17] Shaftesbury, *Characteristicks*, III, 1.

[18] Edward Young, *Night Thoughts*, IX.

NOTES TO CHAPTER IV

[1] Thomas Warton, "The Pleasures of Melancholy."

[2] Joseph Warton, *An Essay on the Writings and Genius* (London, 1756), Dedication.

[3] *Summa Theologica*, Part I, Q. 84, Art. 7, Reply Obj. 3.

[4] *A Treatie of Humane Learning*, stanza 17, in *Poems and Dramas of Fulke Greville*, ed. Bullough (Edinburgh, 1938).

[5] *Ibid.*, stanza 109.

[6] A. G. Baumgarten, *Meditationes Philosophicae de Nonnullis ad Poema Pertinentibus*, ed. and trans. Karl Aschenbrenner and William Holther (Berkeley and Los Angeles, 1955).

[7] James Thomson, *Liberty*, V, lines 23 ff.

[8] Thomas Hobbes, *Treatise of Human Nature*, chap. iv, sec. 3.

[9] *Ibid.*, chap. x, sec. 5.

[10] Rosemond Tuve, *Elizabethan and Metaphysical Imagery* (Chicago, 1947), p. 391.

[11] *Ibid.*, p. 396.

[12] *Remarks on Prince Arthur*, in *The Critical Works of John Dennis*, ed. Hooker (Baltimore, 1939), I, 59.

[13] *Summa Theologica*, II (1) xxvii, 1.

[14] Muratori, *The Perfection of Italian Poetry*, trans. E. F. Carritt, in *Philosophies of Beauty from Socrates to Robert Bridges* (Oxford, 1931).

[15] Perry Miller, *Jonathan Edwards* (New York, 1949), pp. 55–56.

[16] Luis de la Puente, *Meditations upon the Mysteries of Our Holie Faith . . .*, trans. John Heigham (St. Omers, 1619), I, 385.

[17] Rosemond Tuve (see note 10, above) effectively quotes Puttenham to the effect that the good poet is a "representer of the best, most comely and bewtifull images or appearances of thinges to the soule and according to their very truth." She remarks that Puttenham "relates all insight in any field to poetic insight, and in all fields sees imagination as coöperating with judgment"; and, most important: "This connection of the imagination with the matter-finding process, invention, is quite usual. . . . We must simultaneously remember that matter-finding is a preformal stage and that the subject of a poem is an embodied purpose, not a subject matter as such." Dryden's *Of the Original and Progress of Satire* gives an extended exposition of this process.

[18] John Livingston Lowes, *The Road to Xanadu* (Boston and New York, 1927), pp. 59–60.

NOTES TO CHAPTER V

[1] George Santayana, *The Sense of Beauty* (first published, 1896), Part I, sec. 2.

[2] Longinus, *On the Sublime*, trans. W. F. Fyfe, Loeb Classical Library, sec. 35. This version seems to me to come closest to the sense of the original.

[3] William Sanderson, *Graphice* (London, 1658), p. 8.

[4] On the subject of the sublime in the eighteenth century, see the following: Samuel H. Monk, *The Sublime: A Study of Critical Theories in Eighteenth-Century England* (New York, 1935); a review by R. S. Crane of this book in *Philological Quarterly*, XV (1936), 165; Monk's introduction to John Baillie, *An Essay on the Sublime* (1747), Augustan Reprint no. 43 (Berkeley and Los Angeles, 1953).

[5] *Anthologia Palatina*, IX, 577.

[6] Leonard Welsted, trans., *The Works of Dionysius Longinus, On the Sublime . . .* (London, 1712), p. 104.

[7] Josephine Miles has aptly suggested the name "sublime poem" for such works as Thomson's *The Seasons*, Mallet's *The Excursion*, Savage's *The Wanderer*, Akenside's *The Pleasures of Imagination*, Joseph Warton's *The Enthusiast*, Young's *Night Thoughts*, Langhorne's *The Enlargement of the Mind*. See Josephine Miles, *Eras and Modes in English Poetry* (Berkeley and Los Angeles, 1957), chap. iv. Thomson, in a letter of advice to Mallet,

describes a prospectus for a poem consisting of "a description of the grand works of Nature raised and animated by moral and sublime reflections," and concludes that "sublimity must be the characteristic of your piece." Quoted by A. D. McKillop, *The Background of Thomson's Seasons* (Minneapolis, 1942), p. 129. This book is the standard treatment of the materials and methods of the best example of this type of poem, *The Seasons*. Thomson proposes a poem in which ideas and themes are subordinate to the effect—they being chosen, indeed, solely for the effect they produce. It is notable that the "moral and sublime reflections," instead of determining what descriptions are introduced, are secondary elements. The effect has indeed absorbed the genre.

[8] John Donne, *LXXX Sermons* (London, 1640), Sermon XII, p. 117.

[9] On English influence in Germany on aesthetics, see P. O. Kristeller, "The Modern System of the Arts," *Journal of the History of Ideas*, XIII (1952), 27–28.

[10] A. G. Baumgarten, *Meditationes Philosophicae de Nonnullis ad Poema Pertinentibus*, ed. and trans. Karl Aschenbrenner and William Holther (Berkeley and Los Angeles, 1955), esp. sec. 116.

[11] See Kristeller (note 9, above).

[12] Lowth, *Lectures on the Sacred Poetry of the Hebrews*, trans. G. Gregory (Boston, 1815), p. 6.

[13] Joseph Trapp, *Lectures on Poetry*, trans. William Clarke and William Bowyer (London, 1742), Lecture IV. The lectures are dated 1711–1715.

[14] *Essays of John Dryden*, ed. Ker (Oxford, 1900), I, 153.

[15] Albert Gérard, *L'Idée romantique de la poésie en Angleterre*, Bibliothèque de la Faculté de Philosophie et Lettres de l'Université de Liège, Fasc. CXXXVI (1955), p. 173. Cf. M. H. Abrams, *The Mirror and the Lamp*, chap. vii.

NOTES TO CHAPTER VI

[1] The works on this subject are far too numerous to be listed in detail. Some of the most useful studies on which I have drawn may be mentioned, with a blanket acknowledgment of indebtedness. I have already cited Monk's *The Sublime*, the indispensable source book for understanding eighteenth-century British aesthetic theory. My thesis is, to a considerable extent, an expansion and modification of Monk's opinion that eighteenth-century theory evolved toward a realizing of the implications of subjectivism. A comprehensive account of the vicissitudes of the principal aesthetic terms is given by W. J. Hipple, *The Beautiful, the Sublime, and the Picturesque in Eighteenth-Century British Aesthetic Theory* (Carbondale, Ill., 1957). I obviously do not agree, however, with Hipple's apparent view that no pattern emerges from the aesthetic speculations. Another major account of an important aspect of aesthetic theory is by Gordon McKenzie, *Critical Re-*

sponsiveness: A Study of the Psychological Current in Later Eighteenth Century Criticism, University of California Studies in English (1949). Other histories include: W. J. Bate, *From Classic to Romantic: Premises of Taste in Eighteenth-Century England* (Cambridge, Mass., 1946); C. D. Thorpe, *The Aesthetic Theory of Thomas Hobbes* (Ann Arbor, 1940); René Wellek, *A History of Modern Criticism, 1750–1950* (New Haven, 1955), chaps. v, vi. Wellek's account of British critics is incisive and among the most accurate I know. I do not concur, however, with Wellek's ideas about the influence of cultural action in general on literature or on literary theory, and I think he underestimates the influence of British writers on the development of romanticism. I am much indebted to Thorpe.

Shorter studies include: A. O. Aldridge, "Akenside and Imagination," *SP*, 42 (1945), 769 ff.; R. S. Crane, "English Neoclassical Criticism: An Outline Sketch," in *Critics and Criticism, Ancient and Modern* (Chicago, 1952); introduction by E. N. Hooker to *The Critical Works of John Dennis* (Baltimore, 1939); Martin Kallich, "The Association of Ideas and Critical Theory: Hobbes, Locke, and Addison," *ELH*, 12 (1945), 29 ff.; C. D. Thorpe, "Addison's Theory of the Imagination as 'Perceptive Response,'" *Papers of the Michigan Academy of Science, Arts, and Letters*, 21 (1935), 511 ff.

[2] See Caroline Robbins, "'When It Is That Colonies May Turn Independent,' An Analysis of the Environment and Politics of Francis Hutcheson," *William and Mary Quarterly*, 3d ser., 2 (1954), 237.

[3] Francis Hutcheson, *A System of Moral Philosophy, in Three Books.* Published by his son, Francis Hutcheson (Glasgow, 1755), chap. i, sec. iv, art. 12.

[4] *Ibid.*, I, iv, 13.

[5] "To the senses of seeing and hearing, are superadded in most men, tho' in very different degrees, certain powers of perception of a finer kind than what we have reason to imagine are in most of the lower animals, who yet perceive the several colours and figures, and hear the several sounds. These we may call the senses of beauty and harmony, or, with Mr. Addison, the *imagination.*" *Ibid.*, I, ii, 1.

[6] Hutcheson, *An Inquiry into the Original of Our Ideas of Beauty and Virtue* (1726), Treatise I, sec. i, art. 17.

[7] *Works of Thomas Reid,* ed. Sir William Hamilton (Edinburgh, 1863), I, 89.

[8] Hipple, *The Beautiful* . . . , p. 155.

[9] John Baillie, *An Essay on the Sublime*, ed. Monk, Augustan Reprint no. 43 (Berkeley and Los Angeles, 1953), p. 3.

[10] Alexander Gerard, *An Essay on Taste* (Edinburgh, 1780), pp. 145–146.

[11] *Ibid.*, p. 21.

[12] *Ibid.*, pp. 15–16.

[13] *Ibid.*, p. 133.

[14] John Armstrong, "Of Genius," *Miscellanies* (London, 1770), II, 135.

[15] William Duff, *Critical Observations on the Writings of the Most Celebrated Original Geniuses in Poetry* (London, 1770), p. 69.

[16] *Ibid.*, p. 196.

[17] Gerard, *An Essay on Taste*, p. 21. The same ideas, about genius being at home in a relatively primitive society, are repeated by many authors: Blair, for example, in the *Lectures on Rhetoric and Belles-Lettres.*

[18] Henry Home, Lord Kames, *Elements of Criticism* (Edinburgh, 1762), I, 294–295. See Helen W. Randall, *The Critical Theory of Lord Kames* (Northampton, 1944).

[19] Home, *Elements of Criticism*, III, 3.

[20] *Ibid.*, III, 6.

[21] *Ibid.*, III, 43.

[22] *Ibid.*, II, 58–59.

[23] *Ibid.*, III, 101.

[24] *Ibid.*, III, 140.

[25] *Ibid.*, I, 415.

[26] *Ibid.*, I, 265.

[27] *Letters from Mrs. Elizabeth Carter, to Mrs. Montagu, between the Years 1755 and 1800*, ed. Montagu Pennington (London, 1817), III, 251.

[28] MS letter (probably August, 1758) in collection of the Henry E. Huntington Museum and Art Gallery, MO 3021.

[29] MS letter to Lord Bath, August 21, 1762. Huntington Collection, MO 4537 A and B.

[30] Letter to Mrs. Carter, October 3, 1762. Huntington Collection, MO 3084.

[31] Letter (undated, but probably 1762) to Lord Bath, Huntington Collection, MO 4561.

[32] Copy of a letter dated May 26, 1764. Huntington Collection, MO 4576.

[33] Letter to Mrs. Vesey, January 3, 1770, in *A Series of Letters between Mrs. Elizabeth Carter and Miss Catherine Talbot from the Year 1741 to 1770*, ed. Montagu Pennington (London, 1819), III, 142–143.

[34] *Letters from Mrs. Elizabeth Carter, to Mrs. Montagu . . .* , III, 35.

[35] Letter dated June, 1769, in *A Series of Letters between Mrs. Elizabeth Carter and Miss Catherine Talbot . . .* , III, 120.

[36] Letter of 1765, *ibid.*, III, 40–41.

[37] "It is not important that the poet should say some particular thing, but should speak in harmony with nature. The tone and pitch of his voice is the main thing." Entry of April 2, 1858, in Thoreau's *Journal*, ed. Torrey and Allen. It is interesting to observe how many features of the doctrine of imagination as means of grace Thoreau expresses. In the entry for May 23, 1853, we find the "polished mirror" image: "The poet must bring to Nature the smooth mirror in which she is to be reflected. He must be something superior to her, something more than natural. He must furnish equanimity. No genius will excuse him from importing the ivory which is to be

his material." The genius is not superior to nature because he completes her meaning, or because in his humanity he represents a higher reality, but because he brings to nature something she cannot supply—the mirror in which her image is reflected, and the "equanimity," the calmness, necessary to make the reflection. On May 6, 1841, Thoreau wrote that "The poet speaks only those thoughts that come unbidden, like the wind that stirs the trees, and men cannot help but listen. He is not listened to, but heard." The last sentence hits off admirably the difference between poetry as the statement of rational truth and poetry as source of subjective effects.

Other statements of Thoreau reflect a symbolic theory of poetry (to be discussed in chapter vii), especially: "Is it not as language that all natural objects affect the poet? He sees a flower or other object, and it is beautiful or affecting to him because it is a symbol of his thought, and what he indistinctly feels or perceives is matured in some other organization. The objects I behold correspond to my mood." August 7, 1853.

NOTES TO CHAPTER VII

[1] George Santayana, *The Sense of Beauty*, Introduction.

[2] Samuel H. Monk, *The Sublime*, p. 96.

[3] *The Mind of Henry Fuseli: Selections from His Writings with an Introductory Study*, ed. E. C. Mason (London, 1951), p. 56.

[4] *Ibid.*, p. 331.

[5] Dugald Stewart contrasts "invention" and "discovery." The object of the former "is to produce something which had no existence before; that of the latter, to bring to light something which did exist, but which was concealed from common observation." Further, "improvements in the Arts are properly called *inventions;* and . . . facts brought to light by means of observation are properly called *discoveries*." *Elements of the Philosophy of the Human Mind* (Boston, 1836), chap. v, sec. iv. Stewart's attitude is romantic; the discovery of reality does not belong to the arts.

[6] On this subject see my article, "The Importance of Shaftesbury," *ELH*, 20 (1953), esp. pp. 287 ff.

[7] James T. Flexner, *The Light of Distant Skies* (New York, 1954), p. 40.

[8] Stewart, *Elements* . . . , chap. vii, sec. ii.

[9] *Ibid.*, chap. vii, sec. i.

[10] Stewart, *Philosophical Essays* (1810; Edinburgh, 1816), Part II, Essay First, chap. ii.

[11] *Ibid.*, Part II, Essay Second, chap. ii.

[12] *Ibid.*, chap. iii.

[13] On the influence of Alison's *Essays*, especially on Keats, see James R. Caldwell, *John Keats' Fancy* (Ithaca, 1945), chap. ii.

[14] Monk, *The Sublime*, p. 155.

[15] Archibald Alison, *Essays on the Nature and Principles of Taste* (2d American ed.; Hartford, 1821), Introduction. The great influence of this book dates from its second, 1810 edition, and the famous review by Jeffrey which blew the trumpet of praise. Stewart also spoke of Alison's *Essays* with the highest commendation, and took up the point, discussed later, that the effect of beauty is not a single one. The book might be said to have replaced Lord Kames's *Elements* as a kind of textbook of moral philosophy in the field of aesthetics.

[16] On the breakdown of the macrocosmic idea, see Marjorie Nicolson, *The Breaking of the Circle* (Evanston, 1952). Rosemond Tuve, in *Elizabethan and Metaphysical Imagery*, and A *Reading of George Herbert*, has studied the poet's use of the macrocosmic symbolism.

[17] Edmund Wilson, *Axel's Castle* (1931), chap. i.

[18] William Butler Yeats, *Ideas of Good and Evil* (1903).

[19] "The Symbolism of Poetry," *ibid.* (1st ed., 1900). The combination of "indefinable" and "precise" is an important feature of symbolism. Compare the following lines from Verlaine's "Art Poétique":

Il faut aussi que tu n'ailles point
Choisir tes mots sans quelque méprise;
Rien de plus cher que la chanson grise
Où l'Indécis au Précis se joint.

Index

INDEX